Python 3 for Absolute Beginners

Tim Hall and J-P Stacey

Apress®

Python 3 for Absolute Beginners

ISBN-13 (pbk): 978-1-4302-1632-2

ISBN-13 (electronic): 978-1-4302-1633-9

9 8 7 6 5 4 3 2 1

Lead Editor: Matthew Moodie
Technical Reviewer: Duncan Parkes
Additional material: Dr. J. Burton Browning
Editorial Board: Clay Andres, Steve Anglin, Mark Beckner, Ewan Buckingham, Tony Campbell, Gary Cornell, Jonathan Gennick, Michelle Lowman, Matthew Moodie, Jeffrey Pepper, Frank Pohlmann, Ben Renow-Clarke, Dominic Shakeshaft, Matt Wade, Tom Welsh
Project Managers: Beth Christmas and Debra Kelly
Copy Editor: Heather Lang
Compositor: LaurelTech
Indexer: BIM Indexing and e-Services
Artist: April Milne

Distributed to the book trade worldwide by Springer-Verlag New York, Inc., 233 Spring Street, 6th Floor, New York, NY 10013. Phone 1-800-SPRINGER, fax 201-348-4505, e-mail orders-ny@springer-sbm.com, or visit http://www.springeronline.com.

For information on translations, please e-mail info@apress.com, or visit http://www.apress.com.

Apress and friends of ED books may be purchased in bulk for academic, corporate, or promotional use. eBook versions and licenses are also available for most titles. For more information, reference our Special Bulk Sales–eBook Licensing web page at http://www.apress.com/info/bulksales.

The source code for this book is available to readers at http://www.apress.com.

Contents at a Glance

Contents

About the Author

Tim Hall currently provides front–line support for 64 Studio. He has also written newbie tutorials for Linux User and Developer magazine in between more mundane system admin and web authoring jobs.

Tim has released albums and performed as a musician and songwriter, both solo and in collaboration with other artists. He has been further honored as the holder of the Bardic chair of Glastonbury between 2005 and 2007. Tim uses Python as his main programming language, primarily as a means for creative ends, because it is easy to read and fun to learn.

J-P Stacey has been a senior developer at Torchbox Ltd since 2005, building and maintaining (among other things) Python, Django, and Drupal applications.

He organizes the Oxford Geek Nights and gets involved in tuition and seminars at Torchbox. In his spare time he reads and writes fiction and blogs, buys too much music, and tries not to startle Cotswold lions on his bicycle.

About the Technical Reviewer

 **Duncan Parkes** has been coding in Python, both for work and for fun, for roughly a decade. He drifted into programming largely by accident after initially taking a doctorate in Combinatorial Group Theory, a branch of Pure Mathematics. As an ex-mathematician, he loves the clarity and simplicity of Python and needs a bit of persuading to code in anything else. After completing a technical review of this book, he joined Apress as an editor in the Open Source group. He currently splits his time between editing books and coding for mySociety, a charitable organization that runs most of the UK's best-known democracy web sites.

Duncan lives in Oxford, England, with his wife, Ruth. When away from his computer, Duncan enjoys playing the guitar very badly, cycling long distances on a Brompton folding bicycle, and fiddling with old cars.

His friends and colleagues have been known to run sweepstakes on how far these vehicles can get without the assistance of a breakdown service.

CHAPTER 1

■ ■ ■

Introducing Python

So, you want to learn programming. Welcome to one of the great adventures of the twenty-first century. Programming requires little in the way of specialized equipment; the software tools can all be downloaded for free off the Internet, and it can be practiced in the safety and comfort of your own home, without having to ask anyone's permission. This chapter will ease you in gently by introducing you to the software you will need to create your programs: a command-line interface, which allows you to use Python in interactive mode, and a text editor for writing scripts—nothing more complicated than that. I will also show you where to go to find help and documentation, so you can decode the sometimes-impenetrable jargon that seems to surround this, the geekiest of all technical disciplines. To begin with, you will need to make sure that you have a decently recent version of Python installed on your machine or follow the steps later in this chapter to install it (see "Choosing the Right Python Version" for a definition of *decently recent*). This chapter explains how to make sure that you have everything set up correctly and that you have suitable references at hand before you start your journey.

Python is an excellent language with which to learn programming. There are many reasons for this, but the simple explanation is that it's easy to read and fast to write; it doesn't take long to come up with working code that does something meaningful. Python has a very human-friendly syntax, which makes writing elegant code easy. The basic language is fairly simple and therefore easy to remember, and then it has an extensive library of predefined functions that you can use to facilitate most common computer tasks. Writing effective applications in Python can be as simple as playing with conceptual building blocks. It works really well for writing a little two-line application to perform some routine system administration task or to provide interactive functions on a web page, but it has enough power and flexibility to comfortably create much larger and more complex applications with graphic interfaces indistinguishable from the programs you are used to running from your computer's main menu. If you follow the suggestions laid out in this book about writing self-explanatory code, in several months, even years, you will be able to come back to your programs and see immediately what they were supposed to do and what your original intentions were; this makes maintaining programs much simpler too.

OK, let's make sure your system is ready for you to start running Python programs.

Running Python on Various Systems

Python can be installed and run on most operating systems including Windows, Mac OS X, or OS/2, Linux, and Unix. If you are running Mac OS X or a GNU/Linux system, you will probably have it installed by default. I would recommend using a system of this kind, which already has Python set up as an integral part. The book was written using a Debian GNU/Linux system, and therefore, the examples will work exactly the same on any Debian-based system, such as Ubuntu. In fact, the differences between Linux variants are few, so you'll be equally at home with other distributions.

Installing on Windows

If you are using Windows, you will probably have to install Python and configure certain settings correctly before you can get to grips with the examples in this book. For that, you will need to refer to the specific instructions for your operating system on the following Python web pages:

- http://wiki.python.org/moin/BeginnersGuide/Download
- http://www.python.org/doc/faq/windows/
- http://docs.python.org/dev/3.0/using/windows.html

First, you need to download the official installer; alternative versions for Itanium and AMD machines are available from http://www.python.org/download/. You should save this file, which will have a .msi extension, somewhere you'll be able to find again easily. You can then double-click this file to start the Python installation wizard, which will take you through the installation. It's fine to accept the default settings if you're not sure of any answer.

Installing on Other Systems

You may choose to install Python on other systems, particularly if you want to take advantage of newer versions. For Linux and other Unix-like systems, the installation instructions are here:

- http://docs.python.org/dev/3.0/using/unix.html

  If you're using OS X, your instructions are here:

- http://www.python.org/download/mac/
- http://docs.python.org/dev/3.0/using/mac.html

Choosing the Right Python Version

You will find the different installers include a number after the word *Python*. This is the **version number**. When I started writing this book, those numbers ranged from 2.3.7 (old but still usable) through 2.5.2 (the previous stable version) to 3.0 (the new version about to be released). At the same time as version 3.0 was released, the Python team also put out version 2.6, which is an upgraded version of Python version 2 for people who want (or need) to stick with the old way of doing things but still want to benefit from general fixes and some of the new features introduced in version 3.0.

The Python language is continuously evolving; version 3.0 has become the norm and has evolved into version 3.1.1. The *new* version, which I'll refer to as version 3.0 because all 3.x versions are simply refinements on the original plan of 3.0, includes several changes to the programming language that are incompatible with version 2.x (*x* is any number you like), which I will refer to in the rest of this book as the *old* version. Most of the language is the same, however, so the differences between the versions of Python will be noted in the text as those subjects are covered. Examples in this book are for Python 3.0 except where noted.

Further information about the latest version of Python 3.0 (also known as Py3k or Python 3000) is available at `http://www.python.org/download/releases/`.

There may be some differences running Python on other operating systems, which I will do my best to point out where relevant. Otherwise, the examples of code will work the same way. This is one of the many good points of Python. For the most part, this book will concentrate on the fun part—learning how to write programs using Python. The official Python documentation is plentiful, free, and well written, and you should read it alongside this book. It is available on at `http://www.python.org/doc/`.

Understanding the Jargon

Throughout this book, I will be doing my best to demystify, clarify and explain the various bits of technical terminology that you will frequently encounter during the process of learning the art of programming. Technical terms and jargon words that need further explanation will be highlighted in **bold** the first time you encounter them. Any terms not immediately explained in the chapter will be covered in the "Jargon Busting" section at the end of each chapter. You may also wish to study one of the most famous resources on the Internet, the Jargon File, which is part of the *New Hacker's Dictionary* (available at `http://catb.org/~esr/jargon/`).

As an example, here's the definition of the noun "code" from the Jargon File:

"The stuff that software writers write, either in source form or after translation by a compiler or assembler. Often used in opposition to 'data,' which is the stuff that code operates on. Among hackers this is a mass noun, as in 'How much code does it take to do a "bubble sort"?' or 'The code is loaded at the high end of RAM.' Among scientific programmers, it is sometimes a count noun equivalent to 'program;' thus they may speak of 'codes' in the plural. Anyone referring to software as 'the software codes' is probably a 'newbie' or a 'suit'."

For comparison's sake, here's the definition of the verb "code":

"To write code. In this sense, always refers to source code rather than compiled. 'I coded an Emacs clone in two hours!' This verb is a bit of a cultural marker associated with the Unix and minicomputer traditions (and lately Linux); people within that culture prefer v. 'code' to v. 'program,' whereas outside it, the reverse is normally true."

The noun "program" is defined as being:

- "A magic spell cast over a computer allowing it to turn one's input into error messages"

- "An exercise in experimental epistemology"

- "A form of art, ostensibly intended for the instruction of computers, which is nevertheless almost inevitably a failure if other programmers can't understand it"

As the information contained in the Jargon File is more entertaining than strictly informative, I will be providing some simpler definitions at the end of each chapter.

Learning While Having Fun

Having fun is often underestimated in the realm of technical disciplines. We learn best and are most productive when we're having fun. Developing software using Python is often an engrossing and enjoyable experience, partly because you can test out your changes as soon as you have made them without having to perform any intermediary steps.

Python also deals with many background tasks, the household chores of programming, so you don't have to bother with them as you might in languages like C. This kind of immediate gratification makes it easier to stay in the creative flow and keep being inspired.

Python is also easy to read, being closer to natural language than many other programming languages, so you spend less time trying to decode what you have just written, which in turn means more time to think about how you could improve and expand your work.

The other great thing is that you can use Python for pretty much any task you can think of, be it large or small, simple text-driven script or major graphical application. It does have its limitations, but by the time you come up against them, you will already have become a competent programmer and will be able to make an informed choice about where to go next.

Introducing the Interactive Shell

Although this book is primarily aimed at showing you how to write stand-alone scripts and **applications**—that is, fully fledged programs that don't require anything other than having Python installed for them to work—Python also works in **interactive mode**, which allows you to enter Python commands using a command-line interface. This is a great resource for immediate Python gratification. You need to locate and start up your computer's command-line interface, sometimes known as the terminal or terminal emulator, or on machines running Windows, the DOS prompt. This will provide you with a **command line** at which you can start typing commands. Interactive mode can be started up by typing python at the command line. If Python is properly installed, you should see something like this:

```
$ python
Python 3.1.1 (r311:74483, Aug 17 2009, 17:02:12)
[GCC 4.2.3 (Debian 4.2.3-5)] on linux2
Type "help", "copyright", "credits" or "license" for more information.
>>>
```

The details may be different according to your operating system. The first line shows the Python version number and the compilation date of the version you have installed. The last line (>>>) is your Python prompt. This indicates that the Python interpreter is running and waiting for your input. The Python interpreter is the program that reads Python programs and carries out their instructions. Interactive mode can be useful for testing out individual commands line by line, experimenting with new ideas, and getting help (try typing help(), and don't forget the parentheses; they are important). To get out of the interactive Python interpreter on a Linux system, you can use the quit() or exit() functions, or else you must hold down the Ctrl key and the D key at the same time (in Windows, you need to use Ctrl+Z and then press Enter).

Choosing to Code with a Text Editor

My preferred method of creating Python scripts is to use a plain text editor, with a few basic programming features. Programs like notepad (especially notepad2/++), BBedit, gedit, NEdit and Kate are ideal for this task. A variety of editors are available that offer specific enhancements for programmers, such as syntax highlighting, which is useful for showing coding errors immediately as you type. Old-school hackers may prefer to use Vi or Emacs. Python does not dictate what software you use to create the code; the choice is up to you. Do not attempt to use word-processing software, such as Word or OpenOffice for this task; it will mess you up badly. Be warned!

Choosing to Code with an Integrated Development Environment

An integrated development environment (IDE) is a graphical interface with lots of useful features designed to make programming with Python even easier. You still have to type the code in the same way, but you can do all your coding using a single application, and these programming **environments** can provide some useful shortcuts and reminders. There are now several Python-specific IDEs. Popular applications include IDLE (which is bundled with Python itself), Eric (you may notice a theme here, nudge nudge, wink wink, say no more...), Geany, DrPython, and SPE. Python is also supported by more general programming environments like Bluefish and a whole host of others. This book doesn't cover the use of IDEs or any of the alternative distributions of Python, because each of these approaches would require a chapter unto themselves, at the very least. However, the examples contained in this book will still work if you *do* choose to explore these options. This book will take the simplest approach, using tools that come as standard with most operating systems; that is, a text editor and the Python Interactive Shell.

Getting Started with Programming

The process of writing a new program usually starts with a problem. Before you can code anything, you need to have an idea of what you want to create, the problem you wish to solve, and a fairly good idea of how to solve it. Chapter 2 will take you through the process of designing software, known as the **software development cycle**. Usually, this is something that you have to learn separately, as most programming manuals go straight into the details of the language, assuming you will have studied program design at college or in the process of learning some other programming language. This can lead you to create code that is difficult to read and understand and makes fixing problems later a nightmare. Understanding the principles of software design can dramatically speed up the process of creating new software and help ensure that important details are not missed out.

In Chapter 3, you start coding those designs in Python. You will learn about constructing the basic units of data, words and numbers, and how to combine and manipulate them. In Chapter 4, I will show you how to compare values, make choices, and deal with errors. The subsequent chapters go through the process of refining those designs, breaking them down into manageable chunks, and expanding your understanding of the Python programming language so you can turn your ideas into fully fledged, functional computer programs.

Creating Your Own Help Files

Python is described as **self-documenting**. This doesn't mean that it will write your user manual for you, but you can add blocks of text, known as **documentation strings**, to your own code, and these strings will then show up in an online help utility. This information can easily be turned into web pages to provide a useful reference. I will show you how to do this in Chapter 2; it is one of the unique features of Python and is worth learning how to use early on.

Jargon Busting

This chapter introduced several technical terms with which you may not be familiar, these are defined as follows:

- *Command-line interface (CLI)*: This mechanism is for interacting with a computer by typing in commands to a text-based interface such as the terminal or DOS prompt.

- *Compile*: This process turns a sequence of instructions in programming language, which is readable by humans (in theory) into machine code, which can be directly executed by the computer. Python does this automatically in the background when you run your script. In some other languages, this has to be done as a separate step before you can execute the program.

- *Documentation strings*: This block of text on the first line of a *function, module, class,* or *method* definition is also called a "docstring." Docstrings are used by Python's built-in tools for automated testing and to provide help documentation. See Chapter 2.

- *Interpreter*: This program turns a sequence of instructions in a script into something that a computer can execute on the fly, effectively compiling the code as the program is running rather than as a separate step.

- *Natural language*: This is language that humans speak, as opposed to a programming language.

- *Operating system*: This is the software component of a computer system that is responsible for the management and coordination of activities and the sharing of the resources of the computer. The operating system communicates between the applications that are run on the machine and the machine's hardware components.

- *Prompt*: This visual cue tells the user to input something.

- *Script and application*: The terms "script," "application," and "program" are used somewhat interchangeably in this book, though there are some subtle differences in meaning:

  - *Script*: This short but complete piece of code is intended to be run using an interpreter. A script will exist as a text file that you can read.

  - *Application*: This refers to any applied use of a programming language. It usually means a complete, packaged-up, and usable piece of software. It is the preferred term among Linux/Unix users.

- *Program*: This refers to the sequence of instructions involved in a script or application; it is also used as a general term to describe an executable computer file.

- *Software development cycle*: In this structured approach to developing software, each stage can be fed back into previous stages. See Chapter 2.

- *Version number*: This number corresponds to a new development in a piece of software. These numbers may refer to major or minor changes and are generally assigned in increasing order. The method used for assigning these numbers is referred to as a *versioning system*.

Summary

This chapter has explained some of the technical terms that you will encounter as you study the art of programming and has introduced you to some sources of further information to help you as you grow in understanding.

So far, you have made sure that the right version of Python is installed on your system and you know how to get to the Python command prompt. You should have selected a text editor to use for writing and saving your scripts, but you haven't written any code yet. In the next chapter I will show you how to start designing programs from the initial seed of a problem that you wish to solve.

CHAPTER 2

■ ■ ■

Designing Software

If you are anything like me, you impatiently started reading this book at Chapter 3, became really confused about halfway through, and decided to start at the beginning and read it all properly this time. This chapter explains the bit that most manuals leave out: *how to actually turn your problem into a working program*. The first stage of the software development cycle is the creation of a program design. In this chapter, I'll demonstrate how to break down your ideas into manageable chunks, understand each problem that you are trying to solve, build up a sequence of actions, keep track of what you've done, and above all, how to go about the constant refinement and simplification of your ideas that will lead to an effective solution that is easy to understand. I'll be introducing you to pseudocode, the software design language, and showing you how to turn it into Python documentation strings to create a framework around which you can grow an effective and maintainable piece of software.

Your first challenge, which I'll be using as an example for this chapter, is to get the computer to respond to a command and print out some kind of response—fairly basic stuff, which you could probably guess at a solution for. However, it's always good to start as we mean to go on, so I'm going to break this down in terms of the software development cycle. In order to get off the starting blocks, it is necessary to identify the problem through a process of asking the right questions and then begin developing a solution, initially by creating a wish list of the things you want your new program to do and getting feedback from potential users. You will use all this information to create your initial program design.

In the next part of this chapter, you will be able to start turning that design into working code. As soon as the design is coded, you will want to begin refining and testing it, starting with defining the results you expect to get and then figuring out how to detect and correct errors.

In the final stage of the software development cycle, you will discover how to use docstrings to document the solution and see how this then feeds back into the next round of the development cycle.

Designing Your Own Software (Why Bother?)

There are many reasons that you might want to write your own software, the chief one being that the applications you have available don't do what you want in the way that you want. You may already have an idea of something you wish to achieve, which led you to pick up this book in the first place. Perhaps you need a solution for work; maybe you have a killer game idea that you'd like to realize; you might want to organize some data in a web page or perform some system administration task. You might want to control a gadget you just built or automate any number of repetitive jobs. Possibly, you already have the program you need, if only it would do this one extra thing, or maybe you just enjoy the idea that writing your own software is possible. I'm not going to try to tell you why you should want to get involved in this peculiar sport; I'll assume you have worked that out for yourself already.

Let's start by asking some questions. Never be afraid to ask questions. Why bother doing all this? Why not just go straight ahead and start writing code? Coming up with a clear design first, along with a clear idea of what answers you expect to see, cuts down on a lot of wasted effort and makes your programs easier to document, troubleshoot, and maintain. It is important to remember that you are trying to make life easier—not more complicated—for yourself and others.

Asking the Right Questions

"Why bother?" is an important programming question that should be applied to every project, module, function, or line of code before you begin. There is a strong possibility that someone, somewhere has already written the software you need, or at least something very similar, that you could convert to your needs with the addition of a couple of lines of code.

Close on its heels comes the next question, "Isn't there a simpler way to do this?" Laziness is the programmers' ally; you probably won't have to write very much from scratch, and you won't need to learn everything by heart before you begin. Generally speaking, you can look up most things as you go along. The art of programming has much more to do with figuring out a logical procedure to get something done than memorizing lines of code; indeed, one of the most common practices involved in coding is simplification. Your first task is about as simple as it gets, but as the book progresses, you will be facing much more complex problems as well as coming up with ideas of your own.

Using Python to Solve Problems

Python is similar in style to **pseudocode**, the language programmers use to design software, with the difference that you can run it on your computer and actually get results. It's easy to read (being close to English), fun to learn, and doesn't require compiling, that is, you can run your script as soon as you have saved it without having to perform any intermediate steps. Python is also a useful language in that it can be used to deal with a wide range of problems with relative ease, and it has a good selection of preconstructed modules to deal with many of the more common computer tasks. I find it similar to playing with conceptual building blocks: the elements of the language are fairly simple to grasp, but they can be combined in pretty much any way you can think of to create apparently complex and graceful structures.

One of the other great features of Python is that it is self-documenting. You still have to write the documentation yourself, but you can include blocks of help text, known as documentation strings or docstrings, within the structure of the program itself. I will be using this particular feature to keep all the design ideas together in one file at the outset and allow us to think on paper. Subsequently, you will be able to look back over old code and know what you were trying to achieve long after you have forgotten why you wrote it in the first place. Eventually, these docstrings will be used to communicate how your program works to other programmers.

Identifying the Problem

Before you start coding anything, you need to have an idea or a problem that you wish to solve. It is quite useful to start with a familiar repetitive task that you suspect could be performed more efficiently using a simple script. Your first problem is to find out how to communicate with your computer using Python and how to get your computer to communicate back. Using this as an example, I will briefly explain the stages of the software development cycle that most programs will go through in course of their development. You don't have to slavishly follow all the suggestions in this chapter, but you may find that they provide a useful structure for developing more complex applications and to get you back on track if you find yourself getting lost. It is also useful to be able to design your program before having to think about the details of coding it in a formal computer language.

The first stage of writing any new program is to grow a design out of the initial problem, a sequence of actions that will calculate the correct result and create the required output. Once the idea has passed the "Why bother?" test, it is necessary to create a simple framework on which to hang the various bits of code that you come up with. Without such a framework, it is often difficult to know where to begin and virtually impossible to construct anything but the simplest of scripts without it getting messy very quickly. The great news is that no specialized knowledge is required at this stage. The process can be started off by answering a few simple questions:

- What do you want the software to do?

- Who will be using it?

- What system will users be running it on?

What Do You Want the Software to Do?

Open a text editor, and write out what the problem is that you want to solve and, very briefly, what you actually want the software to do. A simple text editor will do for this task (see Chapter 1). It's best to start with some simple jobs that you already know computers can do, like printing out a daft message, adding up some numbers, or updating the prices of items in a catalog. Classically, half the battle is identifying the problem, and once you have done so, the solution will begin to become clear. Save the file as plain text (with the .txt extension) and give it the title of your program-to-be. The first program you're going to write later in this chapter will be called Hello World! It will be designed to solve the problem of getting your computer to print out a friendly, affirmative or daft message when you ask it to, so you may as well save this as hello_world.txt.

■ **Tip** You might want to create a new directory to store all your Python experiments.

Who Will Be Using It?

Next, you need to specify who will be using the application, even if you're just doing it for your own personal gratification and no one is ever going to see the output. Write this down.

What other people will be using the program?

- Friends

- Relatives

- Work mates

- Registered users

- Anonymous clients that you're never likely to meet

How much interaction do you expect them to have with the application?

- Clicking a single button

- Using a text interface

- Answering a complex form

How computer-literate do you expect them to be?

- Will they need to learn the ropes?

- Should the application be self-explanatory?

What System Will Users Be Running It On?

It may make a difference whether your program will be running on a Windows, OS X, GNU/Linux, or some other operating system. It may be running on one kind of operating system and be accessed by clients using a variety of other systems, like with most Internet applications. It may use a standard computer keyboard and mouse for input or have some custom-designed interface. What other software will users need to have installed in order to be able to use your script?

All these questions may have a bearing on choices you make later on in the development process. Answer them now, and you will be better prepared for the challenges to come. At this stage, keep your answers simple and to the point; you want to produce a concise overview that neatly summarizes what the software is intended for to begin with. If you can't answer some of the questions yet, that's fine too. Later in this chapter, you will break this down into detailed steps, but before getting on to that, it's your turn to start asking questions.

Creating Your Wish List

In this first stage of defining what you want the software to do, it can be useful to create a wish-list of the specific things you want this software to achieve. This requires analyzing the procedure that might be required to perform the job in hand a little more deeply. Initially, it is quite useful to examine a task that you know how to do. It could be something that is currently not automated or computerized. The following sections outline some suggestions of things you could do to generate your wish list.

Talking to Potential Users

Interview potential users of your application to find out how they currently perform the task you have in mind. Ask them which parts of the procedure could be usefully automated and which factors they want to be able to control. Find out which aspects are confusing and how they overcome existing difficulties.

Some people find it useful to create a short questionnaire, even if only you will be answering the questions; sometimes, this can help to gain some perspective on the problem at hand. In the questionnaire, you can ask more detailed questions of what your potential users expect the application to look like and how they expect it to behave, what file formats they expect to use to read in information from and save it out to, particularly covering any unique or special considerations that you can imagine. File formats could include plain text, XML, and HTML for text documents, or your users might have images saved as JPEGs or PNGs or WAV audio files that they want to convert to MP3s. A file's extension (the letters after the last dot in the filename) usually provides a clue as to what format a file is in, though there are other ways of finding out this information.

The purpose of this exercise is to find out how this job is usually done and what information is needed before you begin. An example calculation with realistic examples of the type and range of information you are likely to be dealing with is invaluable at this stage. A written procedure could also be useful.

Watching Users Perform the Task at Hand

If possible, watch users carry out the task, and note down any points of interest. Again, you don't need to go into a huge amount of detail at this stage, and you need to cover only the information that is relevant to your software project and your potential users. It can be useful to put yourself in the user's position and walk through the process yourself. Another technique is to collect up all the pieces of paper that go into or come out of the process and use them to create a storyboard. This stage of the design process becomes much more relevant in larger projects, but it's worth getting into the habit of doing it now.

Compiling User Stories

A **user story** consists of one or two lines in everyday language that specifies something that the user wants from the software. The idea is that stories should be brief enough to fit on an index card, on a sticky note, or into one cell of a spreadsheet. A user story should indicate the role of the user, what that user wants the software to do, and what benefit might be gained from it. User stories are prioritized by the user to indicate which features are most important and are then used to work out an estimate of the time it will take to develop those features by the developer. The developer may then create use cases out of these stories and tests to determine whether the requirements have been fulfilled. **Use cases** are longer, more detailed descriptions of features that are required by specific users in specific situations. You just need enough information to work out the basic functionality that will be required from the program you are about to write. Try to keep it concise.

Devising a Solution

Armed with all this information, let's return to the text file to complete the first stage of the software design. The design stage can often be the most time-consuming part of the programming process. It consists of several stages in which the output from one stage becomes the input to the next. Often, the output from one or more stages is fed back through the same process several times. This is known as **recursion** when it happens inside a program. The whole process of software design has a similarly recursive nature. To celebrate this fact, let's go back to the initial problem.

Understanding the Problem

This time around, you're going to fill in a little more detail and turn your text file into a very simple **user requirements document**. In a professional situation, this would become the agreement between the programmer and the client who is paying for the software to be written. For now, you're just going to use it as a means to keep a record of the original purpose of this software. Make sure that the problem is stated clearly and that you have identified the issue you wish to resolve correctly. Often, there can be hidden subtleties in the problem that look straightforward when written down in your natural language but require additional clarification when you come to turn them into programming language, or code. If the problem is not defined well enough to make a decision at that point, you will need to return to this stage and clear up the details before you can make any further progress.

Knowing What the Software Needs to Do

The things you want the software to do are known as **functional requirements** in the trade. Simple examples include printing a message, adding up some numbers up, or sending an e-mail form. You might have additional details to add; for example, maybe the user must be able to input some text, numbers larger than 200 cannot be entered, or the update must be performed over the Internet. Functional requirements specify how a system should *behave*. For your first exercise, Hello World!, you will be asking the software to print out a simple message, so your first functional requirement is that the computer should print out a message.

Considering Other Needs or Limitations

You may also want to include other needs or limitations of the software, which are called nonfunctional requirements. **Nonfunctional requirements** define other constraints and qualities required of the software, such as accessibility, usability by the intended users, cost-effectiveness, compatibility with other systems, security, and performance. You probably won't need to worry too much about such things if you are just programming for your own amusement.

Defining Acceptable Results

You need to give some thought as to how the software will be tested. Early on, it will be enough to simply run the program and see if it works, but as your scripts grow in complexity, you will find it useful to formalize the methods used for testing. It may be worth finding or creating some data to use as an example for testing purposes, and you may find it useful to create a table of values that you expect to find at various points in the process. In Chapter 11, I'll be showing you how to create built-in test suites, which can make a large part of the process automatic. It's generally considered good practice to write your tests before you do any coding, but it often happens that the tests and code actually get written at the same time. For now, a note of the expected output will do fine.

Considering Maintenance

Any piece of software that is going to be used more than once will require some degree of maintenance. Issues that are worth thinking about early on are how the software might need to change in future and how to keep track of issues. You might also consider how the application is going to be kept in working condition while you're integrating new possibilities and responding to new challenges. In many cases, the application will be maintained by the person who wrote it, but it is good practice to organize your project and write your code in a way that makes it easy for someone else to understand what you've done and contribute fixes and new features. One day, you might want to pass on the responsibility of keeping it up to date to someone else.

To facilitate maintenance, the software should include some means of contact, such as the author's e-mail address so that users can get in touch if there are any problems. For now, just note your e-mail address. Later on, I'll show you how you can integrate this information into your code, so you don't have to retype this information every time you want to use it. *Don't Repeat Yourself* is a very sensible principle of programming that states that *every piece of knowledge must have a single, unambiguous, authoritative representation within a system.* No piece of information should ever have to be typed in twice—if you find yourself doing this, it's a sure sign that some part of your script needs redesigning.

Great! You should now have a little text file that looks something like Listing 2-1.

Listing 2-1. *hello_world.txt*

```
Problem: Get the computer to output a message.
Target Users: Me
Target System: GNU/Linux
Interface: Command-line
Functional Requirements: Print out a message.
                         User must be able to input some text.
Testing: Simple run test - expecting a message to appear.
Maintainer: maintainer@website.com
```

Breaking Down the Solution into Steps

Next, you start the process of turning your wish list into a program. In this stage, you will design a logical flow of actions, which will hopefully produce the desired outcome. First, you need to turn the text file into something the Python interpreter can understand by saving it as a Python (.py) file. Use the Save As function in your text editor to save the file with the same name, but this time with a .py extension. This example will become hello_world.py.

Now, the interpreter needs to know what this text is; otherwise, it will attempt to interpret the first thing it finds as a command. There are a variety of ways of marking out blocks of text as comments or text strings so that the interpreter doesn't attempt to execute them.

Comments: The hash symbol, #, is used to mark comments. Comments are completely ignored by the Python interpreter. All text between the # sign and *the end of the line* is ignored. This formatting is a convenience so you, the programmer, can write little notes to yourself to remind yourself what this part of the code is supposed to do or to flag parts of the code that need attention. These comments will only ever be seen by people who are actually reading the code. If you are writing software as part of a team, comments are a great way of communicating your thoughts and intentions to the other programmers. Good code can often contain more comments than actual lines of code—don't be tempted to remove them once you've coded the design. In a month's time, you are likely to have completely forgotten what this script was intended to do, and you will be thankful for these little reminders.

Text strings: Text strings are delimited by quotation marks. *Delimited* means that the text is enclosed between a matching pair of the specified characters. Python uses a variety of forms of quotation marks, principally 'single' and "double" quotation marks. There is a subtle difference between the two forms, which I'll cover in detail in the section on text strings in Chapter 3. The main reason for the different forms is to allow nesting of quotes. **Nesting** means putting one inside the other like this: "What on earth does 'nested delimiters' mean?" she asked.

Like comments, quotation marks only work if the text is all on one line. Fortunately, there are a variety of ways to get the interpreter to ignore line breaks. In this example, I shall use the technique of *triple quoting*. Triple quotes can be either ```'''```single```'''``` or ```"""```double```"""```, and they allow us to mark out an entire block of text along with all the line breaks. I'm going to use triple quotes in a specialized way to create a documentation string

The block of text in Listing 2-1 is going to form the basis of your documentation, so let's enclose it in triple quotes. A text string that occurs as the first statement of any module, function or class becomes a Python docstring, which makes the text available as part of the built-in documentation for this application. It won't do anything yet, but Listing 2-2 is now a legal Python file; the interpreter won't complain if you try to run it.

Listing 2-2. *Creating a Framework for hello_world.py*

```
"""
Problem: Get the computer to output a message.
Target Users: Me
Target System: GNU/Linux
Interface: Command-line
Functional Requirements: Print out a message.
                         User must be able to input some text.
Testing: Simple run test - expecting a message to appear.
Maintainer: maintainer@website.com
"""


# This is just a comment
```

Organizing the Tasks into Steps

Now, you are prepared to start designing your program. The program design is initially sketched out in pseudocode, which is the design language that can be used as an intermediary step to turn the user requirements document into a piece of Python code. There is nothing special about the form of this language; your own natural way of expressing ideas is exactly what is needed in this situation. Pseudocode is simply a series of logical statements in your own words that describe the actions that the program needs to take in order to produce the desired result.

If you are working as part of a team, your company may have a standard way of writing pseudocode, but you don't need to worry about such considerations while you are learning. Over time, you are likely to find that your pseudocode naturally adopts a Python-like syntax. Initially, the important thing is that you can express your ideas clearly without having to worry about the rules of the language yet. The pseudocode is presented in comments # in the order you want it to happen, as shown in Listing 2-3.

Listing 2-3. *Pseudocode Example*

```
# Do the first thing
# Do the next thing
# Do the last thing
```

Each line is commented out so that the interpreter knows not to execute any of these statements. This is your **top-level design**, which is a general description of how you are going to solve this problem. Each statement is referred to as a *step*. When a step is performed, it is said to be *executed*.

Using Indentation and Subgroups

Python is very strict about indentation. Python regards any space or tab at the start of a line as an indentation. Every indentation means something. Without going into too much detail at this stage, pay careful attention to how indentation is used in the examples. The most important thing to remember is not to mix tabs with spaces, as the interpreter thinks these are two different things (even if they look the same to you).

In your text editor's Preferences window, set it to insert four spaces instead of using tabs, and you'll avoid so much future grief by doing this. It is always best to keep your designs clear and readable: use blank lines to separate the different sections of your pseudocode, and use indentation to show how statements are grouped together. As long as each line is a comment preceded by a #, you are free to format it how you like.

■ **Caution** The use of indentation in your actual code follows very specific rules. This is one aspect of Python that takes a little bit of getting used to. I will explain the rules fully in the chapters on control flow statements and functions.

Refining Each Line of Your Pseudocode Until a Solution Is Reached

Each line is then further refined by breaking it down into steps in the same way, until each step comprises a single action and you have a complete design. Subsections should be indented by four spaces, as shown in Listing 2-4.

While you are working in pseudocode, your groupings and indentation can be quite arbitrary; all you are doing is providing a framework for your code to live in. As you learn more about Python, your pseudocode will naturally adopt more Pythonic structures. The process of refining your designs will be covered in greater detail from Chapter 4 onward.

Listing 2-4. *Indentation of Subsections*

```
# Do the first thing.
    # Set the first value.
    # Check whether the first value is some text or not.
    # Print the first value
```

Save it! Every time you sit back from the screen and wonder "What next?" you should save your work. Get into this habit if you haven't already; it will save so much brain-ache and frustration. You may also wish to copy your top-level design along with the finished design back into the original text file, so that you can refer to it when you have finished the coding stage.

Coding the Design

Now, you are ready to start turning your design into proper Python code. Great!

The data your software will be manipulating will take various forms; these values are assigned to things called **variables**, which you can think of as a box or a bucket that contains a single piece of information, often a word or a number. Some people find it useful to think of them as slates that can be written on with chalk. The important thing is that the information in the container can be changed by putting a new value into it; this automatically wipes out the old value and replaces it with a new one. The fact that these values can be changed gives rise to the term *variable*.

There are two stages to creating a variable, the first is to create the container and stick an identifying label on it: this is called **initialization**. The second is to put a value into it: this is called **assignment**. In Python, both these things happen in the same statement. Assignment (and therefore initialization) is performed using the = sign like this: variable = value. One of the specific features of Python is that, once a value has been assigned to a variable, the interpreter will then decide what sort of value it is (i.e., a number, some text, or some other relevant piece of information).

Each variable is referred to by a name, known as an **identifier**, which is rather like a name tag that identifies the variable to the rest of the program. It's a good idea to choose names that give an idea of what sort of values they represent. Python will regard any word that has not been commented out, delimited, or **escaped** in some other way as either a command or an identifier; for this reason, you need to be careful to avoid choosing words that are already being used as part of the Python language to identify your new variables. Details of which words you cannot use will be covered in the next chapter.

Turning the Design into Executable Code

Now, you have to come up with a strategy for solving the problems you have agreed to tackle.

First, you want to print out a message, and you want the user to be able to input some text. OK, so you're expecting your message and users' text to be strings of text. It would be a very good idea to add this information to the Testing section of your docstring at the start of the file. Text strings are represented by enclosing the text in quotes.

Now, you just need to know the function that prints things out to the screen, which is called print() in Python. So your first problem translates fairly easily into executable code as you can see in Listing 2-5. You can print any text you like; "Hello World!" is the default.

Listing 2-5. *First Steps for hello_world.py*

```
"""

Problem: Get the computer to output a message.
Target Users: Me
Target System: GNU/Linux
Interface: Command-line
Functional Requirements: Print out a message.
                         User must be able to input some text.
Testing: Simple run test - expecting a message to appear.
                         - expecting: message == input text
Maintainer: maintainer@website.com
"""
```

```
# 1. Print out a friendly message
print("Hello World!")

# 2. Input some text

# 3. Print out the text we just entered
```

This script can be run by typing

```
$ python hello_world.py
```

on the command line. You did remember to save it, didn't you?

The only line in this script that is actually executed by the interpreter is `print("Hello World!")`. Everything else is either ignored as a comment or assumed to be a docstring, in the case of the block of text at the beginning. If you change the text between the quotes in the call to the `print()` function, the Python interpreter will print out whatever you tell it to.

Well done! You just wrote your first Python program. It's about as basic as can be, but you can now bask in the satisfaction of having got Python to do something.

Further Refining the Design

Constantly editing the script to get it to say something different quickly becomes rather tedious. Wouldn't it be great if the program were interactive? In that case, you would need to find a way to get some user input.

The quick-and-dirty method for doing this is to use the built-in `input()` function. This function takes one argument, a text string that is printed to the screen to prompt the user for input. The function then returns the user's input. All requests for input need a message to tell the user that input is required; this is known as a **prompt**. I assign this input to a variable called `some_text`. Then, I can use the `print()` function to print out the user's input. Notice that this time `some_text` isn't in quotes, because I want the value contained in the variable called `some_text` rather than the literal text string `"some_text"`. Variable names aren't allowed to contain spaces, so you'll notice that I've replaced the space with an underscore. It's worth remembering that variable names can't contain dashes either, because Python will assume that the dash is a minus sign. Details of how to name your variables will be covered fully in Chapter 3.

Using functions

Most of the actual work in programs is performed by functions. You can spot functions quite easily, as they usually have parentheses, (), immediately following the function name. Any information that the function needs to work on is placed inside the parentheses; these pieces of information, called arguments, have to be separated by commas if there is more than one of them.

Again, text strings have to be enclosed in quotes or else the interpreter will treat the string as if it is a variable. Functions often return a value of some kind, so it is usual to catch this value by assigning it to a variable like this: `variable = function()`.

Don't forget the brackets after the function name.

Functions are covered in much greater detail in Chapter 6.

Your final script should look something like Listing 2-6.

Listing 2-6. *A Refined hello_world.py*

```
"""

Problem: Get the computer to output a message.
Target Users: Me
Target System: GNU/Linux
Interface: Command-line
Functional Requirements: Print out a message.
                         User must be able to input some text.
Testing: Simple run test - expecting a message to appear.
                         - expecting: message == input text
Maintainer: maintainer@website.com
"""


# 1. Print out a friendly message
print("Hello World!")

# 2. Input some text
some_text = input('Type in some words: ')

# 3. Print out the text we just entered
print(some_text)
```

■ **Note** The behavior of the `input()` function has changed in Python 3 . You need to use the `raw_input()` function to get the same effect in older versions.

Testing the Design

Now, it's time to save the file again and test it by running the script with the Python interpreter as before. If you get any error messages at this stage, you probably made a mistake typing the script. Common errors include missing quotation marks or spaces in the wrong places. In this case, you will need to go back to the coding stage and correct these errors before you test the code again.

The testing stage involves making sure that the design does what it is supposed to and that it matches the specification that you started with. Compare the actual output from running the program to the output you said you were expecting in your original specification. Are they the same? If not, why not? What could be done better?

Apart from the initial design stage, you will probably spend most of your time cycling around this testing stage. Don't be tempted to view error messages as annoyances or irritations: pay great attention to what they tell you, as they can be one of the most useful aids on the path of learning Python. On some occasions, you will want to deliberately produce error messages to prove that something is working. Try it now. Find out what you have to mess up to get an error message. Take note of what sort of message you get, and fix your script so that it runs cleanly again.

Detecting and correcting coding errors

Let's take a brief tour of a few common errors you're likely to see. For example, the following error indicates that you've left off the quotation marks:

```
$ python hello_world.py
  File "hello_world.py", line 16
    print("Hello World!)
                       ^
SyntaxError: EOL while scanning string literal
```

Turning on the line numbers in the preferences of your text editor will help locate the relevant line. Many editors also allow you to search for the specific line number. The fix for this is easy: go back and add the matching pair of quotation marks. The little arrowhead shows you the place where the interpreter realized all was not well. That won't always be exactly the same place as you made the error, but it will probably have some logical relationship.

The following error means you misspelled some_text the first time you mentioned it:

```
$ python hello_world.py
Hello World!
Type in some words: Some Text
Traceback (most recent call last):
  File "hello_world.py", line 22, in <module>
    print(some_text)
NameError: name 'some_text' is not defined
```

The program runs fine up to that point, but the misspelled word is considered to be an error in your logic. Go back to the Python file, and make sure your logic is sane and that you have spelled the names of your variables consistently.

In the following script, you forgot to put quotes around the argument to input(), your prompt string:

```
$ python hello_world.py
  File "hello_world.py", line 19
    some_text = input(Type in some words: )
                                         ^
SyntaxError: invalid syntax
```

Notice that the interpreter doesn't mind the space between the function name and the parentheses, but it does mind the spaces in between the words in the argument because you didn't enclose them with quotes. Syntax errors mean that you got the punctuation or grammar wrong. The fix for this is usually to go and look up the correct form for this function in the official documentation. It might have been acceptable to have a one-word argument if that word was the name of a variable containing a text string. If no variable of that name existed you would be accused of calling an undefined identifier.

The final example is slightly more obscure. This error was actually caused by leaving off the comment marker # at the beginning of the line and leaving a space:

```
$ python hello_world.py
  File "hello_world.py", line 18
    2. Input some text
    ^
IndentationError: unexpected indent
```

The interpreter wasn't expecting to hit an indented line here; it was expecting another statement at the same level of indentation. I told you Python was fussy about indentation. If the space hadn't been left, you would simply receive a syntax error because 2. isn't a command that Python recognizes.

Noting Modifications, Extensions, and Enhancements

As you read through your code, make notes of any improvements that could be made. I like to use comments in the script for this. It is a useful convention to include the word TODO or FIXME in the line, so you can search the source file later for things that you have decided need doing. You could create a separate TODO file in the same directory if you want to keep track of multiple files.

Documenting the Solution

Documentation is the last good habit I'd like to introduce you to, before I move on to discussing the Python language in depth. As mentioned earlier in this chapter, Python is self-documenting to a certain extent. Modules, classes, and functions may be documented by placing a text string as their first statement, just as I have done with the specification details in this example. The simplest way to test this is to start Python in interactive mode from the same directory as the hello_world.py script:

```
$ python
Python 3.1.1 (r311:74483, Aug 17 2009, 17:02:12)
[GCC 4.2.3 (Debian 4.2.3-5)] on linux2
Type "help", "copyright", "credits" or "license" for more information.
```

The three chevrons are the Python prompt, which means the interpreter is ready to receive your first command. Next, you need to import the script you have just written as a module using the import statement:

```
>>> import hello_world
Hello World!
Type in some words: Some Text
Some Text
```

You will see that the program runs in exactly the same way. However, this method allows us to easily access the documentation you have created. help() is a built-in function that takes one argument—the name of the module, class, function, keyword or topic that you want to find out about. Notice that I didn't use the .py extension or enclose the name of the module in quotes; this is because it became a

Python object when I imported it, so I need to refer to the script as a module, the way Python sees it, rather than using the operating system's filename. I will cover modules, classes and objects in Chapters 9 and 10.

```
>>> help(hello_world)
```

This should give us a result that looks like this:

```
Help on module hello_world:

NAME
    hello_world

FILE
    /home/me/lib/python3.0/hello_world.py

DESCRIPTION
    Problem: Get the computer to output a message.
    Target Users: Me
    Target System: GNU/Linux
    Interface: Command-line
    Functional Requirements: Print out a message.
                             User must be able to input some text.
    Testing: Simple run test - expecting a message to appear.
                             - expecting: message == input text
    Maintainer: maintainer@website.com

DATA
    some_text = 'Some Text'
```

If you need more assistance you can use the

```
>>> help()
```

function to get a basic explanation of most aspects of the Python language.

The output from the help() function provides us with a minimal sort of programmers' documentation, which is probably more than adequate for this example. Larger software projects would produce additional documentation at this stage such as a design document and a user manual. The *design document* is for the benefit of people who will be maintaining the software; it should minimally consist of a statement of the problem, a top-level design, the final design (possibly with an explanation of how it was arrived at), and a data table. A data table for the hello_world.py script from Listing 2-6 would be very simple as illustrated in Table 2-1.

***Table 2-1.** An Example Data Table*

Identifier	Description	Type
some_text	User input text	Text string

This information could be copied into the original .txt file (hello_world.txt, in this instance) if all you need is to provide yourself with a reference for future modifications. Complex applications often come with several text files and extensive user documentation (I'll come back to these later).

The form and content of the user manual is really up to you. The important point to keep in mind is that the software design cycle does not end until all the documentation has been brought up to date.

Jargon Busting

Here are the terms introduced in this chapter:

- *Argument*: This is a value you pass to a function or to a procedure, so it has some data to work with.

- *Assignment*: This is the operation of setting a variable to a value.

- *Delimiter*: This punctuation mark is typically used to separate a text string or other piece of data from surrounding characters.

- *Escape*: This is a method of indicating that the next character in a text string should be processed in a different way.

- *Function*: A function is a block of code that performs a calculation, accepts zero or more arguments, and returns a value to the calling procedure when it is complete.

- *Indentation*: This refers to the use of spaces and tabs at the start of a line of code or text; except you want to use spaces rather than tabs, remember?

- *Identifier*: This is a user-defined name; both function names and variable names are identifiers. Identifiers must not conflict with keywords.

- *Initialization*: This process sets the initial value of a variable. Initialization is done only once for each variable, when that variable is created.

- *Module*: A module is a Python program that can be imported by another program. Modules are often used to define additional functions and classes.

- *Nesting*: Put one piece of code inside another similar construct.

- *Nonfunctional requirements*: These are needs or limitations of the software that are not specifically about what the software will *do*.

- *Program implementation*: This is the actual realization of the program, as opposed to the design.

- *Prompt*: This string of text or punctuation marks indicates that the user needs to input some information or commands.

- *Pseudocode*: This program design language is intended to be read by humans, not performed by a computer.

- *Return*: This refers to the process of transferring execution from a function back to the place from which that function was called in the main program. The return statement can also pass a value back to the main program for use in further calculation.

- *Statement*: This instruction to do something in a programming language manipulates a piece of data, performs a calculation, or produces some output.

- *String*: This refers to a line of text or other characters intended to be displayed or processed as a single item.

- *Top-level design*: This is the first stage of a design, and it provides a summary or general description of the actions that the software is intended to perform.

- *User story*: A user story consists of one or two lines in the everyday language of the user that specifies something desired from the software.

- *Validation*: This process tests whether a value is what the programmer expects it to be.

- *Variables*: Use variables as a means of referring to a specific item of data that you wish to keep track of in a program. It points to a memory location, which can contain numbers, text, or more complicated types of data.

Summary

Congratulations! You have completed your first turn around the software design cycle and produced your first Python program. In the process, you have discovered how to identify and analyze problems and have created a simple framework by breaking the problem down into simple steps. You wrote your first lines of Python code and learned how to assign values to variables. You also obtained user input using your first function and then tested it out, and you learned how to use error messages to help detect and correct coding errors. Finally, you learned about the importance of documenting your intentions, expectations, and results. This chapter has concentrated mainly on preparing ideas in order to turn them into effective applications. In the rest of this book, I will focus on the specifics of the Python programming language, and you will learn how to construct more complex applications.

CHAPTER 3

■ ■ ■

Variables and Data Types

In the previous chapter, you learned that a variable is a unit of data with an identifier, which is held in your computer's memory; it can be changed by putting a new value into it or modifying the value that is already there. In this chapter, I will be introducing some of the different types of variable that are available for you to use in your programs, and I'll be showing you how to build them into the expressions and statements of Python that will allow you to turn your designs into working code. This is where you start to do some real programming. You will be creating two programs from scratch in this chapter: one to manipulate and format simple text strings and a script that performs a mathematical calculation. All this is made possible by using variables.

Using variables allows you to specify a calculation or method for getting a result without having to know what values those variables will refer to beforehand. Any information that is put into the system must be turned into a variable before you can do anything to it, and it will be the contents of a variable that finally get sent back to the user that called the program.

Choosing Good Identifiers

Identifiers are the names used to *identify* things in your code. Python will regard any word that has not been commented out, delimited by quotation marks, or escaped in some other way as an identifier of some kind.

An identifier is just a name label, so it could refer to more or less anything including commands, so it helps to keep things readable and understandable if you choose sensible names. You need to be careful to avoid choosing names that are already being used in your current Python session to identify your new variables. Choosing the *same* name as something else can make the original item with that name inaccessible.

This could be particularly bad if the name you choose is an essential part of the Python language, but luckily Python does not allow you to name variables after any essential parts of the language. Therefore, the next section contains an overview of the most important words used in Python, so you can avoid this problem; this is the territory that you will be exploring and learning to work with over the course of this book.

Python Keywords

The following words are the **keywords**, which form the basis of the Python language. You are not allowed to use these words to name your variables, because these are the core commands of Python. They must be spelled exactly as written here for the interpreter to recognize them as keywords. The words True, False and None have a special meaning, which will be covered later.

• False	• elif	• lambda
• None	• else	• nonlocal
• True	• except	• not
• and	• finally	• or
• as	• for	• pass
• assert	• from	• raise
• break	• global	• return
• class	• if	• try
• continue	• import	• while
• def	• in	• with
• del	• is	• yield

Following the Naming Rules

So, let's talk about what you *are* allowed to call your variables. Variable names must begin with either a letter or an underscore. Although they can contain numbers, they must not start with one. If the interpreter encounters a bunch of characters starting with a numeral, rather than a letter or a quotation mark, it will assume that it is a number.

You should not use anything other than letters, numbers, or underscores to identify your variables. Also, you should be aware that Python is generally **case-sensitive**, which means that lowercase and uppercase letters are treated as being different characters; therefore, true and True are interpreted as completely different entities, as are myvariable, MYVARIABLE, and MyVariable.

It is also a good idea to keep your own record of names you have already used. I recommend keeping a table of variables at the start of the program file, so you can easily find your list when you want to look something up.

Creating Variables and Assigning Values

In many programming languages, there are two stages to creating a variable: The first is to create the container and stick an identifying label on it; this is called initialization. The second is to put a value into it; this is called assignment. Initialization and assignment are performed with a single command in Python, using the = sign. So, you would assign a value to a variable by typing the following:

```
variable = value
```

■ **Note** Every variable has a value; there's no such thing as an empty variable in Python.

A section of code that *does* something, such as an assignment, is known as a **statement**. The part of the code that can be evaluated to produce a value is known as an **expression.** The right-hand side of an assignment can be an expression, like the assignment to total_price in the following list of simple assignment statements:

```
number = 0
roll_width = 1.4
price_per_metre = 5
filename = 'data.txt'
trace = False
sentence = "this is a whole lot of nothing"
total_price = roll_width * price_per_metre
```

Each statement should have its own line. If this looks like a shopping list to you, or a list of materials or ingredients, then you're on the right track. A recipe usually begins with a list of ingredients:

```
eggs = 2
butter = 0.5oz
salt = pinch
pepper = pinch
```

The recipe might specify a list of tools that you will need—knife, fork, bowl, frying pan—and then follow on with the method, often in numbered steps. The same happens in a Python program; you define your variables and then carry out tasks on them.

Recognizing Different Types of Variables

Python recognizes several different *types* of variables: **string literals** (words), numbers, **sequences** (lists), **mappings** (dictionaries), and **Booleans** (true or false values). These are the staple ingredients of all Python programs. The value None has a type all of its own, NoneType. The rest of this chapter will introduce you to words and numbers. However, first we need to talk about Python's dynamic typing features.

Working with Dynamic Typing

In Python, once a value has been assigned to a variable, the interpreter will then decide what sort of value it is (i.e., a number, some text, or some other relevant quality). This is known as **dynamic typing** (it has nothing to do with how many words per minute you can input from the keyboard). Unlike some other languages, it is not necessary to declare what your variables are before you use them. This is both a blessing and a curse. The main advantage is that you don't really have to worry exactly what type an item of data is, so long as it behaves the way you want it to.

Dynamic typing makes it much easier to handle different types of unpredictable user input. The interpreter can accept user input in many different forms, to which it assigns a type dynamically. This means that a single piece of code can be used to deal with words, numbers, or any other data type, and that the programmer doesn't need to decide what type the data will be in order to assign it to a variable.

Not needing to declare variables before you use them makes it tempting to introduce variables at random places in your scripts. Beware: Python won't complain unless you try to use a variable before you have actually assigned it a value, but it's really easy to lose track of what variables you are using and where you set up their values in the script.

There are two really sensible practices that will help keep you sane when you start to create large numbers of different variables. One is to set up a bunch of default values at the start of each section where you will be needing them, keeping all the variables you are going to use together in one part of the text like an ingredients list. The other is to keep track of the expected types and values of your variables, keeping a data table in your design document for each program that you are writing.

Python needs to keep track of the type of a variable for two main reasons. Chiefly, the machine needs to set aside enough memory to store the data, and different types of data take up different amounts of space, some more predictably than others. The second reason is that keeping track of types helps to avoid and troubleshoot errors. Once Python has decided what type a variable is, it will flag up a TypeError if you try to perform an inappropriate operation on that data. Although this might at first seem to be an unnecessary irritation, you will discover that this can be an incredibly useful feature of the language; as the following command-line example shows:

```
>>> b = 3
>>> c = 'word'
>>> trace = False
>>> b + c
Traceback (most recent call last):
  File "<stdin>", line 1, in <module>
TypeError: unsupported operand type(s) for +: 'int' and 'str'
>>> c - trace
Traceback (most recent call last):
  File "<stdin>", line 1, in <module>
TypeError: unsupported operand type(s) for -: 'str' and 'bool'
```

Here, I attempted to perform operations on incompatible types. You're not allowed to add a number to a word or take a yes/no answer away from it. It is necessary to convert the data to a compatible type before trying to process it. You can add words together or take numbers away from each other, just like you can in real life, but you can't do arithmetic on a line of text. The tracebacks are Python's way of alerting you to a potential error in your logic, in this case a TypeError. This tells me that I need to rewrite the code to make it clear what type of information I want to put in and get out of the equation.

The purpose of data types is to allow us to represent information that exists in the real world, that is, the world that exists outside your computer, as opposed to the virtual world inside. We can have the existential conversation about what is real and what is not some other time. The previous example uses variables of type int (whole numbers) and type str (text). It will quickly become apparent that these basic data types can only represent the simplest units of information; you may need to use quite a complicated set of words, numbers, and relationships to describe even the simplest real-world entity in virtual-world terms.

Python provides a variety of ways of combining these simple data types to create more complex data types, which I'll come to later in this book. First, you need to know about the fundamental building blocks that are used to define your data and the basic set of actions you can use to manipulate the different types of values.

In the Beginning Was the Void

Python has a special predefined value called None, which represents nothing, zilch, nada. The value None has its own type and is useful where you want to create a variable but don't want to specify its value (and therefore its type) just yet. Assigning values such as 0 or "" to a variable will create an int or str type variable. You can assign the value None like this, which produces a NoneType variable. Don't forget it starts with a capital *N*.

```
information = None
```

For the next few examples, the real world information that I'll be attempting to model in virtual form will be fantasy characters for a role-playing game. To create some continuity in my fantasy world, I need to be able to keep track of the characters' names, plus some descriptive information, such as what kind of fantasy creature each is. I also need to create some statistics to represent strength, speed, and so on, to provide some data for the combat system to use, and I need to be able to keep a record of how much money each character has. I'm sure you'll be itching to learn how to automate your accounts and database your stock records, but please try to temper your enthusiasm while I take a brief excursion in order to introduce you to the inhabitants of Cloud-Cuckoo Land.

Joining Up Text Fragments

In hello_world.py, you learned how to get some basic output by using the print() function. You can use it to print out a literal string of characters or the value of a variable. Normally, each print statement starts on a new line, but it is possible to print several values on a single line by separating them with commas; print() will then concatenate them into a single line, separated by spaces.

```
>>> Race = "Elf"
>>> Gender = "Female"
>>> print(Gender, Race)
Female Elf
```

There are many ways to combine separate pieces of information into a single line, some more efficient than others. Two adjacent strings (not separated by commas) will automatically be concatenated, but this doesn't work for variables.

```
>>> print("Male" "Gnome")
```

will give the output

```
MaleGnome
```

The following line

```
>>> print("Male" Race)
```

results in this

```
File "<stdin>", line 1
    print("Male" Race)
                 ^
SyntaxError: invalid syntax
```

This approach doesn't work for variables because writing two adjacent strings is just a different way of writing a single string. In other words, you can't write a string using a string and a variable together like this.

■ **Note** It is possible to join strings together using the + sign. In the context of strings, this is called the **concatenation operator**; an **operator** is a command that often consists of a symbol or combination of symbols, placed between two variables, known as operands, just like you would write a mathematical equation. The situation is further complicated because the + sign is also used to add numbers together, as you will see in the next section (this is called **overloading**). Using the + sign to concatenate words can slow down the execution of your program to an alarming degree. For this reason, I recommend that you don't use this method if you need to join lots of strings; some more efficient ways of joining strings together will be covered in Chapter 7.

Using Quotes

Character is the term used to describe a single letter, number, or punctuation mark. Strings of characters intended to be displayed as text are known as **string literals** or just **strings**. If you want to tell the interpreter that a block of text is meant to be displayed literally as text, you have to enclose the text in quotation marks; these can take several different forms:

```
"A text string enclosed by double quotes and all on one line."
'A text string enclosed by single quotes, all on one line again.'
'''A text string including multiple lines of text
    line breaks
    and other formatting
can be enclosed in triple quotes.
'''
"""or even:
 triple double quotes.
"""
```

```
'Single and double-quoted lines can be continued on to the next line by placing a \
(backslash) at the end of the line.'
```

■ **Note** The backslash \ escapes the new-line character, which means it tells the interpreter to ignore any special meaning that the next character might have. All the unescaped characters after that are treated normally.

A value created using text in quotes will be given the type str (string).

Nesting Quotes

Sometimes, you will want to include literal quotation marks within your text. It is possible to nest quotes. That is, have one set of quotation marks inside another, so long as you use a different sort of quotation mark, like this:

```
>>> text = "She quoted 'the rules' at him"
```

In this instance, the interpreter will assume that it has reached the end of the text when it hits the second double quote ", so the substring 'the rules' is considered to be part of the main string including the single quotes. This way, you can only have one level of nested quotes. Inside triple quotes, """ or ''', it is possible to use both normal single and double quotes without confusing things; the interpreter will wait until the second set of triple quotes before it decides that the string has come to an end. The best way to understand how they work is to experiment with assigning and printing out lots of different sorts of strings.

```
>>> boilerplate = """
... #===(")===#===(*)===#===(")===#
... Egregious Response Generator
... Version '0.1'
... "FiliBuster" technologies inc.
... #===(")===#===(*)===#===(")===#
... """
>>> print(boilerplate)

#===(")===#===(*)===#===(")===#
Egregious Response Generator
Version '0.1'
"FiliBuster" technologies inc.
#===(")===#===(*)===#===(")===#
```

This can be very useful if you want to format a whole page or block of text. In Chapter 7, I'll be looking at more sophisticated methods of string formatting.

Escaping Sequences

There will be times when nesting different types of quotes will not be sufficient; in those cases, you can include further literal quotation marks by escaping them, so \' or \". If you need to print a literal backslash, you have to escape the backslash itself, like this: \\.

The input() function, which I used to get user input in hello_word.py, stores the string with extra escapes where necessary, so the string will print out exactly the way it was typed.

```
>>> variable = input('Type something in: ')
Type something in: String, with lot\'s of \bad\ punct-uation (in it);
>>> variable
"String, with lot\\'s of \\bad\\ punct-uation (in it);"
>>> print(variable)
String, with lot\'s of \bad\ punct-uation (in it);
```

Using Special Whitespace Characters

It is also possible to specify whitespace characters using a character sequence that begins with a backslash, as shown in Table 3-1. \n produces a linefeed (LF) character; this is subtly different from the \r carriage return (CR): On a mechanical typewriter, the linefeed would just give you a new line, while the carriage return would properly start a new paragraph. One of the instances where you might need to know the difference is translating text files from one operating system to another: OS X uses the CR character at the end of lines, whereas Unix and Linux use the LF character, and Windows uses both.

The meaning and usage of some of these sequences is somewhat lost in the mists of time. Mostly, you'll want to use the \n escape. The other most useful one is \t, which produces a tab character that can be useful for quick-and-dirty indentation of text. Most of the other whitespace characters are only likely to be useful in very specialized situations (see Table 3-1).

Table 3-1. *Escape Sequences*

Sequence	Meaning
\n	Newline (LF)
\r	Carriage return (CR)
\t	Tab
\v	Vertical tab (VT)
\e	Escape character (ESC)
\f	Formfeed (FF)
\b	Backspace
\a	Bell (BEL)

The following example allows you to nicely format your output for the screen:

```
>>> print("Example Heading\n\nFollowed by a line\nor two of text\n \
... \tName\n\tRace\n\tGender\nDon\'t forget to escape \'\\\'."
)
```

```
Example Heading


Followed by a line

or two of text

    Name

    Race

    Gender

Don't forget to escape '\'.
```

The More Strings Change the More They Stay the Same

The other thing you need to know about strings is that they are **immutable**; this means they can't be changed. In practice, it is possible to use some fairly simple functions to create a new string with an edited value.

Creating a Text Application

It's time to put all this information into practice on our role-playing game example. Strings are quite simple to use; for the most part, you just need to make sure that you enclose your strings in matching quotes properly. The top-level design for an RPG character-description generator script is correspondingly simple.

```
# Prompt user for user-defined information
# Output the character sheet
```

The minimum information I need is a name for each character. I'd also like to keep a note of each person's gender and fantasy race, and I'd like some space for a short description, so I have created variables named Name, Desc, Gender, and Race to hold each of those values as a string. I can then print out those values in a pretty format using the print() function, as shown in Listing 3-1.

Listing 3-1. *chargen.py*

```
"""
chargen.py
Problem: Generate a description for a fantasy role-playing character.
Target Users: Me and my friends
Target System: GNU/Linux
Interface: Command-line
Functional Requirements: Print out the character sheet
            User must be able to input the character's
            name, description, gender and race
Testing: Simple run test
Maintainer: maintainer@website.com
"""

__version__ = 0.1

Name = ""
Desc = ""
Gender = ""
Race = ""

# Prompt user for user-defined information
Name = input('What is your Name? ')
Desc = input('Describe yourself: ')
Gender = input('What Gender are you? (male / female / unsure): ')
Race = input('What fantasy Race are you? - (Pixie / Vulcan / Gelfling / Troll): ')

# Output the character sheet
fancy_line = "<~~==|#|==~~++**\@/**++~~==|#|==~~>"
print("\n", fancy_line)
print("\t", Name)
print("\t", Race, Gender)
print("\t", Desc)
print(fancy_line, "\n")
```

Listing 3-1 is just a fancy version of hello_world, but the output looks a bit more exciting. You can run this from the command line in the same way; you will see all the values you enter displayed as a character sheet and formatted by the escape sequences.

```
$ python chargen.py
```

■ **Note** If you are in a different directory to your script, you will have to supply the full path to its location.

The one new thing I've added is the line __version__ = 0.1 at the beginning. This is a **magic variable**: the name __version__ (with two underscores on either side) is a predefined variable with a special meaning to Python's documentation tools. For now, I'm just going to use this to record the version number of this program; as I edit and refine the design, I will increment this number.

Next, I need to generate some vital statistics to represent the different attributes that the characters will need to interact with the game world. This involves tackling the realm of numerical information.

Working with Numbers

First, assigning numbers to variables is fairly straightforward:

```
muscle = 10
brainz = 4
```

As I mentioned earlier, if the interpreter encounters a bunch of characters starting with a numeral, rather than a letter or a quotation mark, it will assume that it is a number. This is why you can't start variable names with a number. So far, so good. There are a few things that you need to know before you start trying to do math with computers.

Using Binary: Computers Can Only Count to One

All information is stored inside the computer as a series of ones and zeros, that is, in **binary** or base 2. Your computer stores and processes data using a huge collection of tiny little switches, and these switches can be either off (0) or on (1). This has led to the old programmers' joke that "there are only 10 sorts of people in the world—those who understand binary and those who don't" (10 in binary notation represents two rather than ten).

Using Python, you don't really need to know much more than this.

Bits and Bytes

You will frequently encounter the terms bits and bytes in computer literature. Bit is short for "binary digit" and refers to one of these tiny switches that can only hold a "yes" or "no" answer. It is the smallest possible unit of computer information. A byte is theoretically the amount of memory needed to store a single character; this became standardized as 8 bits during the late twentieth century, even though modern computers often use more than 8 bits to store characters.

Using Booleans: Truth or Dare

It follows from the preceding discussion that the simplest type of numerical value that exists on a computer is one that has only two possible values: True (equal to 1) or False (equal to 0). These true/false values are known as **Booleans**, named after a system devised by English mathematician and philosopher, George Boole. They can be manipulated using logical operators such as AND, OR, and NOT. I'll explain the meaning and use of these operators in Chapter 4. You can assign Boolean values by using the True and False keywords:

```
beauty = True
illusion = False
```

■ **Note** True and False are always spelled with capital first letters.

Using Whole Numbers (Integers)

Whole numbers are known as **integers** in programming terms. Integers don't have decimal points but can be positive, negative, or zero. These are used to refer to numbers of things in much the way you'd expect, like the eggs in the recipe example at the start of the chapter. It may be reassuring to know that most of the time you can use numbers like these.

Performing Basic Mathematical Operations

You have learned how to store data inside variables, so let's start manipulating that data. Integers can be added, subtracted, and multiplied, the same as in the real world using the +, -, and * **operators** (the * is the multiply sign). This creates an expression. An **expression** is a piece of code that has to be evaluated (i.e., worked out) before you can discover its value. You can assign expressions to variables using statements like this:

```
>>> muscle = 2 + 3
>>> brainz = 7 - 3
>>> speed = 5 * -4
>>> strangeness = muscle + brainz * speed
>>> strangeness
-75
```

■ **Note** When you are using Python in interactive mode, you don't need to use the print() function to see the value of a variable. You will need print() if you want to get output from a script.

All this works much as expected until the last line, where strangeness equals –75. How did that happen? Surely 5 + 4 = 9, multiplied by –20 would give –180? But no, what happens here is this:

```
(2+3) + ((7-3) * (-4*5))
```

How does Python decide that the arguments to the + are muscle and brainz*speed rather than just muscle and brainz? What happens here is that Python works out the arguments to * before it works out the arguments to +, and it picks as these arguments the smallest bits of the expression that make sense, in this case, brainz and speed. The multiplication operator * is said to **bind tighter** than +, the addition operator.

Understanding Operator Precedence

What you have just seen is an example of something much more general: given an expression to evaluate, how does the Python interpreter decide which parts go with what, and how can you know what its decision is going to be? The answer is that there is a predefined order called **operator precedence**, which tells the interpreter which operators bind tightest. To see this order, you can look in the python documentation at http://docs.python.org/3.0/reference/expressions.html#evaluation-order, or if you're unsure for a particular pair of operators, have a go in the interpreter with some values that will let you distinguish the precedence: you can see from the output of 5 + 4 * –20 previously that * binds tighter than +.

If you want the arguments to be grouped in a different way from Python's default, you can get this to happen using brackets, so in this example, you would type the following:

```
>>> charm = (muscle + brainz) * speed
>>> charm
-180
```

Dividing Numbers

Division is performed using the / operator.

```
>>> print(13 / 5)
2.6
>>> print(13.75 / 4.25)
3.23529411765
```

If you want to do integer division, where the fractional part of the answer is dropped (also known as floor division), you can use the // operator instead of /. The remainder is obtainable by using the modulo % operator.

```
>>> print(13 // 5)
2
>>> print(13 % 5)
3
```

You may encounter results you don't expect when doing integer division with negative numbers:

```
>>> print(-13 // 5)
-3
>>> print(-13 % 5)
2
```

This is because floor division returns the largest whole number that is less than the result of the fractional division. So, –13/5 is –2.6 and the largest whole number less than –2.6 is –3. Now consider the remainder: the result of // multiplied by the divisor gives us the figure to work from to calculate the remainder, as it would in all other remainder calculations:

```
-13 = -3 * 5 + remainder
```

Consider another example:

```
>>> print(-13 // -5)
2
>>> print(-13 % -5)
-3
```

Here, 2 is the largest whole number less than 2.6, and –3 is calculated as follows:

```
-13 = 2 * -5 + remainder
```

Alternatively, you could avoid using this operator with negative numbers.

Working with Fractions and Floats

Fractional numbers are expressed using numbers before and after a decimal point using the float type. Like integers, these numbers can be positive or negative. You don't have to do anything particularly special to assign a float to a variable; if you use a decimal point in the number, Python will assume that it's a float.

```
muscle = 2.9
brainz = -13.678
speed = 0.0
```

Even if the part after the decimal point is zero, the number is considered to be a float. Floats can be manipulated using the same operators as integers, returning any fractional part as well.

Converting One Type into Another

Python has several convenient built-in functions that allow you to convert values from one type to another. These are the most useful ones to start with:

- int(x) converts number x to an integer.
- float(x) converts number x to a float.
- str(object) converts more or less anything into a printable string.

Functions have a very different syntax from operators: the value to be acted upon goes inside the brackets after the function name:

```
>>> float(23)
23.0
>>> int(23.5)
23

>>> float(int(23.5))
23
```

There are a few gotchas when it comes to converting types; notice that float(int(x)) in the preceding example loses its fractional part. Not all conversions are reversible, and the result of the conversion may not be equal to the input value any more.

Working with Base 8 (Octal) and Base 16 (Hexadecimal)

It is possible to input and display integers in other formats such as base 16 (hexadecimal) or base 8 (octal). Integers can be entered in octal form by putting a 0o in front of the octal number (that's the number zero followed by the letter o) and in hexadecimal by putting 0x (zero followed by x) in front of the hexadecimal number. In hexadecimal, you use the letters A to F to represent the decimal numbers 10 to 15.

```
>>> octal_number = 0o12
>>> hexadecimal_number = 0xFC6
>>> print(octal_number)
10
>>> print(hexadecimal_number)
4038
```

Let's break things down to see what's going on here. In a decimal number, the positions of the digits represent: units, tens, hundreds, thousands and so on—in reverse order. In hexadecimal and octal numbers, the positions represent exponents of the numerical base. In octal, these positions would represent units, 8s and 64s, for example, because 8 is the numerical base of octal.

You can work out the decimal value by multiplying the digits according to the value of their position and adding the results together, as shown in Tables 3-2, 3-3, and 3-4. The first row in these tables is the value of the position in the number, the second the multiplication sign to show that the value of the position is multiplied by the digit in that position, the third the number in question, and the fourth the results of the multiplication. Table 3-2 shows a decimal to give you the idea.

Table 3-2. Decimal 2037

1000		100		10		1		
*		*						
2		0		3		7		
2000	+	0	+	30	+	7	=	2037 (decimal)

Table 3-3. *Octal 0o3765*

512		64		8		1		
*		*						
3		7		6		5		
1536	+	448	+	48	+	5	=	2037 (decimal)

Table 3-4. *Hexadecimal 0x7F5*

256		16		1		
*		*				
7		F (15)		5		
1792	+	240	+	5	=	2037 (decimal)

All three representations give 2037 as the resultant decimal value. Octals are encountered in situations such as specifying file permissions and hexadecimals are used to specify colors, so it's worth familiarizing yourself with this notation if you have not encountered it before.

```
>>> permissions = 0o755
>>> gold = 0xFFCC00
```

The octal number assigned to permissions is an array of information where each bit has a distinct meaning: each octal digit sets read, write, and execute permissions for the user, group, and others respectively. The color value set for gold represents a mix of three values, red, green, and blue, which can range from 0x00 to 0xFF according to intensity.

It's important to note that there is only one integer type here: what you get when you enter 0x10, 0o20, or 16 is exactly the same integer. If you want to get back the hexadecimal or octal string representation of an integer, you can use the following functions.

- hex(x) displays integer x in hexadecimal format.
- oct(x) displays integer x in octal format.

```
>>> x = 0xaa + 0x33
>>> hex(x)
'0xdd'
>>> o = 0o77 + 0o33
>>> oct(o)
'0o132'
```

Creating a Number Application

In order to take the character generation script any further, you will need to be able to compare values and store the results. This will require knowledge of conditional statements (which I will move on to in Chapter 4) and the use of more complex data types (see Chapter 5), so I will return to Cloud-Cuckoo Land once you have had time to study these more advanced incantations. To demonstrate the use of mathematical data types right now, let's consider a simpler problem: calculating how much fabric you would need to buy to make a pair of curtains.

To start, you need to define the problem again: calculate how much material to buy, given the size of the windows. The functional requirements are that the user must be able to input the measurements of the window and get back the required length of fabric in meters and the total price of the fabric to be bought. To get a proper idea of how you might go about making a pair of curtains, you might want to talk to real curtain makers, watch them in action, or at least get them to show you how they calculate the amount of material they need. It might also be worth investigating your local fabric shop.

Following some research, my top-level design looked like this:

```
# Prompt the user to input the window measurements in cm
# Add a bit for the hems
# Work out how many widths of cloth will be needed
# and figure out the total length of material for each curtain (in cm still)
# Actually there are two curtains, so we must double the amount of material
# and then divide by 10 to get the number of meters
# Finally, work out how much it will cost
# And print out the result
```

Before any calculation is possible, you will need to know how wide the roll of material is and how much it costs per meter. I have assumed a width of 140 cm and a price of 5 units of currency per meter for this example. I can use the input() function to get the window_height and window_width from the user. The input() function returns a string, so I need to convert that into something Python recognizes as a number using float(). Once I have assigned the four starting values as suitable types, the calculation that follows is fairly straightforward as explained in the comments of Listing 3-2.

Listing 3-2. *curtains.py*

```
"""
curtains.py
Problem: Calculate how much material to buy, given the size of the windows.
Target Users: My friend who wants to make some curtains
Target System: GNU/Linux
Interface: Command-line
Functional Requirements: Print out the required length of fabric in meters
            Print out the total price of the fabric
            User must be able to input the measurements of the window
Testing: Simple run test
Maintainer: maintainer@website.com
"""
```

```python
__version__ = 0.1

# To start with, all the measurements will be in cm
# Assume that the roll of material is going to be 140cm wide
# and that the price per meter will be 5 units of currency
roll_width = 140
price_per_metre = 5

# Prompt the user to input the window measurements in cm
window_height = input('Enter the height of the window (cm): ')
window_width = input('Enter the width of the window (cm): ')

# Add a bit for the hems
# First we must convert the string into a number
# otherwise we will get an error if we try to perform arithmetic on a text string
curtain_width = float(window_width) * 0.75 + 20
curtain_length = float(window_height) + 15

# Work out how many widths of cloth will be needed
# and figure out the total length of material for each curtain (in cm still)
widths = curtain_width / roll_width
total_length = curtain_length * widths

# Actually there are two curtains, so we must double the amount of material
# and then divide by 10 to get the number of meters
total_length = (total_length * 2) / 10

# Finally, work out how much it will cost
price = total_length * price_per_metre

# And print out the result
print("You need", total_length, "meters of cloth for ", price)
```

Any of you who have actually set about making curtains will know that this is a gross oversimplification of the process. Those of you who can add numbers better than I can will realize that I have made a couple of dumb mathematical errors, so this script will return some crazy values, which won't be of much use. Clearly, this is going to need some work, so let's examine the problems.

Unless the width of each curtain is less than the roll_width, you will end up buying much more fabric than you need. However, there is no way of working this out until you know what the initial window measurements are. If the length of the curtains is less than the roll_width, you could turn the whole thing on its side and just use one width of fabric (I'm assuming you're using unpatterned fabric). But if the curtains need to be both longer and wider than the roll_width, there is a problem: if the extra material required is less than half the roll_width, you would need to buy an additional width of material at the same length; if it is more than half, you would need to buy two additional widths, taking into account the extra material needed for the joins. Still with me? Good. The script needs to take into account that fabric is sold by the meter (or half-meters) in whole widths, so I will need to round up the widths to the nearest whole number and the final length to the nearest meter.

To deal with this using Python, it will be necessary to compare values and then execute different calculations based on those conditions. This, incidentally, is what the next chapter is all about.

Jargon Busting

You encountered a lot of new terms in this chapter, so here are some more useful definitions:

- *Binary (base 2)*: Binary arithmetic uses the digits 0 and 1. This corresponds to the electric current in a wire, which can only be on (value 1) or off (value 0)

- *Bit*: A bit is a digit in the binary number system. It can have two values, 0 or 1. The word is derived from *binary digit*.

- *Boolean*: Variables of this type can take only one of two values, True and False. These correspond to 1 and 0. This is the most appropriate return type for a function that uses its return value to report whether some condition holds or not.

- *Built-in*: Anything built-in is innate part of the programming language, as opposed to something that has to be imported from a module. A built-in element is part of Python's standard library.

- *Byte*: A byte is the smallest unit of storage that can be accessed in a computer's memory. It holds exactly 8 bits.

- *Case-sensitive*: In case-sensitive text, uppercase letters are treated as completely different characters from their lowercase counterparts. Treating uppercase and lowercase variants as the same character is known as **case-insensitive**.

- *Characters*: These are letters, digits, punctuation marks, and spaces—basically anything that can be typed in using a single key on the keyboard, even if it doesn't cause anything to be printed on the screen.

- *Concatenate*: When you create a string by joining together copies of two or more text strings without any spaces in between, you concatenate the string.

- *Decimal (base 10)*: Decimal numbers are what you probably think of as normal numbers.

- *Dynamic typing*: Python determines the type and checks the correct usage of variables of different types during execution of a program rather than during compilation. Some other programming languages, like C, are **statically typed**: the compiler will not allow the use of a variable or function unless that function or variable has already been initialized and declared to be of a certain type. You don't need to bother with declaring the type of your variables in Python.

- *Expression*: This refers to a section of code that can be worked out to produce a value.

- *Flag*: A flag is a Boolean variable used to record whether or not something has happened.

- *Float*: Float is short for "floating point" and is a fundamental type used to define numbers with fractional parts.

- *Hexadecimal (base 16)*: Hexadecimal is base 16 arithmetic where each digit is a value from 0 to 15, rather than the 0 to 9 of base 10. The decimal numbers from 10 to 15 are represented by the letters A to F. Hexadecimal is a very convenient way of showing binary numbers, as every four binary digits can be shown as one hexadecimal digit.

- *Integer*: An integer is a fundamental (i.e., built-in) type used to define numeric variables holding whole numbers.

- *Immutable*: An immutable value cannot be modified.

- *Logical operator*: These commands perform basic manipulations on Boolean values.

- *Mapping*: In Python, a mapping is a data type that relates a set of keys to a set of values. It has nothing to do with planning your car journey.

- *Octal (base 8)*: In octal arithmetic, each digit has a value of 0 to 7.

- *Operator*: These are commands, often represented by mathematical symbols, that perform simple manipulations on data, known as **operands**. Expressions take the following form: operand1 operation operand2.

- *Operator precedence*: This is the order in which operators are assigned their arguments when Python evaluates an expression. Where there is ambiguity, the operator with the higher precedence is assigned as arguments the smallest expressions on either side of it that make sense.

- *Sequence*: In Python, a sequence is an instance of a data type that consists of more than a single item. It does not refer to a series of statements to be executed one after another as in some other languages.

- *Statement*: This refers to a section of code that *does* something such as manipulate a piece of data, perform a calculation, or produce some output.

- *String literal*: This refers to words and sentences, and text composed of these, that is, any form of literal text.

- *Truth testing*: Evaluate whether a condition is True or False.

Summary

In this chapter, you have learned how to assign different types of values to variables, how to manipulate simple text strings and perform basic mathematical operations using expressions and statements. Now, you know how to construct and run a simple Python script that can perform a useful calculation. In the next chapter, I will show you how to make decisions that can alter the way the program runs based on those calculations.

CHAPTER 4

■ ■ ■

Making Choices

So far, you have learned how to enter commands and information and get some output returned, using fundamental data types: text strings, numbers, and Booleans. You have learned how to use Python as a pocket calculator, but most importantly, you have learned how to start designing your own software. Now, it is time to begin the process of refining your designs. As you learn more about Python and practice your logic juggling skills, you are likely to find simpler and more effective ways of coding your designs, and you will want to update your old scripts. This is a normal and natural part of the process of program design and a good discipline to develop early on.

Following this train of thought, in this chapter we're going to see some techniques to improve our previous work. I'll explain how to compare values in your code so that you can make decisions and take appropriate actions based on the comparison. This approach to controlling the flow of your application will allow your applications to be more flexible and able to deal with changing input. With this flexibility, however, comes complexity, so I'll go over how to manage increasingly complex code.

The final part of the chapter covers loops, which are another way to alter the flow of your application. With loops, you can iterate over a large set of data and perform the same operations on each member of the set.

Comparing Things

The curtain-making exercise at the end of the previous chapter needs some **refining**. It is too simplistic to provide accurate answers and contains some logical errors that need fixing. In order to generate more accurate answers, you need to know how to compare values and specify different courses of action based on the results. The code construction that allows us to do this is called a **conditional statement**. Conditional statements transform the script from being just a list of instructions to something that can make decisions on the fly based on the information that it receives. It would be useful to be able to tell the program to perform different actions according to whether certain conditions are satisfied. You could write this out in pseudocode like this:

```
if one condition is true:
        then perform one set of actions;
if another condition is true:
        then perform another set of actions.
```

Each if-then pair is a conditional statement. Before we get into that, let's look at how to specify conditions.

Values can be compared using the following **comparison operators**:

- <: Less than
- <=: Less than or equal
- >: Greater than
- >=: Greater than or equal
- ==: Equal
- !=: Not equal

These affect the fundamental data types in different ways, each time giving us an answer of True or False. **Operands** are the bits of data on the left and right of the operator in an expression. The operands on either side of the comparison operator must be of types that can be compared. The operands and the comparison operator together are a conditional expression.

Python might not throw an error if you compare illogical types, so it is a good idea to test your conditional expressions thoroughly and check the data that goes into them. The results obtained from comparing numbers using conditional expressions in interactive mode are fairly self-explanatory.

```
>>> -2 < 5
True
>>> 49 > 37
True
>>> 7.65 != 6.0
True
>>> -5 <= -2
True
>>> 7 < -7
False
>>> 23.5 > 37.75
False
>>> -5 >= 5
False
>>> 3.2 != 3.2
False
```

You can also create conditional expressions using variables.

```
>>> variable = 3.0
>>> variable == 3
True
```

■ **Caution** The single equals sign (=) assigns a value, whereas the double equals sign (==) compares two values and returns True if they are *equal in value*. These two operations are commonly confused in the early stages of learning programming. If you use the assignment operator when you mean to compare two values, you will probably get a syntax error. If you use a comparison operator when you intended to assign a value, the statement may well silently fail, and you won't find out about it until you get some weird value occurring later on in the execution of your script.

Also, strings can be compared alphabetically using the same comparison operators:

```
>>> "alpha" < "omega"
True
>>> "case" == "Case"
False
>>> "net" < "network"
True
>>> "Same" != "Same"
False
```

Notice that uppercase characters don't count the same as their lowercase counterparts. All of the uppercase letters come before any of the lowercase. If you are not familiar with this method of sorting, the order is laid out in Figure 4-1.

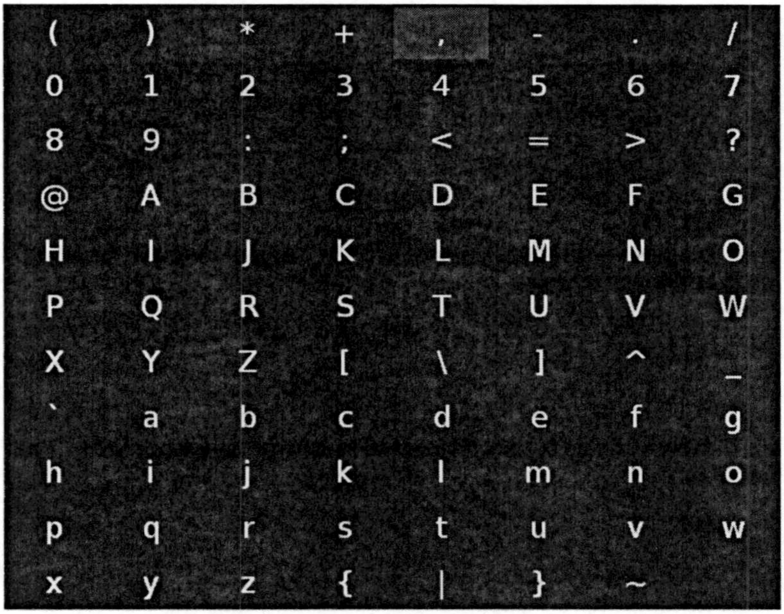

(	)	*	+	,	-	.	/
0	1	2	3	4	5	6	7
8	9	:	;	<	=	>	?
@	A	B	C	D	E	F	G
H	I	J	K	L	M	N	O
P	Q	R	S	T	U	V	W
X	Y	Z	[	\	]	^	_
`	a	b	c	d	e	f	g
h	i	j	k	l	m	n	o
p	q	r	s	t	u	v	w
x	y	z	{	|	}	~	

Figure 4-1. Case-sensitive alphabetical ordering

If you want to compare strings according to their lengths, you would need to use the built-in len() function.

```
>>> len("alpha") < len("omega")
False
>>> len("case") == len("Case")
True
>>> len("net") < len("network")
True
>>> len("Same") != len("Same")
False
```

Manipulating Boolean Values

Before moving on to conditional structures, no discussion of fundamental data types would be complete without covering the manipulation of True and False values (recall from Chapter 3 that these are called Boolean values). This used to be the subject with which computer students began their education, and as it is essential to understanding the way computers work, I won't skip the details.

While I'm sorting things, I may as well organize my audio and video collection. I started off by creating a bunch of Boolean values to represent various bits of information about my collection. Here I set the values of a particular CD:

```
>>> is_emo = True

>>> is_country = False

>>> is_techno = False

>>> is_CD = True

>>> is_DVD = False
```

This is a task in which I may need to make several comparisons at once. I might want to be notified if the album is a particular genre, such as emo or country.

```
>>> is_emo or is_country
```

```
True
```

The or operator will return True if either variable is true. If I wanted to narrow my search to find out if an item is a techno CD, I would use and.

```
>>> is_techno and is_CD
```

```
False
```

Both conditions have to be true for and to return True. If you want to be totally contrary and test whether the opposite of a condition holds true, use not. This will return True if the value you are testing is false; otherwise, it will return False.

```
>>> not is_techno
```

True

```
>>> not is_techno and not is_DVD
```

True

All these comparisons boil down to a single True or False answer, which can then be used to tell the program in which direction to go next. Boolean operators have a lower precedence than all the other mathematical operations: not first, then and, and or last. This means that in the preceding example, the expression is actually evaluated as if it is bracketed like this:

```
(not is_techno) and (not is_DVD)
```

Comparisons can be used to set flag variables. A flag is used to record whether an event happened or a test was passed, so that information can be used later on in the program.

```
>>> is_cool = not is_techno and not is_country and not is_emo
```

Combining Conditional Expressions

Conditional expressions can be combined to produce relatively complex conditions using the logical operators, and and or. For example, we can check if two conditions are true:

```
(var1 < 6) and (var2 > 7)
```

This will return True only if var1 is less than 6 and var2 is greater than 7. We can also use or:

```
(var1 < 6) or (var2 > 7)
```

This returns True if either of the conditions are satisfied.

Using Assignment Operators

You are already familiar with the basic **assignment operator** (=), which you use when you want to put a value into a variable. Python allows you to use some neat typing and time-saving tricks with assignments. The humble equals sign can unpack sequences, which will be covered fully in the next chapter. The simplest form of this can unpack a string into its constituent characters.

```
>>> char1, char2, char3 = 'cat'
>>> char1
'c'
>>> char2
'a'
>>> char3
't'
```

In addition, you can swap the values of two variables using the following technique:

```
height, length = length, height
```

You can also assign the same value to several different variables.

```
x = y = z = 1
```

The assignment operator can be used in conjunction with most arithmetic operators to modify a variable in place. For example, you could type

```
counter += 1
```

which is the same as `counter = counter + 1`. Some other possible combinations are `-=`, `*=`, `/=`, which decrease the value of the variable by the specified amount, multiply the value of the variable by the specified amount, and divide the value of the variable by the specified amount.

Understanding Operator Precedence

As discussed in the previous chapter, the order in which you use operators *does* matter. The best way to avoid confusion or unwanted results in your scripts is to use parentheses to dictate which order the subexpressions should be evaluated.

```
>>> 2 + 3 * 6 + 4 / 2 + 3
```

25.0

```
>>> (2 + 3) * (6 + 4) / (2 + 3)
```

10.0

```
>>> 2 + (3 * (6 + 4) / 2) + 3
```

20.0

The interpreter will evaluate the expression in the innermost set of brackets first. Otherwise, operators will be evaluated in the order shown in Table 4-1, which includes some additional operators that will be discussed later in this book. The important thing to note here is that arithmetical operators have a higher precedence than comparison operators, so the sums are done first, before they are compared, and only then are the effects of not, and, and or evaluated. Expressions that are equal in precedence are evaluated from left to right, except for comparisons, which are chained: `2 + 3 + 4` evaluates as `(2 + 3) + 4`, but `2 < 3 < 4` evaluates as `(2 < 3)` and `(3 < 4)`.

Table 4-1. *Operator Precedence*

Operator	Description
,, [...], {...}, and `...`	Creates a tuple, list, and dictionary and converts a string
s[i], s[i:j], s.attr, and f(...)	Indexes and slices, assigns attributes, and calls functions
x**y	Elevates to the power of
+x, -x, and ~x	Performs unary operations
x*y, x/y, and x%y	Performs multiplication, division, and modulo operations
x+y and x-y	Performs addition and subtraction
x<y, x<=y, x>y, x>=y, x==y, and x!=y	Makes comparisons
x is y and x is not y	Ascertains identity
x in s and x not in s	Ascertains membership
not x	Performs Boolean negation
x and y	Returns True if both x and y are True. Returns False otherwise.
x or y	Returns True if either x or y are True. Returns False if both x and y are False.

Taking Control of the Process

Sometimes, you need to make a choice about what happens next during the execution of the program using what is known as a control flow statement. In your scripts, you can now use the results of comparisons to create conditional statements. They are a form of control flow statement that allow different actions to be performed based on whether certain conditions hold true. In Python, conditional statements are constructed using the if, elif, and else keywords. If you are used to other languages, you will notice that Python doesn't use the keyword then. The syntax for conditional statements is very specific, so pay close attention to the punctuation and layout:

```
if condition:
    # Perform some actions
    print "Condition is True"
elif condition != True:
    # Perform some other actions
    print "Condition is not True"
else:
    # Perform default or fall-through actions
    print "Anomaly: Condition is neither True nor False"
```

Here, the first line begins with the keyword if, which must be followed with a conditional expression that gives a True or False answer and a colon (:). The colon could be considered to mean *then*.

It is not usually considered good style to explicitly state condition == True; if whatever condition is gives a value of True or False, you can simply write if condition: or elif not condition:. This advice particularly applies to Boolean variables, but don't forget you can perform comparisons on anything because anything in Python evaluates to either True or False.

■ **Note** Variables assigned values such as " ", 0, or None will return False if you test them as shown previously. Any number is True.

The statements that follow must start on a new line and be indented. The number of spaces doesn't strictly matter so long as all the instructions after the colon are indented by the same amount, though it's good practice to use the same number of spaces to indicate control flow throughout your code. The statements following after the colon are known as a **suite**.

You can include further conditional sections using the elif keyword (an abbreviation of *else-if*, which is not a Python keyword); statements following elif will be evaluated only if the previous test fails (i.e., the conditional expression is False).

You can also include a final else: statement, which will catch any value that did not satisfy any of the conditions; it doesn't take any conditional expression at all. This can be used to specify a default set of actions to perform. In our previous example, things would have to go very wrong for us to ever see the final anomaly warning, as the preceding if and elif statements would have caught either of the two possible results. It is possible to nest if statements to allow for more possibilities, and you can leave out the elif or else statements if you don't want anything to happen unless the condition is satisfied. In other words, sometimes you want to do something if a condition is satisfied but do nothing if it is not satisfied.

After the final statement, the indentation must go back to its original level: this will indicate to the interpreter that the conditional block has come to an end. Python marks out blocks of code using indentation alone; it doesn't use punctuation marks like the curly braces you may see in other languages. This unique feature of Python means you have to be extra careful about indentation. If you do get it wrong, you'll find out soon enough, as the interpreter will complain loudly.

```
>>> if c:
...     print(c)
...     c += 1
...   indent = "bad"
  File "<stdin>", line 4
    indent = "bad"
             ^
IndentationError: unindent does not match any outer indentation level
```

Conditional statements provide a powerful way of checking that your data is what you expect it to be; this is called **validation**. Validation is usually performed when the data is first fed into the computer and also when that information is written out to a file or database record. Checks could include making sure that all boxes have been ticked and all questions answered, that the input contains the correct number of characters of the correct type and format, that numbers are within a specified range, and that the information is consistent with other records.

Testing and validation are such important parts of programming that I'll be presenting several ways of doing it at various levels of sophistication over the course of this book.

Dealing with Logical Errors

As your applications become more complex, you will need more formal methods of testing your designs. One of the ways of doing this is to construct a **trace table**, like the one shown in Table 4-2. I'm going to use this method to get some clues as to what is wrong with curtains.py.

To find out what is up with the script, I am going to **trace** the values of all the variables and conditional expressions over the course of the program's execution. The variable names and test conditions form the headers of the table columns and each step is given a new line.

Table 4-2. *Trace Table Template*

	var1	var2	condition1	condition2
step2		x		
step4				x

A trace should be performed with as many different sets of data as is necessary to make sure that all the possible alternatives get tested. Most errors in programming don't occur if the values lie within some expected range, but they often occur for unusual values (also called **critical values**). Critical values are values that lie outside the tolerances of the program, such a number that the application is not equipped to deal with.

Critical values should be worked out early on in the design process, so that the program can be properly tested against them. In my curtain calculation, the value that most needs taking into account is that of the roll_width, which has been set at 140 cm. Allowing 20 cm for hems means that the maximum width of curtain I can make out of a single length is 120 cm before I have to start thinking about sewing widths together. Each curtain has to be three-fourths of the width of the window, so the maximum width of window I can cover with two single widths of material (one for each curtain) is 160 cm. If the window is 320 cm wide, I will need four widths to cover the window, and if I were really clever, I could probably do a 240-cm-wide window with three widths.

If the window is much wider than it is deep, it might be possible to turn the cloth the other way. Allowing for a 15-cm hem, it would be possible to do this if the window_height was less than 125 cm. To represent these different conditions, I could use a set of arbitrary values for the window size, such as 100×100, 100×200, 200×100, 200×200, 200×300, and 300×200.

I also need to work out some expected results for these values by hand, so I can find out whether they tally up with the script's output:

- The first case (100×100 cm) could be measured either way against the material width; each curtain needs a piece of material 1.15×0.95 m, due to the allowance needed for hemming. I would need 2.3 m of material if I measured it lengthways, but I would use less material if I measured it along the width, which would give 1.9 m. I know the roll of material is 1.4 m wide (I will probably want to round the length up to the nearest half-meter when I go to buy it).

- In the second case (100×200 cm), each curtain needs to be 150 cm wide (0.75×200). However, because that is greater than the material width, I will have to allow an extra 20 cm for the join as well as 20 cm for the hems, making 190 cm, so each curtain has to be 1.15×1.9 m. If I measure the material lengthways, I would need 4.6 m. But I could get away with measuring it along the width, so 3.8 m would be the minimum length required.

- If the window is twice as deep as it is wide (200×100 cm), it would only make sense to measure it lengthways, giving an answer of 4.3 m.

- The fourth case (200×200 cm) is interesting, because either way round, it requires two widths of material. Measuring it along with width would seem more efficient (requiring only 6.8 m of material), except that I will end up with a very funny looking pair of curtains with a horizontal seam in the middle. By measuring lengthways, I could get away with only buying three lengths of cloth, which would give a measurement of 6.45 m.

- I can't use this material to make curtains in the fifth case (200×300 cm): each curtain has to be 2.15×2.25 m, so I would need 8.6 m of cloth to make a pair of curtains to fit a window measuring 2×3 m.

- However, if the measurements were reversed (300×200 cm), I could get away with only 9.45 m using the same method as the fourth case for the last case. It would make the logic much simpler, however, to decide that horizontal seams are going to look ugly and go and buy 12.6 m of material to do this window.

This analysis brings up a couple of issues, which I want to bear in mind as I refine the design. First, it doesn't look like measuring material along the width is going to provide many advantage unless the window is wider than it is deep and less than 1.25 m deep and unless the material has no pattern. One of the programming decisions I now need to make is whether to bother pursuing an option to measure material along its width at all. Second, there is a minor issue of accuracy; I actually need an answer rounded up to the nearest half-meter. This only really applies to the final output, as the figures used in the calculations need to keep their fractional parts to maintain accuracy.

Now, let's see how this compares to the trace produced by the existing calculations. The simplest way to create a trace table is to insert a bunch of print statements into your code, as you can see in Listing 4-1.

Listing 4-1. *Tracing Variables*

```
# print headers for the basic trace table
print()
print('\twidth\theight\twidths\ttotal\tprice')

# I need to add a bit for the hems.
# First, I must convert the string into a number.
# Otherwise, I will get an error if I try to perform arithmetic on a text string.
curtain_width = (float(window_width) * 0.75) + 20
```

```
print('\t', curtain_width)
curtain_length = float(window_height) + 15
print('\t\t', curtain_length)

# Now, I need to work out how many widths of cloth will be needed
# and figure out the total length of material for each curtain (in cm still).
widths = curtain_width / roll_width
print('\t\t\t', widths)
total_length = curtain_length * widths
print('\t\t\t\t', total_length)

# Actually, I have two curtains, so I must double the amount of material
# and then divide by 10 to get the number of meters.
total_length = (total_length * 2) / 10
print('\t\t\t\t', total_length)

# Finally, I need to work out how much it will cost.
price = total_length * price_per_metre
print('\t\t\t\t\t', price)
```

Each different variable is preceded by a different number of tab stops '\t', so the information goes into a separate column. Now, I can properly test the design. Here are the results of the first test I ran:

```
Enter the height of the window (cm): 100
Enter the width of the window (cm): 100

        width  height   widths   total   price
        95.0
                115
                        0.678571428571
                                78.0357142857
                        15.6071428571
                                78.0357142857
You need 15.6071428571 metres of cloth for  78.0357142857
```

Immediately, several things become apparent. I was expecting an answer of something more like 1.9 m. What happened? The conversion from centimeters to meters is off by a factor of ten, as shown in the fourth column, total, which is fairly easy to fix. I also have far more numbers after the decimal point than I really need. This can be fixed using the built-in round() function, which takes two arguments inside the brackets: the number I want to remove the excess digits from and the number of decimal places I want to run to. Two will probably do us fine right now. The edited portion of the code looks like Listing 4-2.

■ **Caution** Notice that we only round numbers when displaying them. If you round the numbers you are actually calculating with, that change will affect the results of your calculations, and depending on the calculation, the error introduced could be bigger than you expect.

Listing 4-2. *Rounding the Tesults to Two Decimal Figures*

```
# Actually, I have two curtains, so I must double the amount of material
# and then divide by 100 to get the number of meters.
total_length = (total_length * 2) / 100
print('\t\t\t\t', round(total_length, 2))

# Finally, I need to work out how much it will cost
price = total_length * price_per_metre
print('\t\t\t\t\t', round(price, 2))

# And print out the result
print("You need", round(total_length, 2), "meters of cloth for ", round(price, 2))
```

Now the design needs to be tested again with the same values. Here is a different sample of the results:

```
Enter the height of the window (cm): 100
Enter the width of the window (cm): 200

        width  height   widths  total   price
        170.0
                115
                        1.21428571429
                                139.642857143
                                2.79
                                        13.96
You need 2.79 metres of cloth for   13.96
```

And here are the results of another test:

```
Enter the height of the window (cm): 200
Enter the width of the window (cm): 100

        width  height   widths  total   price
        95.0
                215
                        0.678571428571
                                145.892857143
                                2.92
                                        14.59
You need 2.92 metres of cloth for   14.59
```

And these are the results of our final test:

```
Enter the height of the window (cm): 200
Enter the width of the window (cm): 300

        width   height   widths   total    price
        245.0
                  215
                           1.75
                                   376.25
                                   7.52
                                            37.62
You need 7.52 metres of cloth for   37.62
```

From this sample of test data, I can tell that I am getting closer to the right sort of results, but if I went out and bought some material on the basis of these results, I would find that I didn't have quite enough. Somehow, I've managed to consistently calculate results that are too small.

Knowing what results to expect is the only way of really telling whether our program is working or not. The difference between our expectations and the actual output can often help in finding the point where the calculation went wrong. Before reading any further, try to figure out why this version of the program is still returning the wrong length and, most importantly, where it is going wrong. In order to refine this design further, I will need to know about the relationship of the curtain_height and curtain_width to the roll_width.

Using Conditional Code in the Application

Now you can apply your knowledge of conditional statements to allow for different ways of measuring up the material. If the length of the curtains is less than the roll_width, it is possible to turn the whole thing on its side and just use one width of fabric. However, if the curtains need to be both longer and wider than the roll_width, there is a further problem: If the extra material required is less than half the roll_width, I would need to buy an additional width of material at the same length. If it is more than half, I would need to buy two additional widths.

Somehow, I need to come up with some code that reflects these conditions. The first step is to translate the preceding statements into pseudocode:

```
if curtain width < roll width:
        total_length = curtain width
else:
        total_length = curtain length
if (curtain width > roll width) and (curtain length > roll width):
        if extra material < (roll width / 2):
                width +=1
        if extra material > (roll width / 2):
                width +=2
```

I will need to work out how many whole widths there are in the curtain width and how much extra material will be needed to make up the whole width.

```
widths = int(curtain_width/roll_width)
extra_material = curtain_width%roll_width
```

I have used the built-in int() function to drop the fractional part of the calculation and used the modulo operator to calculate how much would be left over. The final script is shown in Listing 4-3.

Listing 4-3. *curtains-0.2.py*

```
#! /usr/bin/env python

"""
Calculate how much material to buy, given the size of the windows.

Target Users: My friend who wants to make some curtains
Target System: GNU/Linux
Interface: Command-line
Functional Requirements:
        Print out the required length of fabric in metres
        Print out the total price of the fabric
        User must be able to input the measurements of the window
Testing: Trace table
Test values:  100x100, 100x200, 200x100, 200x200, 200x300 and 300x200
Expected results: 1.9, 3.4, 4.3, 6.45, 9.8, 9.45
"""
__version__ = 0.2
__maintainer__  = "maintainer@website.com"
__status__  = "Prototype"

# To start with, all the measurements will be in cm.
# I will assume that the roll of material is going to be 140cm
# and that the price per metre will be 5 units of currency.
roll_width = 140
price_per_metre = 5

# Prompt the user to input the window measurements in cm.
window_height = input('Enter the height of the window (cm): ')
window_width = input('Enter the width of the window (cm): ')

# Print headers for the rather basic trace table.
print()
print('\twidth\theight\twidths\ttotal\tprice\tshorter?\twider?')

# I need to add a bit for the hems.
# First, I must convert the string into a number.
# Otherwise, I will get an error if I try to perform arithmetic on a
# text string.
curtain_width = (float(window_width) * 0.75) + 20
print('\t', round(curtain_width, 2))
curtain_length = float(window_height) + 15
print('\t\t', round(curtain_length, 2))

# Now. I need to work out how many widths of cloth will be needed
# and figure out the total length of material for each curtain (in cm still).
```

```
# If the length of the curtains is less than the roll_width, I can turn the
# whole thing on its side and just use one width of fabric, but if the curtains
# need to be both longer and wider than the roll_width, then I have a further
# problem: If the extra material required is less than half the roll_width, I
# would need to buy an additional width of material at the same length. If it
# is more than half, then I would need to buy two additional widths.
print('\t\t\t\t\t\t', curtain_length < roll_width)
print('\t\t\t\t\t\t\t', curtain_width > roll_width)
if curtain_length < roll_width:
        total_length = (curtain_width * 2) / 100
elif curtain_width > roll_width:
        widths = int(curtain_width/roll_width)
        extra_material = curtain_width%roll_width
        if extra_material < (roll_width / 2):
                widths +=1
        if extra_material > (roll_width / 2):
                widths +=2
        print('\t\t\t', widths)
        total_length = (curtain_length * widths) / 100
else:
        total_length = (curtain_length * 2) / 100

print('\t\t\t\t', round(total_length, 2))

# Finally I need to work out how much it will cost
# Rounded to two decimal places using the built-in round() function
price = total_length * price_per_metre
print('\t\t\t\t\t', round(price, 2))

# And print out the result
print("You need", round(total_length, 2), "meters of cloth, costing: ",
      round(price, 2))
```

The following results represent three tests of the new script:

```
Enter the height of the window (cm): 200
Enter the width of the window (cm): 200

        width   height  widths  total   price   shorter?        wider?
        170.0
                215.0
                                                False
                                                        True

                        2
                        4.3
                                21.5
You need 4.3 metres of cloth, costing:  21.5
```

```
Enter the height of the window (cm): 200
Enter the width of the window (cm): 300

        width   height  widths  total   price   shorter?        wider?
        245.0
                215.0
                                                False
                                                        True
                        3
                                6.45
                                        32.25
You need 6.45 metres of cloth, costing:  32.25


Enter the height of the window (cm): 300
Enter the width of the window (cm): 200

        width   height  widths  total   price   shorter?        wider?
        170.0
                315.0
                                                False
                                                        True
                        2
                                6.3
                                        31.5
You need 6.3 metres of cloth, costing:  31.5
```

This new version of the program almost gets there. The tests on 200×200 cm and 200×300 cm produce expected results, which shows that I'm on the right track. But the last test, for 300×300 cm, still underestimates the amount of material I'd need. This is probably because I haven't properly accounted for the additional material required for joins. If you are familiar with the process of curtain-making or even good at algebra, you could refine the process further to produce an even more accurate result. It may be necessary to redesign all or part of the program from scratch; for this, you have to go back to the drawing board: start again with the top-level design, sketching the process out in pseudocode again, translating that into Python code, rerunning the script, and testing it against the same set of values as before, until there are no longer any discrepancies.

Notice that I have bumped up the version number to 0.2; every time you refine your design, you will be creating a new *minor* revision of your application, so you should increment the number after the decimal point to reflect this. The number before the decimal point is the actual version number. The standard practice is to increment this number to 1 once the program is ready to release into the world at large. Some larger projects use three numbers separated by points, so version 1.3.2 would be the second *minor* revision of the third *major* revision of version 1 and so on.

Now that you've seen conditional statements and used them in our application, let's consider another type of control flow statement: loops.

Now Repeat That

Often, you will want to repeat the same process over a range of different values. Writing this out longhand is not only tedious but contrary to the principles of good programming. Ideally, you should have to write out a set of instructions or piece of information only once. This can be achieved using a **loop**, which means that certain statements are executed repeatedly.

There are two main methods of creating a loop in Python: the while and for statements. Let's look at the while statement first.

Looping with the while Statement

Listing 4-4 uses the while keyword, which will execute the indented statements that follow after the colon while the given condition is True. The indented statements after the colon are referred to as the **loop body**. They are indented in the same way as the if statements covered previously in this chapter.

Listing 4-4. *Looping Using a while Statement*

```
result = 1
while result < 1000:
    result *= 2
    print result
```

Recall that result *= 2 is the same as result = result*2, so the number printed is doubled during each iteration. This is the same as starting with 2^1 and raising the power by one during each iteration (i.e., 2^2, 2^3, 2^4, and so on).

■ **Note** An **iteration** is one repetition of a series of statements such as those found in a loop body.

To control the number of times the loop is processed, it is necessary to specify a conditional expression; as long as this conditional expression is True at the beginning of an iteration, the loop continues. In the preceding example, our conditional expression is result < 1000. So, as long as the value of result is less than 1,000, the loop will continue processing. Once result reaches 1,024 (2^{10}), the program will stop processing the loop body.

The variables used in the conditional expression are often expendable entities, which are only required for as long as the loop is active. Rather than keep thinking up different names, this kind of integer counter is usually named i or j by convention.

■ **Caution** Be very careful about reusing variable names. It is often better to come up with a unique and more explanatory name.

Here is what this simple program prints:

```
2
4
8
16
32
64
128
256
512
```

Two things are important to remember in this sort of construction: Any variable used in the conditional expression must be initialized before the execution of the loop. Also, there must be some way of updating this variable within the loop; otherwise, the loop will just go round and round forever, which is called an infinite loop.

■ **Caution** Python won't warn you if you have created an infinite loop, and you will have to find some way of killing the running program if you make this mistake. In text mode, this is as simple as pressing Ctrl+C (or Ctrl+Z), but killing the program might not always be so simple. You have been warned.

It is possible to use different sorts of variables in the conditional expression. Let's consider the problem of calculating the average of several numbers input by the user. The main problem here is that I don't know how many numbers will be input. The solution is to use what is called a **sentinel** value to control the loop. Rather than using the counter in this instance, the script checks the value of the user input number. While it is positive (i.e., >= 0) the loop processes as normal, but as soon as a negative number is entered, the loop is broken, and the script goes on to calculate the average. An example is shown in Listing 4-5.

Listing 4-5. *averages.py*

```
counter = 0
total = 0
number = 0
while number >= 0:
        number = int(input("Enter a positive number\nor a negative to exit: "))
        total += number
        counter += 1
average = total / counter
print(average)
```

Because I don't know what sort of value the user is going to input, the value returned by input() is immediately converted to an integer. If you try to enter text here, the result will be a value error, and the program will abort. I will show you how to catch and use errors in Chapter 10.

Listing 4-5 has a serious flaw in that the negative number, which has to be input last, gets included in the calculation and, therefore, messes up the final result. See if you can figure out how to avoid this problem before moving on to the next section. There are usually many ways of arriving at a good design, but sometimes, messing around with the details can lead to greater complication and create more problems. In these cases, it may be better to go back to the top-level design and start again. Fortunately, there are still a few more weapons in our armory.

Now Get Out of That

There are several methods of getting out of loops cleanly, the chief ones being the use of the break and continue keywords: If you want to get out of a loop without executing any more statements in the loop body, use break. If you just want to get out of this particular iteration of the loop, continue immediately takes you to the next iteration of the loop. The difference between the two is shown clearly in the **flowchart** in Figure 4-2.

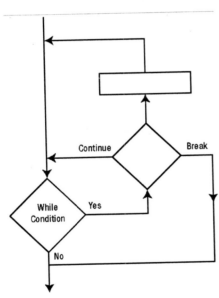

Figure 4-2. Flowchart for a while loop

At times, you will want the interpreter to recognize a condition but do nothing. In this case, the pass keyword can be useful; it creates a **null statement**, which simply tells the interpreter to move on to the next instruction.

```
while True:
    this_input = int(raw_input("#? :-> "))
```

```
        if this_input > 0:

                pass

        else:

                print("Input is negative")
```

```
#? :-> -1

Input is negative

#? :-> 17

#? :->
```

Like the if statement, while can also be followed with an else suite. In this case, the else suite is only executed after the loop has finished, as long as you didn't break out of it. An example of break and continue is shown in Listing 4-6.

Listing 4-6. *Using break and continue*

```
counter = 0
sum = 0
while True:
    this_input = float(input('#? :~> '))
    if this_input < 0:
        if counter == 0:
            print("You haven't entered any numbers yet!")
            continue
        break
    sum += this_input
    counter += 1
    print(counter, ':', sum)
```

```
#? :~> -3
You haven't entered any numbers yet!
#? :~> 5
1 : 5.0
#? :~> 7
2 : 12.0
#? :~> 3
3 : 15.0
```

```
#? :~> 8
4 : 23.0
#? :~> -1
>>>
```

Nesting Conditional Statements

You are allowed to nest loops and other conditional statements in Python, probably infinitely, but it is best to keep the number of levels of nesting to a minimum. For one thing, it's very easy to get confused about which option the program is taking at any particular point. Also, having lots of indented blocks within other indented blocks makes your code difficult to read, can slow down the program's execution, and is generally considered bad style. If you have come up with a design that involves two or three layers of looping, you should probably start thinking about redesigning it to avoid the excessive depth of nesting.

Using the for Statement

The other control flow statement I want to introduce is the for statement, which is constructed in a similar manner to the if and while statements. Its construction is for element in sequence: followed by an indented suite of instructions. During the first iteration of the loop, the variable element contains the first element in the sequence and is available to the indented suite. During the second iteration, it contains the second element in the sequence, and so on.

To understand how this statement works, you need to know about sequences. The simplest sequence in Python is a string, which is a sequence of individual characters including spaces and punctuation. Other forms of sequence are tuples and lists. Tuples and lists are sequences of data items, the chief difference between them being that lists are editable in place, whereas tuples are not (the distinction will be fully explained in Chapter 5). It's possible to use either in a for statement. They are constructed as follows:

```
# tuple
sequence1 = (1, 2, 3)
# list
sequence2 = [1, 2, 3]
```

I'll show you how to use and construct lists and tuples fully in the next chapter. The for statement, then, makes it possible to process several pieces of data in only a couple of lines of code. So in the example below, the variable banana contains each element in the splits sequence in turn, as the for loop goes through each iteration.

```
>>> splits = ['Fleagle', 'Beagle', 'Drooper', 'Snorky']

>>> for banana in splits:

...     print(banana)

...

Fleagle
```

Beagle

Drooper

Snorky

Using a for statement allows us to dispense with variables in loop conditions and means we can simply go through a sequence and do the same actions on each member of the sequence in turn. This turns out to be incredibly useful; for example, we can go through a line of text and print each character out on a separate line of its own.

```
text = input("Type in some words: ")
for character in text:
    print(character)
```

Or we can iterate through a list of items of data and process each one separately.

```
sequence = ['Just','a','list','of','words']
for word in sequence:
    print(word)Application
```

■ **Note** Like while, for can take an else statement, which is executed at the end unless the loop is exited with a break statement.

For the final example in this chapter, I want to take the problem of removing all the punctuation from a line of text input by the user. This is going to be a simple command-line application again. The top-level design, sketched out in pseudocode, might look like this:

```
Enter a text string
Loop through characters in text string
        if character not one of #()*+,-/:;<=>?@\^_`{|}~[]
                write out character
        elif character == '.'
                new line
```

To test out this example, I will need to come up with a suitable text string that contains all the available punctuation. Something along the lines of the following will probably do the job nicely:

```
"(One long string)*+with various punctuation - like this / this: and a list; of
< arithmetic = and comparison symbols> including, dubious? email@addresses and
[Stuff \ that] might be ^ Python_code, which `evaluates` as {something|other}~
you don't want. Another sentence. Blah97635o98q6v4ib5uq."
```

The first problem with our design is that if the character is a period, it will get written out rather than translated into a new line, so I need to reverse the order of the if and elif statements. Second, it would be much neater if I could replace all the punctuation with spaces; there is an easy way to do this, but I would end up with strange numbers of spaces in between words, and I want only one. I have to come up with some method of checking whether the last character was a space. For this example, I have chosen to set a flag as True if a space is written out and as False if any other character is written. I then check whether this flag is set or not before writing out a space character. The refined design turns out as follows:

```
Enter a text string
Loop through characters in text string
        if character == '.':
                new line
        elif character == ' ':
                if space_flag:
                        do nothing
                else:
                        add character to output string
                        space_flag = True
        elif character not one of #()*+,-/:;<=>?@\^_`{|}~[ ]:
                write out character
                space_flag = False
        else:
                if space_flag = False
                        add space to output string
                        space_flag = True
```

The else section should catch all the characters in the set of punctuation marks, so I want to check whether the last character was a space, if not I can add a space to the output. In fact, the design is slightly repetitious, with a little ingenuity it may be possible to merge the elif character == ' ': and else: suites.

```
Enter a text string
Loop through characters in text string
        if character == '.':
                new line
        elif character not one of #()*+,-/:;<=>?@\^_`{|}~[ ]:
                write out character
                space_flag = False
        else:
                if not space_flag:
                        add space to output string
                        space_flag = True
```

That's neater, so now it's time to code the design (see Listing 4-8).

Listing 4-8. *stringclean.py*

```python
#! /usr/bin/env python

"""

Clean up text string, replacing punctuation with spaces.
```

```
    Target System: GNU/Linux
    Interface: Command-line
    Functional Requirements:
            Loop through the characters in a string
            Removing all non-alpha-numeric characters
            Lines break at full stops
            It would be great to have a single space between each word.
    Testing: Run test
    Test values:
    (One long string)*+with various punctuation - like this / this: and a list; of <
    arithmetic = and comparison symbols> including, dubious? email@addresses and
    [Stuff \ that] might be ^ Python_code, which `evaluates` as {something|other}~
    you don't want. Another sentence. Blah97635o98q6v4ib5uq. test
    Expected results:
            One long string with various punctuation like this this and a list of
        arithmetic and comparison symbols including dubious email addresses and
        Stuff that might be Python code which evaluates as something other you
        don't want
            Another sentence
            Blah97635o98q6v4ib5uq
"""


__version__  = "0.1"
__maintainer__ = "maintainer@website.com"
__status__   = "Prototype"
punctuation = "#()*+,-/:;<=>? \\@^_`{|}~[]"
print()
print("***")
print()

input_string = input("Enter a text string: ")

output_string = ' '
space_flagged = False

for char in input_string:
    if char == '.':
        print(output_string)
        output_string = ' '
    elif char not in punctuation:
        output_string += char
        space_flagged = False
    else:
        if not space_flagged:
            output_string += ' '
            space_flagged = True

print(output_string)
print()
print("***")
print()
```

The variable `punctuation` is a string containing all the punctuation marks that I want to remove including spaces. I will use this to contain all the values that I want to be replaced by spaces. I need to initialize `output_string` and `space_flagged` at the start, so the interpreter knows what they are when it gets to them. Next, the program prompts the user for input and loops through the string checking for punctuation and spaces. The heavy lifting here is done by the conditional construction `char not in punctuation`. This conditional expression checks to see if the character `char` matches up with any of the individual contents of the `punctuation` string, printing out a space if it does or adding the string to the `output_string` if it doesn't.

This is a rather long-winded way of analyzing a sentence. Python has various methods of making this sort of task a lot simpler. In the next chapter, I'll show you how to refine this script to make use of Python's list manipulation facilities. Even using the limited commands that you have learned so far, it would be possible to refine the design in Listing 4-7 further or customize it to deal with other special punctuation cases in different ways.

Jargon Busting

The terms presented in this chapter follow:

- *Assignment operator*: The single equals sign (=) is the assignment operator. It can be combined with other operators to perform more complex assignment operations.

- *Built-in*: A built-in element is an innate part of the programming language, as opposed to something that has to be imported from a module. Built-in elements are part of Python's standard library.

- *Comparison operators*: These operators compare two values:

    - `<`: Less than

    - `<=`: Less than or equal

    - `>`: Greater than

    - `>=`: Greater than or equal

    - `==`: Equal

    - `!=`: Not equal

    - `is`: Tests object identity

    - `is not`: Tests object identity

- *Conditional statement*: This section of code is performed if a certain condition evaluates as `True`. A conditional statement is a form of control flow statement.

- *Critical values*: These values exist at the edges of the permissible ranges set for an application. In particular, these are values that would cause changes or unexpected results from the normal running of the program.

- *Flowchart*: This is a graphical method of designing and analyzing the control flow of a program.

- *Iteration:* An iteration is single run through a loop.

- *Loop:* A loop is code construction that repeats.

- *Loop body:* The body is the suite of instructions to be repeated in a loop.

- *Null statement:* The pass keyword creates a null statement, which tells the interpreter to move on to the next statement.

- *Operands:* These are the expressions on either side of an operator.

- *Refining:* This refers to the process of improving and simplifying a program design.

- *Sentinel:* This loop condition control variable has a value that is the result of the process needing to be controlled, such as user input.

- *Suite:* A suite is a group of commands executed in a conditional statement and are all indented the same amount.

- *Trace:* This refers to the process of checking the state of the internal values and conditions of a program over the course of its execution.

- *Trace table:* This data table is output by performing a trace.

- *Validation:* This refers to the process of checking that your data is what you expect.

Summary

You now know how to get your programs to actually do something. Much of the fundamental action of a program is controlled by the use of comparison operators, logical operators, assignment operators combined with the arithmetical operators that were covered in the previous chapter, and in accordance with the rules of operator precedence.

You have learned about the fundamental control structures used for decision making (if, elif, else) and looping (while, else, and for...in...else) as well as how to get out of loops cleanly using break and continue. You have also started to learn how to refine the design and deal with logical errors using trace tables and flowcharting.

In the next chapter, I will introduce the first of several more complex data types—the list—and show you how you can manipulate entire sequences of data at once.

CHAPTER 5

■ ■ ■

Using Lists

In this chapter, you will learn how to deal with multiple items of data by processing them in sequence. First, I'll give you an overview of the data structures that Python provides that can contain more than one item. These include Strings, tuples, lists and dictionaries. There are a few actions that you can perform on all of these data types, so I'll cover those before going into the details of creating and manipulating each type separately. In the second half of this chapter, you'll be making a simple role-playing combat game. You will use these data structures to contain your player's statistics and inventory and to translate the numerical results of the combat calculations into descriptive phrases. You'll be using what you learned about loops in the previous chapter to work with the individual items in those data structures. In the process, I'll cover some of the design and development issues you may have to face when creating more complex applications, and you'll see how Python can be used to make repetitive number-crunching and text manipulation not only fast and painless but also entertaining!

Working with Python Data Structures

So far, you have learned to work with individual pieces of data to produce some simple results. Real-world data is usually in lumps or groups, and it would be useful to work with such groups without having to make lots of repetitive statements in our code. Fortunately, Python provides a variety of data types that can make handling groups of data much simpler.

The data types that are most used in Python are strings, tuples, lists and dictionaries. These are collectively called data structures.

Strings are just pieces of text. Tuples and lists are ordered groups of individual data items. Dictionaries are groups of key-value pairs.

Strings, tuples, and lists are examples of a particular data model called sequences. The methods used for accessing the data in a sequence are same, which you will see later in this chapter.

There is another way of looking at these data types—according to whether they can be modified or not, which is called mutability. Strings and tuples are immutable, which means that we cannot modify an existing string or tuple, although we can use them to create new strings and tuples, respectively. Lists are **mutable**, which means we can add or remove items from a list.

Accessing the items in a sequence

We can fetch an individual item from a sequence using an **index**, which is the position of the element. The index is specified as an integer (a whole number) in square brackets immediately following the variable name. So s[i] will retrieve the item at position i of sequence s. This allows you to access a single character in a string:

```
>>> fruit = 'apple'
>>> fruit[0]
'a'
```

or an item in a list or tuple:

```
>>> fruits = ['avocados', 'bananas', 'oranges', 'grapes', 'mangos']
>>> fruits[2]
'oranges'
```

The first thing you will notice is that indexing is zero-based; that means you start counting at 0. An index of [2] accesses the third item in the list, the first item would be referenced with [0]. So you can use integers 0 through to the number of elements in the sequence minus one (0 to n - 1) as indices. Negative indices count backward from the end:

```
>>> fruits[-1]
'mangos'
```

You can grab sections of a sequence using **slices**. Slicing is used to fetch multiple items from a sequence. Slices are written using the same notation as an index, but this time with two or three integers separated by colons. The first value is the inclusive starting point and the second number is the exclusive end point of the slice. So s[0:2] means that the slice will start from index 0 and stop just before index 2, (i.e., fetch items at positions 0 and 1).

The third value is optional and specifies an additional step value, which may be negative, so instead of picking out a sequential list, you can retrieve every other, or every *n*th item, and you can also retrieve them backward if you need to. So s[i:j:step] will retrieve a slice of s starting from i and up to, but not including j, and taking the specified step.

```
>>> fruits = ['avocados', 'bananas', 'oranges', 'grapes', 'mangos']
>>> fruits[2:-2]
['oranges']
>>> fruits[2:4]
['oranges', 'grapes']
>>> fruits[1:4:2]
['bananas', 'grapes']
```

If the starting point, i, is equal to or greater than end point, j, the slice you get back will be empty.

```
>>> fruits[4:4:2]
[]
```

If you leave out the starting point, the slice will start at the beginning of the original sequence, and if you leave out the end point, the slice will run to the end of the original sequence.

Indexing and slicing do not modify the original sequence; they make a new sequence from the original. However, the actual individual data items are the same. So if you modify an individual item in a sequence, you will see the item change in a slice from the sequence as well.

> ■ **Note** list_alias = sequence does not make a copy of the list. Instead, list_alias and sequence are the same (i.e., they are two names—references—pointing to the same list). So, if you perform any operation on list_alias, you will see the change in sequence as well. If you do new_sequence = sequence[:], then operations on new_sequence won't affect sequence. Beware of this difference!

If You're Not on the List, You Can't Come In

Often, you will want to find out whether a particular piece of data is in a sequence or not. This is achieved in Python using the keyword in, which is a Boolean operator that tests for membership in a sequence. The test x in s will return True if x is in sequence s; otherwise, it will return False.

```
>>> 'apple' in fruits
False
```

It is possible to use not in conjunction with in to produce the opposite answer.

```
>>> 'apple' not in fruits
True
```

You can also use this operator on strings to find out whether x is contained in (i.e., is a substring of) string s.

```
>>> 'ana' in 'banana'
True
```

You can use the + operator to combine sequences to make a new sequence.

```
>>> 'pine' + 'apple'
'pineapple'
```

You can also use the * operator on sequences to create multiple copies glued together.

```
>>> 'heart'*5
'heartheartheartheartheart'
```

The best method for joining strings in a sequence is separator.join(seq). It uses an apparently bizarre notation, which deserves a little further explanation. You will have gathered by now that the different data types all have a different set of operations that can be used with them. These operations can be carried out by *operators* or *methods*.

Operators are commands written as a symbol (+, -, etc.) or keyword (in, and, or, etc.) between two operands. **Methods** are accessed using a command that follows the variable name immediately after a period (dot) and terminates in parentheses, which may or may not contain further arguments. In separator.join(seq), join() is the method. Methods are like functions that are specific to an object, such as a data type in this instance (objects are covered in Chapters 9 and 10). For now, objects are specific instances of data types.

The string type has the method join(), which takes a sequence as an argument and returns a single string made up of the elements of the sequence joined together with copies of the original string between them. It might seem more logical to write sequence.join(separator), but that would be a method belonging to the **separator** type. Try reading the statement backward if you have trouble making sense of this:

```
>>> ", ".join(fruit)
'avocados, bananas, oranges, grapes, mangos'
```

You could pretty this up by assigning sep = ", " first and then calling sep.join(fruit) if you prefer; this could be useful if you are using the same separator elsewhere and you want to make sure that you are splitting and joining all your lists with the same separator. Readability of code is an important consideration. The assignment in the following example could be to vegetables.split(sep) in this case.

Splitting up a string to form a list can be done with stringToSplit.split(separator,max), which is much more logical to write. This is a string method, so it works on a string variable. This method takes an additional argument that specifies the maximum number of splits allowed.

```
>>> vegetables = "carrots, potatoes, onions, leeks, celery"
>>> vegetables = vegetables.split(", ")
>>> vegetables
['carrots', 'potatoes', 'onions', 'leeks', 'celery']
```

The preceding code allows to you process each word in a sentence separately, which can prove to be a useful technique.

There are a few useful built-in ways to convert sequences into different types of sequences. First, list(seq) turns any sequence into a list; if you do this with a string, you'll get a list of the individual characters:

```
>>> list('banana')
['b', 'a', 'n', 'a', 'n', 'a']
>>> list(vegetables)
['carrots', 'potatoes', 'onions', 'leeks', 'celery']
```

If you want to turn a sequence into a tuple, the same rules apply to tuple(seq).

```
>>> tuple(vegetables)
('carrots', 'potatoes', 'onions', 'leeks', 'celery')
```

Converting a list into a string will make a readable text representation of the list.

```
>>> str(vegetables)
"['carrots', 'potatoes', 'onions', 'leeks', 'celery']"
```

If you want to know how many elements a sequence has, use len(seq).

```
>>> len(vegetables)
5
```

The number of items in a sequence that are equal to x can be counted up with sequence.count(x). In other words, it counts each item where x == item is true.

```
>>> vegetables.count('carrot')
1
```

If you want to retrieve the greatest item in a sequence, use max(seq).

```
>>> max(vegetables)
'potatoes'
```

The least item can be accessed similarly with min(seq).

```
>>> min(vegetables)
'carrots'
```

It may be worth taking a moment to consider the results of the last two examples. Were they what you expected? The results came out based on alphabetical order. It seems that sequences have some kind of implicit sort order, even if they haven't been sorted yet. It turns out that it is possible to use this implied order to compare sequences using the same comparison operators that are used to compare the fundamental data types.

```
>>> fruits > vegetables
False
>>> vegetables > fruits
True
>>> vegetables == fruits
False
```

The sequences fruits and vegetables both contain five members. Nevertheless, the Python interpreter is able to determine that the two sequences are not the same and decide that one is greater, as a whole, than the other.

Note that empty sequences will always return False in when tested in Boolean expressions.

This is where the similarities between strings, tuples, and lists end.

Tuples

A tuple is an immutable ordered group of items or elements. Think of tuples as useful little sealed packets of information.

A tuple is specified as a comma-separated list of values, which may be enclosed in parentheses. On certain occasions, the parentheses are required, so when in doubt, use parentheses. The values need not all be of the same type. A value can also be another tuple.

Creating a Tuple

You can create a tuple with zero items using an empty pair of round brackets ().

```
>>> blank_tuple = ()
```

If you want to make a tuple that only contains one item, you must follow the item with a single comma (item,).

```
>>> single_tuple = ('item',)
```

Tuples are normally created by assigning a sequence of comma-separated values to a variable, which is known as **sequence packing**. Notice that we don't need parentheses in this example, because it is unambiguous that it is a tuple:

```
>>> t = 'blah1', 'blah2', 'blah3'
```

The sequence can be unpacked by doing the reverse:

```
>>> blah1, blah2, blah3 = t
```

Changing the Values in a Tuple

You can't. That's not what they're meant for. Remember when we said they are useful little *sealed* packets of information? They are used mostly in situations where a set of values has to be passed on to another place without worry of having them messed about. You can also use them to provide dictionary keys. If you want a sequence of data that you can change, then you need a list.

Lists

A **list** is an ordered, comma-separated list of items enclosed in square brackets. Items need not all be of the same type. An item can also be another list.

Lists can be sliced, concatenated, and indexed the same as any other type of sequence. It is possible to change individual items in a list, as opposed to immutable strings and tuples. Where a tuple is rather like a fixed menu, lists are more flexible. It is possible to assign data to slices, which can change the size of the list or clear it completely.

Creating a List

Lists are easy to create:

```
>>> inventory = ['pole', ['another', 'list'], 'silver mirror', '10 gold coins',
 'potion']
```

Modifying a List

New values can be assigned to list items using the assignment operator sequence[i] = x.

```
>>> inventory[1] = 'wax'
>>> inventory
['pole', 'wax', 'silver mirror', '10 gold coins', 'potion']
```

You can replace a slice of your list with another sequence using list[i:j:step] = sequence.

```
>>> inventory[::2] = ['shield', 'scroll', 'oil']
```

```
>>> inventory
['shield', 'wax', 'scroll', '10 gold coins', 'oil']
```

Here, I have specified a slice with no start or end point and a step size of two, so every other item in the whole list is affected by this change.

You can add elements to a list by using the append() or extend() methods, the append() method adds individual items; the extend() method is used to add items from another list:

```
>>> inventory.append('skull')
>>> inventory
['shield', 'wax', 'scroll', '10 gold coins', 'oil', 'skull']
>>> inventory.extend(['sword', 'oil'])
>>> inventory
['shield', 'wax', 'scroll', '10 gold coins', 'oil', 'skull', 'sword', 'oil']
```

The keyword del can be used to remove entire variables or slices of a list. Remember that this only removes references from the list; the actual item itself is not affected if they are still being used in other data structures.

```
>>> del inventory[4:]
>>> inventory
['shield', 'wax', 'scroll', '10 gold coins']
```

You can get the index position of the first item that corresponds to x using list.index(x).
```
>>> inventory.index('scroll')
2
```

You can insert an item x at position i with list.insert(i,x).

```
>>> inventory.insert(2,'wand')
>>> inventory
['shield', 'wax', 'wand', 'scroll', '10 gold coins', 'emerald', 'pole', 'potion']
```

You can also remove the first item that is equal to x in list s using list.remove(x).

```
>>> inventory.remove('wax')
>>> inventory
['shield', 'wand', 'scroll', '10 gold coins', 'emerald', 'pole', 'potion']
```

Sometimes, you may want to remove and return a value from the list at the same time. This can be done using list.pop(i). This method takes an index position as an argument. If the index is not specified, it defaults to the last item in the list.

```
>>> inventory.pop(-2)
'pole'
>>> inventory
['shield', 'wand', 'scroll', '10 gold coins', 'emerald', 'potion']
```

Stacks and Queues

Because lists are an ordered type of data, it is possible to use them to store and retrieve data items in a particular order. The two main models for doing this are described in traditional programming-speak as "stacks" and "queues."

A **stack** is a last in, first out (LIFO) structure, used rather like the discard pile in a card game. You put cards on the top of the pile and take them back off the top. You can push items onto the stack with list.append() and pop them back off with pop(). Note that there is no additional index argument, so it will be the last item of the list that is popped.

```
>>> inventory.append('ring')
>>> inventory.pop()
'ring'
>>> inventory
['shield', 'wand', 'scroll', '10 gold coins', 'emerald', 'potion']
```

The other approach involves creating a first in, first out (FIFO) structure called a **queue**. This works more like a pipe, where you push items in at one end and the first thing you put in the pipe pops out of the other end. Again, we can push items into the pipe using append() and retrieve them using pop(0)—this time with an index of 0 to indicate that the data items should be popped from the start of the list.

```
>>> inventory.append('ring')
>>> inventory.pop(0)
'shield'
>>> inventory
['wand', 'scroll', '10 gold coins', 'emerald', 'potion', 'ring']
```

■ **Note** There is also another data type known as a deque (pronounced "deck"), which works very similarly to a list but has been designed with extra features to facilitate double-ended stacking and queuing operations.

Sorting Lists

You can sort lists either using a list method list.sort(), which directly modifies the original list, or using sorted(list) which returns a new sorted list and thus doesn't modify the original.

```
>>> sorted(inventory)
['10 gold coins', 'emerald', 'potion', 'ring', 'scroll', 'wand']
>>> inventory.sort()
```

Reversing the order of your list can be done using the list.reverse() method, which reverses the original list.

```
>>> reversed(inventory)
<listreverseiterator object at 0x81abf0c>
>>> inventory.reverse()
>>> inventory
['wand', 'scroll', 'ring', 'potion', 'emerald', '10 gold coins']
```

Many sequence manipulation functions, rather than returning another sequence, return another object, in the above example, an **iterator** object is returned. This object can be used in a for loop just the same as a sequence. The reversed() function returns a new reversed list iterator object.

```
>>> for item in reversed(inventory):
...     print item
...
wand
scroll
ring
potion
emerald
10 gold coins
```

Multidimensional Lists

Lists can be multidimensional, that is to say, nested inside other lists. Lists containing other lists can be used as a way of storing a **matrix**, or table of information. A 3×3 matrix could be created by assigning a list of lists to a variable.

```
>>> matrix = [[11,12,13],[21,22,23],[31,32,33]]
```

Processing Large Amounts of Data Easily

It is common practice to **iterate** through a list using a for loop. This construction for var in list is known as a list **traversal**. It is appropriate to use a for loop because even if you don't know how long your list is, your computer sure does—using the built-in len() function. A matrix like the one in the preceding example, incidentally, would require two nested for loops, one for each dimension of the matrix.

The positional index and value can be both retrieved at once using enumerate(), another built-in function.

```
>>> for i, value in enumerate(fruits):
...     print i, value
...
0 avocados
1 bananas
2 oranges
3 grapes
4 mangos
```

Let's do the same for our matrix example:

```
>>> for row in matrix:
...     for i, value in enumerate(row):
...             print i, value,
...     print
...
0 11 1 21 2 31
```

```
0 21 1 22 2 32
0 31 1 32 2 33
```

To loop through two or more sequences at a time, entries can be paired with zip().

```
>>> for fru, veg in zip(fruits, vegetables):
...     if fru < veg:
...             print fru, "are better than", veg
...     else:
...             print veg, "are better than", fru
...
avocados are better than carrots
bananas are better than potatoes
onions are better than oranges
grapes are better than leeks
celery are better than mangos
```

List Comprehensions

The last nifty tricks to cover in this list of things you can do with lists are list comprehensions. List comprehensions evaluate an expression for each item in a list and return a list of the results. Think of this as a shortcut to apply an operation to every element in a list and get back a new list, without the pain of creating a temporary list.

List comprehensions usually result in clearer code than using built-in functions like map() or filter() but can also lead to the construction of unwieldy one-liners if you include too many additional for loops and if statements.

The most basic construction is [expression for var in list[for...|if...]]. This means that you can have multiple for and if statements after the initial construction. If the expression part is a tuple, this is one occasion where it *must* be in parentheses.

```
>>> [fruit.upper() for fruit in fruits]
['AVOCADOS', 'BANANAS', 'ORANGES', 'GRAPES', 'MANGOS']
```

Let's look at two for statements. Here, we extract each integer and pair it with each letter:

```
>>> int_list = [0, 1]
>>> char_list = ['a', 'b', 'c']
>>> [(an_int, a_char) for an_int in int_list for a_char in char_list]
[(0, 'a'), (0, 'b'), (0, 'c'), (1, 'a'), (1, 'b'), (1, 'c')]
```

Note that (an_int, a_char) is the pairing expression that operates on the results of the two for expressions.

List comprehensions are cool and very powerful. The expression part can be any expression you can code, and you can also make the evaluation of that expression conditional. If the matrix were modified to include different values, it would be possible to retrieve only the changed values using a list comprehension. Note the way data is assigned to the cells of a nested list.

```
>>> matrix = [['data', 'data', 'data'], ['data', 'data', 'data'],
              ['data', 'data', 'data']]
>>> matrix[0][0] = 'one'
>>> matrix[1][1] = 'two'
>>> matrix[2][2] = 'three'
>>> matrix
[['one', 'data', 'data'], ['data', 'two', 'data'], ['data', 'data', 'three']]
>>> [value for row in matrix for value in row if value is not 'data']
['one', 'two', 'three']
```

The for statements within the list comprehension have to come in the same order you would put them if you were using nested loops. So for row in matrix comes before for value in row, which gives a rather counter-intuitive reading. It is the *resultant* value of the left-hand expression that becomes the item of data in the new list, the for and if statements that follow it should run in the order they are to be processed. If you get confused, try to find ways you can reduce the level of nesting required.

Sets

Sometimes, you may need to use a data structure to test for membership. For example, we are processing a group of names, how do we know if we've already come across the same name? This is where we can use sets, using the if item in set statement. Notice that creating a set automatically removes any duplicate entries.

Similarly, it is also useful to find out what is common or different between two sets of items.

```
>>> a = set(['apples', 'oranges', 'bananas', 'apples', 'oranges'])
>>> b = set(['avocados', 'mangos', 'apples', 'grapes', 'mangos'])
>>> a
set(['apples', 'oranges', 'bananas'])
>>> b
set(['avocados', 'apples', 'grapes', 'mangos'])
>>> a-b # what is in 'a' that is not in 'b'?
set(['bananas', 'oranges'])
>>> b-a # what is in 'a' and not in 'b'?
set(['avocados', 'grapes', 'mangos'])
>>> a|b # what is in either 'a' or 'b'?
set(['apples', 'grapes', 'mangos', 'avocados', 'oranges', 'bananas'])
>>> a&b # what is common between 'a' and 'b'?
set(['apples'])
>>> a[1]
Traceback (most recent call last):
  File "<stdin>", line 1, in <module>
TypeError: 'set' object is unindexable
```

As the members of a set are not in any particular order, you can't reference them with an index.

▨ **Note** You can also create sets using curly braces. So you could type b = {'avocados', 'mangos', 'apples', 'grapes', 'mangos'}. You still have to use set() to create an empty list because {} makes a new dictionary (see the "Dictionaries" section).

Dictionaries

Dictionaries are like address books: if you know the name of the person, you can get all of that person's details. The name is technically referred to as a key, and any corresponding detail is referred to as the value.

The key must be of an immutable type, that is, a string, number or tuple; the value can be more or less anything you like. The dictionary itself is a mutable data type, which means you can add, remove, and modify key-value pairs. The keys are said to be mapped to objects, hence dictionaries are referred to as "mappings" to remind us that their behavior is somewhat different to sequences.

▨ **Note** Dictionary-like structures are referred to in some other languages as associative arrays or hashes, because the values used to define the keys must be hashable values. **Hashed** keys are small values calculated from the actual key and are an efficient way of storing potentially large keys. This makes value lookup much quicker. Python organizes the information in the dictionary according to these hashes rather than an alphabetical list. It follows that if you change the contents of a hashable value, the resultant hash would also change, and the computer would no longer be able to locate the value it contains. Now you know why keys have to be of an immutable data type.

Defining Dictionaries

Dictionaries are created by specifying key-value pairs (separated by colons) inside curly braces ({}).

```
>>> profile = {'Name':"",'Desc':"", 'Race':"",
    'Gender':"",'Muscle':0,'Brainz':0,'Speed':0,'Charm':0}
>>> profile['Name'] = "Adam"
>>> print profile['Name'], "has", profile['Brainz'], "Brainz"
Adam has 0 Brainz
```

You can refer to items in a dictionary using the familiar square bracket notation. Remember we accessed items in a list as item[i], where i is the position of the item. In dictionaries, there are no positions, because all we have are keys and their respective values. Hence, we just use the key itself to access its corresponding value in the dictionary: dictionary[key] = value. Don't forget to enclose the key name in quotes or the interpreter will treat it as if it is a variable.

Dictionaries can also be traversed using a for loop, but the loop will iterate only through the keys.

```
>>> for key in profile:
...      print key,
...
Brainz Name Gender Race Charm Muscle Speed Desc
```

If you want the value, use profile[key] as you have seen before. However, if you need to ensure that the key exists in the dictionary, you can check using key in profile, which returns True or False. Otherwise, Python will throw an error.

If you do not know whether the key exists already, the best approach is to use the get(key,default) method. This method takes two arguments, the key that you're looking for and a default value if that key is not found.

```
>>> profile.get('Name')
'Adam'
>>> profile.get('Gender','not known')
''
>>> profile.get('Life','not present')
'not present'
```

Note that if the key is present, but only contains an empty string, you'll get the empty value returned rather than the default message.

```
>>> for item in profile:
...      profile.get(item,'not present')
...
0
'Adam'
''
''
0
0
0
''
```

We can access the dictionary's contents as a whole using the keys(), values(), and items() methods, which return the keys, the values, and the key-value pairs respectively. You'll notice that the items are presented in an apparently random yet consistent order (see the note on hashes).

```
>>> profile.keys()
['Brainz', 'Name', 'Gender', 'Race', 'Charm', 'Muscle', 'Speed', 'Desc']
>>> profile.values()
[0, 'Adam', '', '', 0, 0, 0, '']
>>> profile.items()
[('Brainz', 0), ('Name', 'Adam'), ('Gender', ''), ('Race', ''), ('Charm', 0),
 ('Muscle', 0), ('Speed', 0), ('Desc', '')]
```

■ **Note** These three methods return *views* instead of lists. Views can be iterated over and support membership tests in much the same way as lists.

Dictionaries can also be created using the built-in `dict()` function. Without arguments, the function will create an empty dictionary. Also, the function will accept arguments to create dictionaries out of other iterable entities, such as lists, keyword arguments, or other dictionaries. It is also possible to create a blank copy of a dictionary using the `dict.fromkeys(iterable, value=None)` method.

```
>>> new_profile = profile.fromkeys(profile)
>>> new_profile
{'Brainz': None, 'Name': None, 'Gender': None, 'Race': None, 'Charm': None,
    'Muscle': None, 'Speed': None, 'Desc': None}
>>> profile
{'Brainz': 0, 'Name': 'Adam', 'Gender': '', 'Race': '', 'Charm': 0, 'Muscle': 0,
    'Speed': 0, 'Desc': ''}
```

Dictionaries also respond to the built-in functions `len()`, `max()` and `min()`.

```
>>> max(profile)
'Speed'
>>> min(profile)
'Brainz'
>>> len(profile)
8
```

Deleting Items

To remove an individual item from a dictionary, use `del`:

```
>>> profile
{'Name': 'Adam', 'Gender': '', 'Race': '', 'Charm': 0, 'Muscle': 0,
    'Speed': 0, 'Desc': ''}
>>> del profile['Gender']
>>> profile
{'Name': 'Adam', 'Race': '', 'Charm': 0, 'Muscle': 0, 'Speed': 0, 'Desc': ''}
```

If you want to fetch the value and remove it from the dictionary, you can use `dict.pop(key[, default])`.

Alternatively `dict.popitem()` will remove a random item from the dictionary and returns the key-value pair as a tuple.

```
>>> profile.popitem()
('Brainz', 0)
>>> profile
{'Name': 'Adam', 'Gender': '', 'Race': '', 'Charm': 0, 'Muscle': 0, 'Speed': 0,
    'Desc': ''}
```

If you want a clean slate, `dict.clear()` removes all items from the dictionary.

```
>>> profile.clear()
>>> profile
{}
```

Sorting Dictionaries

You can sort the output from any of the dictionary methods using the built-in `sorted()` function.

```
>>> sorted(profile.items())
[('Brainz', 82), ('Charm', 64), ('Desc', 'Tall'), ('Gender', 'female'),
 ('Muscle', 43), ('Name', 'Ez'), ('Race', 'Pixie'), ('Speed', 76), ('gold', 109),
 ('life', 45), ('magic', 73), ('prot', 63)]
```

Using Dictionaries

Dictionaries are used anywhere we want to store attributes and values that describe some concept or entity. For example, we can use a dictionary to count instances of particular objects or states. Because each key has to have a unique identifier, there cannot be duplicate values for the same key. Therefore, we can use the key to store the items of input data, leaving the value part to store the results of our calculations. For example, suppose I wanted to find out how many times each letter turns up in a sentence like "The quick brown fox jumps over the lazy dog." I could iterate through the characters of the sentence and assign each one to a key in a dictionary.

```
>>> sentence = "The quick brown fox jumps over the lazy dog."
>>> characters = {}
>>> for character in sentence:
...         characters[character] = characters.get(character,0) + 1
...
>>> characters
{' ': 8, '.': 1, 'T': 1, 'a': 1, 'c': 1, 'b': 1, 'e': 3, 'd': 1, 'g': 1, 'f': 1,
 'i': 1, 'h': 2, 'k': 1, 'j': 1, 'm': 1, 'l': 1, 'o': 4, 'n': 1, 'q': 1, 'p': 1,
 's': 1, 'r': 2, 'u': 2, 't': 1, 'w': 1, 'v': 1, 'y': 1, 'x': 1, 'z': 1}
```

A Simple Role-Playing Combat Game

For this chapter's special guest application, I will introduce a really simple role-playing combat game to demonstrate dictionaries and sequences in action. This is an expansion of `chargen.py`, the role-playing character generation script that I started to design in Chapter 3. Starting with the top-level design, there will be three main sections to this program.

- Generate character statistics.
- Buy some equipment.
- Fight.

Each step needs to be refined separately:

1. We need a container for our character statistics; a dictionary would be perfect for this. We want the user to define the 'Name', 'Desc', 'Gender', and 'Race' fields. The main statistics 'Muscle', 'Brainz', 'Speed', 'Charm', and 'gold' need to be randomly generated. The combat statistics 'life', 'magic', and 'prot' (protection) need to be derived from the main statistics. For generating random numbers, I will have to use the random module. As I don't cover modules until Chapter 9, I should explain that **modules** are collections of extra functions that you can call on to do specific jobs. They need to be imported at the start of the script, and then the contained functions can be used, with a similar syntax to the object methods we have been using to manipulate strings and lists so far.

2. Next, I want the characters to be able to buy some equipment with their gold. This means I'll have to set up shop. I can do this by creating a dictionary called stock, where the names of the stock items are keys and the corresponding values are the prices.

3. Finally, we get to the combat phase. Each character must choose a weapon and take turns attacking opponents. Rather than having some boring numerical score, I want to translate the damage results into descriptive text. For this, I'm going to create some more tuples containing suitable phrases. I need to work out how to calculate whether each blow meets its mark and, if so, how much damage it does. To help this calculation, I want to add two more items of data to my already existing stock list to represent weapon damage and weapon speed. In order to do this, each value in the stock dictionary will be represented by a tuple of three values (price, damage, and speed). These calculations can all be set up at the start of the script, because I don't want these values to change. Finally, I want the combat section to loop until one or other combatant is defeated.

Next, I sketched the whole thing out in pseudocode as you can see in Listing 5-1.

***Listing 5-1.** The Role-Play Game's Pseudocode*

```
rpcombat.py
Purpose: Simple Role-Playing Combat Game.
Target System: GNU/Linux
Interface: Command-line
Functional Requirements: The user must be able to generate more than one
  character profile, equip those characters with suitable weapons,
  and model hand-to-hand combat between characters.
Test values: (Ez, Tall, Pixie, female), (Inkon, Small, Troll, male)
Expected results: All statistics should be integers in the (1-99) range.
Limitations: Too many to mention.

# set up constant data.
# Set up shop = {}
```

```
#1 loop while players < 2
        #1.1 Create profile dictionary
        #1.2 Prompt user for user-defined information
            #      (Name', 'Desc', 'Gender', 'Race')
        #1.3 Validate user input
        #1.4 Generate stats ('Muscle', 'Brainz', 'Speed', 'Charm')
        #1.5 Work out combat stats ('life', 'magic', 'prot', 'gold')
        ## And modify according to user-defined info
        #1.6 Validate stats
        #1.7 Output the character sheet

        #1.8 Prompt user to buy some equipment.
        #1.9 loop while purchase not 'no'.
                #1.9.1 Display shop stock list with prices.
                #1.9.2 Prompt user to make a purchase.
                #1.9.3 If the item is in stock and the player has enough gold, buy it.
        #1.10 Add new player to list of players

## Combat
# Set up descriptive lists
## hits = (), misses = (), damage_report = (), life_changing = ()

#2 Prompt user to enter into combat
## Prompt user to choose a weapon
## The weapon must be in player's inventory.
## Default to fist if weapon not available.

#3 Loop while attacker[health] > 0 and target[health] > 0:
        #3.1 for player in players:
                #3.1.1 Calculate velocity of blow
                #3.1.2 Calculate damage inflicted by blow
                #3.1.3 Print damage report
                #3.1.4 if attacker[health] > 0 and target[health] > 0: break
        #3.2 Print progress report

#4 Print winner
```

This translates fairly easily into Python, as shown in Listing 5-2. Immediately after the docstring and the magic variables at the beginning of Listing 5-2 is the import random statement. We can now use random methods, just the same as any built-in object. The following block are the **constants**: all the salable items in a dictionary called stock; each item containing a (price, damage, speed) tuple; a set containing the items, which are some sort of armor; and four tuples containing verb phrases for the hits and misses and noun phrases for the damage_report and life_changing output. It's important to have the form of the final output in mind when designing these phrases. Each phrase in the set needs to be of a compatible grammatical structure, mood, and tense; otherwise, the final output won't sound right.

The preferences section is minimal; most important is the trace variable, which controls output of the trace table during execution. Set this variable to True, and you will get the workings out printed to the screen as you run the script. I needed to set up an empty list to contain the character profiles; it is called players. The character profile is held in a temporary dictionary called profile.

The first four fields are input by the user. I have provided a very basic form of validation: in cases of choices from a fixed list, the script guesses the correct answer on the basis of the first letter, and the other fields are capitalized.

The next four statistics are generated using the random module; the method random.randint(start, end) will return a pseudorandom integer between the start and end of the specified range, much like rolling polyhedral dice. The combat stats are worked out from the random values returned and are checked to be within the range 1 to 100; if not, the value is rerolled. Finally, this section prints out the completed character profile.

I moved the shopping section into the character-generation loop for simplicity, and the stock list is displayed using a for loop. Notice how the price is extracted from the tuple values using an additional index stock[item][0]. The user is prompted to make a choice; the choice is added to the current player's inventory; and the price is deducted from the player's gold supply. Finally, the user is prompted to choose a weapon, and if that weapon is not in the player's inventory, a fist is provided instead. Actually, what happens is the player gets the relevant tuple from the stock dictionary loaded into the weapon stat. The inventory is checked against the armour_types set, and the resulting tuple gets loaded into the player's armour stat. The complete profile is then written out to the player's list.

The combat takes place continuously inside a while statement that checks both players' statistics to make sure neither player is dead. Nested within that is a for loop that toggles between the players giving each a chance to play by setting one as the attacker and the other as target. It does so by getting the player's index from players, using the enumerate() function, and then turning that into a Boolean value. When the player's turn ends, the Boolean is reversed with the not operator and assigned to target.

Now, I can use the target and attacker indices to refer to both members of the players list. In some places, I have to refer to values nested three deep in players, whether dictionaries, lists, or tuples. The syntax is fairly straightforward so long as you can remember which structure is nested inside which—so making some notes is probably worth your time.

Next, the velocity is calculated. If the value is positive, the attack counts as a hit; a negative value is a miss. The value is set with a rather arbitrary calculation designed to produce a value somewhere between 0 and 7 and then deliberately *constrained* if it is greater than 7 to prevent unnecessary errors. This value is then looked up in the hits or misses tuple, and a message is printed about the success or failure of the blow.

This result is fed into the equation to calculate the amount of damage, which works in a similar manner to produce a weighted random value, which is then constrained. These underlying values are required merely to produce some plausible output, which is hopefully fun to play.

Finally, the damage score is subtracted from the target's life, and the target's life score is checked. If it is less than or equal to 0, the game ends with a break statement and a declaration of the winner. This momentarily ejects the program's execution into the while loop, which checks both players life stats. As you already know, one of them does not have a life score above 0, so the while loop terminates too, and the program should exit cleanly.

Listing 5-2. rpcombat.py

```
#! /usr/bin/env python

"""

rpcombat.py
Purpose: Simple Role-Playing Combat Game.
Target System: GNU/Linux
Interface: Command-line
Functional Requirements: The user must be able to generate more than one
 character profile, equip those characters with suitable weapons,
```

and model hand-to-hand combat between characters.
Testing methods: trace table and play testing.
Test values: (Ez, Tall, Pixie, female), (Inkon, Small, Troll, male)
Expected results: All statistics should be integers in the (1-99) range.
        Apart from that, this script needs play-testing.
Limitations: Too many to mention.
"""

```python
__version__ = 0.1
__maintainer__ = "maintainer@website.com"
__status__ = "Prototype"

# Import modules

import random

# set up constant data.

stock = {'shield':(15,20,50),
               'sword':(60,60,40),
               'dagger':(25,30,50),
               'halberd':(80,80,30),
               'club':(15,30,30),
               'flail':(50,70,45),
               'hammer':(99,100,20),
               'cuirass':(30,45,20),
               'armour':(101,100,0),
               'lantern':(10,5,30),
               'pole':(10,5,50),
               'rope':(10,5,70)}
armour_types = set(['shield','cuirass','armour'])
hits = ('hits','bashes','smites','whacks',
               'shreds','mutilates','lacerates','annihilates')
misses = ('misses', 'nearly hits', 'fails to connect with',
               'swipes wildly at', 'flails ineffectually at',
               'gets nowhere near', 'nearly decapitates self instead of',
               'hits self on the foot, to the amusement of')
damage_report = ('small insult','flesh wound','deep slash','ragged gash',
               'savage laceration','fractured rib-cage',
               'smashed-up face','split skull')
life_changing = ('a scar.','bruising.','serious blood-loss.',
               'total debilitation.', 'chronic concussion.','a severed limb.',
               'multiple fractures.','an amputated head.')

# Preferences
# Set to 'True' to trace variables.
trace = False
max_players = 2

# This is a global variable.
players = []
```

```
# Generate characters
while len(players) < max_players:
        print()
        print("New Character")
        print()
        # Create empty profile dictionary
        profile = {'Name':"", 'Desc':"", 'Gender':"", 'Race':"", 'Muscle':0,
                        'Brainz':0, 'Speed':0, 'Charm':0, 'life':0, 'magic':0,
                        'prot':0, 'gold':0, 'inventory':[]}

        # Prompt user for user-defined information (Name, Desc, Gender, Race)
        name = input('What is your name? ')
        desc = input('Describe yourself: ')
        gender = input('What Gender are you? (male/female/unsure): ')
        race = input('What Race are you? - (Pixie/Vulcan/Gelfling/Troll): ')

        # Validate user input
        profile['Name'] = name.capitalize()
        profile['Desc'] = desc.capitalize()
        gender = gender.lower()
        if gender.startswith('f'):
                profile['Gender'] = 'female'
        elif gender.startswith('m'):
                profile['Gender'] = 'male'
        else:
                profile['Gender'] = 'neuter'
        race = race.capitalize()
        if race.startswith('P'):
                profile['Race'] = 'Pixie'
        elif race.startswith('V'):
                profile['Race'] = 'Vulcan'
        elif race.startswith('G'):
                profile['Race'] = 'Gelfling'
        elif race.startswith('T'):
                profile['Race'] = 'Troll'
        else:
                profile['Race'] = 'Goblin'

        # Generate stats ('Muscle', 'Brainz', 'Speed', 'Charm')
        profile['Muscle'] = random.randint(3,33) + random.randint(3,33) \
                                        + random.randint(3,33)
        profile['Brainz'] = random.randint(3,33) + random.randint(3,33) \
                                        + random.randint(3,33)
        profile['Speed'] = random.randint(3,33) + random.randint(3,33) \
                                        + random.randint(3,33)
        profile['Charm'] = random.randint(3,33) + random.randint(3,33) \
                                        + random.randint(3,33)

        # Work out combat stats (life, magic, prot, gold)
        life = (profile['Muscle'] + (profile['Speed']/2) + random.randint(9,49))/2
        magic = (profile['Brainz'] + (profile['Charm']/2) + random.randint(9,49))/2
```

```
prot = (profile['Speed'] + (profile['Brainz']/2) + random.randint(9,49))/2
gold = random.randint(9,49) + random.randint(9,49) + random.randint(9,49)

# Validate stats
if life > 0 and life < 100:
      profile['life'] = life
else:
        life = random.randint(9,99)
if magic > 0 and magic < 100:
      profile['magic'] = magic
else:
        magic = random.randint(9,99)
if prot > 0 and prot < 100:
      profile['prot'] = prot
else:
        prot = random.randint(9,99)
if gold > 0:
      profile['gold'] = gold
else:
        gold = random.randint(9,99)

# Output the character sheet
fancy_line = "<~~==|#|==~~++**\@/**++~~==|#|==~~>"
print()
print(fancy_line)
print("\t", profile['Name'])
print("\t", profile['Race'], profile['Gender'])
print("\t", profile['Desc'])
print(fancy_line)
print()
print("\tMuscle: ", profile['Muscle'], "\tlife: ", profile['life'])
print("\tBrainz: ", profile['Brainz'], "\tmagic: ", profile['magic'])
print("\tSpeed: ", profile['Speed'], "\tprotection: ", profile['prot'])
print("\tCharm: ", profile['Charm'], "\tgold: ", profile['gold'])
print()

# Prompt user to buy some equipment.
purchase = input('Would you like to buy some equipment? ')
while purchase != 'done':
        # Display shop stock list with prices.
        print()
        print("<==|#|==\SHOP/==|#|==>")
        for item in stock:
                print("\t", item, stock[item][0])
        print("<==|#|==\@@@@/==|#|==>")
        print()
        print("You have", profile['gold'], "gold.")
        # Prompt user to make a purchase.
        purchase = input('Please choose an item or type "done" to quit. ')
        # If the item is in stock and the player has enough gold, buy it.
        if purchase in stock:
```

```
                        if stock[purchase][0] <= profile['gold']:
                            print("You buy a", purchase, "for",stock[purchase][0], \
                                                    "gold pieces.")
                            profile['gold'] -= stock[purchase][0]
                            profile['inventory'].append(purchase)
                            print("You have a", " ".join(profile['inventory']), \
                                                    "in your bag.")
                            print("You have", profile['gold'], "left.")
                        elif purchase == 'done':
                            break
                    else:
                            print("You don't have enough gold to buy that.")
                else:
                        print("We don't have", purchase, "in stock.")
            print("You own a", " ".join(profile['inventory']))

            # Prompt user to enter into combat and choose a weapon
            print(profile['Name'], "Are you ready for mortal combat?")
            weapon = input("Then choose your weapon: ")
            # The weapon must be in player's inventory.
            # Default to fist if weapon not available.
            weapon = weapon.lower()
            if weapon in profile['inventory']:
                    profile['weapon'] = stock[weapon]
            else:
                    profile['weapon'] = (0,20,50)
            # See if player has any armour
            profile['armour'] = (0,0,50)
            for armour_type in armour_types:
                    if armour_type in profile['inventory']:
                            profile['armour'] = stock[armour_type]

            print(profile['Name'], "is now ready for battle.")
            # Add new player to list of players
            players.append(profile)

# Combat

print()
print("Then let the combat begin!")
print()

vel_max = 23
vel_min = 1
dam_max = 23
# Loop while both players are still alive
while players[0]['life'] > 0 and players[1]['life'] > 0:
        for attacker, player in enumerate(players):
                target = int(not bool(attacker))
                life_left = players[target]['life']
                # Calculate velocity of blow
```

```
attack_speed = players[attacker]['Speed']
weapon_speed = players[attacker]['weapon'][2]
attack_chance = random.randint(1,players[attacker]['Brainz'])
attack_velocity = attack_speed + weapon_speed + attack_chance
target_prot = players[target]['prot']
armour_speed = players[target]['armour'][2]
target_velocity = target_prot + armour_speed
velocity = (attack_velocity - target_velocity) / 2
if trace:
        print("\t", velocity)
if velocity > 0:
        if velocity > vel_max:
                vel_max = velocity
        hit_type = int(7 * velocity / vel_max)
        if hit_type > 7:
                hit_type = 7
        if trace:
                print("\t\tHit#", hit_type)
        print(players[attacker]['Name'], hits[hit_type], \
                players[target]['Name']),

else:
        if velocity < vel_min:
                vel_min = velocity
        miss_type = int(velocity / vel_max)
        if miss_type > 7:
                miss_type = 7
        if trace:
                print("\t\tMiss#", miss_type)
        print(players[attacker]['Name'], misses[miss_type], \
                        players[target]['Name'])

        continue

# Calculate damage inflicted by blow
attack_strength = players[attacker]['Muscle']
weapon_damage = players[attacker]['weapon'][1]
attack_damage = attack_strength + weapon_damage + velocity
target_strength = players[target]['Muscle']
armour_strength = players[target]['armour'][1]
target_chance = random.randint(9,players[target]['Brainz'])
target_defence = target_strength + armour_strength + target_chance
potential_damage = (attack_damage - target_defence)
if potential_damage < 1:
        potential_damage = 2
damage = random.randint(1,potential_damage)
if trace:
        print()
print("\t\tDamage:", damage)
if damage > dam_max:
        dam_max = damage
# Print damage report
```

```
                    damage_type = int(7 * damage/dam_max)
                    if damage_type > 7:
                                damage_type = 7
                    if trace:
                            print("\t\t\tDamage#", damage_type)
                    change_type = int(5 * damage/life_left)
                    if change_type > 7:
                                change_type = 7
                    if trace:
                            print("\t\t\t\tChange#", change_type)
                    print("inflicting a", damage_report[damage_type], \
                                "and", life_changing[change_type])

                    # Inflict damage on target.
                    players[target]['life'] -= damage
                    # Check whether target is still alive or not.
                    if players[target]['life'] <= 0:
                            # Print winner
                            print()
                            print(players[target]['Name'], "collapses in a pool of blood")
                            print(players[attacker]['Name'], "wins the fight.")
                            print()
                            break

if trace:
        print()
        print("\t\tmax", dam_max, vel_max, ":: min", vel_min)
        print()
```

There are several things to be said about Listing 5-2. It is very long and repetitious, and by far the longest script you have encountered so far in this book. The first thing that needs to be done is to get rid of all unnecessary repetitions. This is always true in situations *where removing repetition makes the code easier to read.*

Also, some of its methods are rather brutal and rely on receiving the right data in the first place. How could the error checking and validation be improved to make sure the internal values stay within useful ranges? The output is rather gruesome and not particularly grammatical, so how could the output be improved? Perhaps it could describe a magical battle, a war of rhetoric and wit, or something silly and fun. I'm sure you could improve it.

Development on this version (0.1) of the script stopped as soon as it fulfilled the test requirements that I had set. Any improvements, new features, or fixes mean going back to the pseudocode stage and sketching out the changes, as well as setting new tests to check whether the new code works—before you do any further coding. When you do get that far you need to bump up the version number, because you are now working on version 0.2.

If you feel adventurous, you could adapt the script to allow more player characters to fight, by upping the max_players count. The toggling of attacker and target is rather ungraceful too. Perhaps something could be done to reorder the players list, so each character gets to fight all the others. The methods of hit and damage calculation could also be improved; currently, the game gives too much weight to the weapon statistics for example.

One of the ways we could simplify things would be to have containers for commands, like the data containers we have explored in this chapter. Fortunately, we can create these; and in the next chapter, I'll be introducing you to building your own functions.

Jargon Busting

As usual, here is the roundup of new words in this chapter:

- *Arbitrary:* In this instance, anything defined by the programmer is arbitrary.

- *Complex data types:* These are structured or compound types constructed from a sequence of other types of data.

- *Constant:* A constant value does not change during the execution of the program.

- *Constrain:* Ensure that the results of a calculation fall between a specified range.

- *Hash:* A hash is number calculated from a dictionary key to help with storage. This number is designed to be smaller than the key to aid efficiency.

- *Immutable:* An immutable value that cannot be edited in place.

- *Index:* An index is a token of an immutable type in square brackets immediately following the variable name, used to point to a specific item in the sequence.

- *Iterable:* This refers to a code object that can be iterated.

- *Iterate:* When you loop through items in a sequence one item at a time, you iterate it.

- *Iterator:* This construct is designed to allow looping.

- *Mapping:* This refers to a sequence that maps hashable values to arbitrary objects.

- *Matrix:* A matrix is a multidimensional sequence.

- *Method:* A method is a function specifically attached to an object or class of objects.

- *Mutable:* A mutable value can be changed.

- *Operation:* This action is performed on two variables (operands), usually of a mathematical or logical nature.

- *Queue:* A queue is a first in, first out (FIFO) structure. You push things in at one end and pop values out of the other.

- *Resultant:* This value is returned as the result of a process.

- *Separator:* This text string is used to distinguish between items of data.

- *Sequence:* A sequence is the simplest sort of complex data type in Python. Lists, strings, and tuples are the types of sequences.

- *Sequence packing:* Sequence packing is the action of assigning a sequence of comma-separated values to a variable.

- *Slice:* This refers to a smaller segment of a sequence.

- *Stack:* This is a last in, first out (LIFO) structure, used rather like the discard pile in a card game.

- *Traverse:* When you go through the items in a sequence in order, you traverse them.

Summary

You have taken on a lot of new information in this chapter, culminating in developing the ideas from previous chapters to create a much more complex program that processes several related pieces of information and returns a rather verbose human readable response. This level of sophistication was made possible using Python's data structures—strings, tuples, and lists (which are all kinds of sequence) and dictionaries (a mapping).

You have also learned that some of these structures (i.e., strings and tuples) are immutable, whereas others like dictionaries and lists are mutable, which means they can be modified. You know how to access items of a sequence using indexes and slices; you can test for membership of a structure using the in keyword or iterate through an entire sequence using the for keyword or a list comprehension. You have encountered several different uses of lists as stacks, queues and matrices of information and you know how to create dictionaries out of key-value pairs.

You also now have at your disposal a number of methods you can use to manipulate your data to produce useful output. Combined with looping techniques, these data structures provide the logical building blocks with which you can process your data. In fact, using what you have already learned, you could probably write a program that will do most things you can think of. However that code will be very long-winded, possibly difficult to read, and not really reusable. So, in the next chapter, I will introduce the next stage of program development, known as *abstraction*, which means you get to create your own functions.

CHAPTER 6

■■■

Functions

In the previous chapters, you have learned how to assign variables, do sums, perform comparisons, set conditions, and make choices. In the preceding chapter, I showed you how to store, process, and retrieve greater amounts of information by grouping the data into lists and dictionaries. You have learned enough vocabulary to enable you to design programs that can solve a wide variety of problems. Now, it's time to up the game to a new level.

The skills you have acquired so far are more than enough for writing top-down scripts like the examples in the previous chapters. No matter how long the scripts become, execution still starts at the top of the page and stops at the bottom. The only problem is that if you want to do something more than once, the section has to be repeated verbatim. This also means that modifying the code will become difficult, as you can often find yourself having to rewrite the whole script to change one small thing. It would be great to be able to break down the program into manageable pieces of functionality, and luckily, Python gives us a way to do this, using functions.

In this chapter, I'll cover how to write functions and segment your code into manageable pieces. In the process, I'll explain how to refactor one of our example applications.

Accessing Privileged Information

The first design considerations in making a new function are what kind of input it needs and what information the function will return. Of close importance are the type and structure of the data that will be fed in and retrieved. Data supplied to a function are called parameters, and the final information that is returned is known as **results**, or output. Our initial specification for the function design should also include a general description of the function's specific purpose.

■ **Note** An important effect of using functions is that their internal working can be changed without affecting the other parts of the program.

Defining Functions

Functions are defined using a def statement. The word def is followed by the name of the function with an optional list of parameters in parentheses, and the line ends with a colon, which indicates that the next lines must be indented as a block or suite of instructions. Let's start with a function that takes no parameters:

```
>>> def generate_rpc():
...     """Role-Playing Character generator

    """
...     profile = {}
...     print "New Character"
...     return profile
```

This block of instructions proceeds in exactly the same way as a complete script. So, in essence, we give a name to each piece of functionality, and they are called functions.

If you want to provide some notes on what the function does, you can do so in the docstring, which must be the first thing in the function. The docstring is then followed by a series of statements that are the core functionality.

The function can also return some data using a return statement. The function's last line specifies which variables get returned to the main program. If there is nothing to return, you do not have to use a return statement, and Python will assume None as the default return value.

■ **Note** The convention is to name functions in a similar way to variables: using lowercase letters with underscores. The main difference is that functions should have names that suggest actions (verbs) rather than things (nouns).

Up to this point, the block of code in our function has not yet been run; it has simply been assigned to the **function definition**. To get the code to run, you need to call the function from the main body of the program. (This is called a **function call**.) Since we have given names to functions, we can call those functions any number of times:

```
>>> generate_rpc()
New Character
{}
```

We haven't specified any parameters in this example, hence the empty parentheses after the function name.

Sending Out Invitations

Most functions work on some data that they have been given by the main program. In order for the function to receive data, it needs to set up some empty containers to hold the data. These become variables unique to the function and are known as **formal parameters**, and it's best if they don't use the same names as in the main program. These formal parameters have to be specified in the parentheses after the function name on the first line of the function definition.

```
import random
def roll(sides, dice):
    result = 0
    for rolls in range(0,dice):
        result += random.randint(1,sides)
    return result
```

This function might be called from the main program in the following way:

```
muscle = roll(33,3)
```

The values in parentheses in the function call are known as arguments; they correspond to the formal parameters in the function definition. In this case, the first argument, 33, is bound to the parameter sides, and the second argument, 3, is bound to the parameter dice. This effectively creates two variables, sides and dice, to be used inside the function. If you just send the function values like this, there must be the same number of arguments as parameters, and they have to be in the right order, so these are known as **positional arguments**. You could substitute the actual values in the function call with variables if you prefer. Just remember that the function is going to refer to that value by the name of the parameter that receives it, and the original variable will remain unaffected; only the value gets passed on.

Note The variables sides and dice only exist inside the function roll(). If you try to use them outside the function, you'll get a name error. See the "Understanding Scope" section later in this chapter.

You can set default values for your parameters in the function definition:

```
def roll(sides = 6, dice = 1):
```

This would allow you to call roll() with no arguments, which would return a random number between 1 and 6, as if you had called roll(6,1).

Another option is to call the function using **keyword arguments**, where we can specify which parameter gets which value. Although this involves a little more typing, the benefit is that the order no longer matters, and it the function call is easier to understand.

```
>>> roll(dice = 3, sides = 33)
35
```

Passing an Unknown Number of Values into the Function

Sometimes, you may want your function to accept an unknown number of arguments. To do this, you precede the name of the parameter with an asterisk (*). This syntax collects all the remaining positional arguments into a tuple that it assigns to the parameter name following the asterisk.

```
>>> def collect_args(*args):
...     print args
...
>>> collect_args('one', 'two', 'three')
('one', 'two', 'three')
```

You can also collect keyword arguments using a double asterisk, and you will get a dictionary.

```
>>> def collect_kwargs(**kwargs):
...     print kwargs
...
```

```
>>> collect_kwargs(one = 1, two = 2, three = 3)
{'three': 3, 'two': 2, 'one': 1}
```

You can use these two concepts together in a single function, but you must be careful to specify positional parameters before keyword arguments.

Also, parameters that are to gather up any remaining arguments go at the end in the same order: positional first and then keywords. In big applications, it's best to avoid mixing keyword and positional arguments.

```
>>> def collect_args(b, e, a = 432, c = 512, *args, **kwargs):
...     print a, b, c, e
...     print args
...     print kwargs
>>> collect_args(486, 648, 432, 512, 576, 682, 768, first = 729, second = 546, third
= 819)
432 486 512 648
(576, 682, 768)
{'second': 546, 'third': 819, 'first': 729}
```

Note that you can use any name you like after the asterisks (* or **), but the convention is to call them *args and **kwargs.

You can also use the argument-gathering asterisks in the function call, which basically expands the tuple or dictionary in line, so that the function sees the tuple or dictionary's contents as normal positional arguments and keyword arguments.

```
>>> args = (486, 648, 432, 512, 576, 682, 768)
>>> kwargs = {'first': 729, 'second':546, 'third':819}
>>> collect_args(*args, **kwargs)
432 486 512 648
(576, 682, 768)
{'second': 546, 'third': 819, 'first': 729}
```

Notice that args in the function call does not contain the same values as args in the function. You can use this technique to pass arguments through one function into another, which can sometimes be useful.

Using docstrings to Document Your Function

Once a function is fully coded and passes the tests you have set for it, it is a good time to edit its docstring to fit with the expectations of Python's documentation tools.

Docstrings are expected to follow convention: The first line of a docstring should be a short description of the function that makes sense by itself and fits on only one line (usually a maximum of 79 characters, including any indentation). The next line should be left blank. After that, the body of the docstring should contain a description of the function's parameters, a longer description of the function, notes about the algorithm used, and an example of how to use the function that includes details of optional arguments, keyword arguments, and its return values. You might also want to include information about possible **side-effects**, **exceptions**, and restrictions on when the function can be called (these matters will be covered later in this book). In short, all the information that another programmer would need to be able to use the function. It is very important to update your docstrings and comments every time the code changes.

Working with Variable Scope

One way of conceptualizing functions is to think of them as black boxes that take in source data, process it, and pass it back. The code in the main program that sends the source data and receives the result is known as the **calling procedure**. It doesn't need to know what is inside the black box, so long as the **source data** and results are clearly identified.

Understanding Scope

When you write a function, you should not have to worry about using names that will clash with names used in the other parts of the program. This is why we have the concept of **scopes**.

When any program is run, the interpreter keeps track of all the names that are created and used in the program. These names are tracked in a table referred to as a **symbol table** and can be viewed as a dictionary using the built-in vars() function. The variables created in the main program's symbol table are known as **global** variables, because any part of the program can access these variables. These can be viewed with the built-in globals() function. You will notice that the result of running vars() with no arguments inside the main program is the same as running globals(). So far, the script examples in this book have only used global data.

▓ **Caution** Do not attempt to modify the dictionary returned by vars(), locals(), or globals(). Doing so may not have the effect you want.

Any variable that is created in a function is stored in a symbol table unique to that function; this data is known as **local** data and can be accessed within that function using the locals() function. The main body of the program (global scope) cannot access the variables set inside the function (local scope). The function, however, is still able to access names in the main body, that is, **globals**. Hence, you have two ways to get at a function to process some data: The correct way is to take that data as a parameter for the function; the function will process it and then return the result, which will be collected by the main program. The other way is to let the function directly access and process the global data, but this second way is discouraged because the function works with only particular variable names and cannot be reused anywhere else.

Listing 6-1 shows a simple example of this behavior.

Listing 6-1. *dave.py*

```
#! /usr/bin/env python

"""Dave the cardboard box.

A simple scope example.
"""
fred = 1
pete = 2
def cardboard_box():
    dave = fred + pete
    return vars()
```

```
print("Outside the box:")
print(vars())
print("Inside the box")
print(cardboard_box())
```

This program gives the following output:

```
Outside the box:
{'pete': 2, '__builtins__': <module '__builtin__' (built-in)>, '__file__':
'test.py', 'fred': 1, 'cardboard_box': <function cardboard_box at 0xb7ddf224>,
'__name__': '__main__', '__doc__': 'Dave the cardboard box\n\nA simple scope
example.\n'}
Inside the box
{'dave': 3}
```

You can see that, although fred and pete are global citizens, and dave can borrow freely from them, dave is the only *local* and does not exist in the *global* scope. If I try to access dave outside the cardboard_box function, I get NameError: name 'dave' is not defined.

If dave was defined alongside fred and pete in the outer scope, the opposite problem could occur. If I tried to access dave from inside the cardboard_box(), I would only be able to access the value set inside the cardboard_box(). The global dave value would remain inaccessible. Variables in this situation are known as shadowed globals and are demonstrated in Listing 6-2. If this is ever a problem, you can usually get round it by passing the global value to the function under a different name.

Listing 6-2. Dave's Shadow Side

```
print "dave\tfred\tpete"
dave = 0
fred = 1
pete = 2
def cardboard_box():
    global fred, pete
    dave = fred + pete
    print("Inside the box:")
    print(dave, '\t', fred, '\t', pete)
cardboard_box()
print("Outside the box:")
print(dave, '\t', fred, '\t', pete)
```

```
dave      fred       pete
Inside the box:
(3, '\t', 1, '\t', 2)
Outside the box:
(0, '\t', 1, '\t', 2)
```

■ **Tip** The vars() function can also return a symbol table, for which you need to provide the name of the object as an argument.

Using the global Statement

Although you can access global variables from inside functions, it is always recommended to declare that you are using these variables using the global statement (see Listing 6-3). If you ever need to change a global variable from inside a function, using the global statement is a must.

Listing 6-3. *Dave Goes Global*

```
#! /usr/bin/env python

"""Dave the cardboard box

A simple scope example.
"""

fred = 1
pete = 2

def cardboard_box():
    global dave
    dave = fred + pete
    return vars()

print("Inside the box")
print(cardboard_box())
fred = dave
print("Outside the box:")
print(vars())
```

And here's the output:

```
Inside the box
{}
Outside the box:
{'pete': 2, '__builtins__': <module 'builtins' (built-in)>, '__file__': 'test.py',
'fred': 3, 'dave': 3, 'cardboard_box': <function cardboard_box at 0xb7c4d86c>,
'__name__': '__main__', '__package__': None, '__doc__': 'Dave the cardboard box\n\nA
simple scope example.\n'}
```

Manipulating Lists and Dictionaries

Parameters to a function are passed by value. However, in the case of **objects** (unlike simple types such as integers and strings), if you modify the parts of an object, including items in a list or a dictionary, the changes are reflected outside the function as well. This means that a function can be used to modify a mutable data type such as a dictionary or list. Technically, such a **modification procedure** is not a **pure function**, as it neither needs a return value or indeed, any input parameters.

In order to avoid strange side-effects, a good general policy is to send and return immutable values from functions and keep any modification procedures for your mutable types separate. If you send a list or dictionary to a function, all you are doing is sending it a **pointer** to the same global instance of that object, just as if you had written local_list = global_list. Please review Chapter 5 if you've forgotten how this works.

```
>>> global_list = []
>>> def modify_list(local_list):
...     local_list.extend( ['dave', 'pete', 'fred'] )
...
>>> result = modify_list(global_list)
>>> print(global_list)
['dave', 'pete', 'fred']
>>> print(result)
None
```

Here, the local symbol table for modify_list() will contain only local_list, as the function doesn't create any variables itself and doesn't return any either.

Refactoring rpcombat.py to Reduce Repetition

Now that you understand global and local scopes, you are ready to start **refactoring**. Refactoring is the process of rewriting your application to make it easier to maintain or more efficient, but keeping the same behavior.

Let's go back to rpcombat.py and examine the refactoring possibilities. The first bits of code that stand out are the repeated calls to random.randint(). This particular function gets called several times in different ways with different values. The trick here is to come up with a function that will work in all these instances and be flexible enough to work with future changes. As these future changes are as yet unknown, the only way we can cater for them is to make write a generic piece of functionality that can replace these individual pieces of code with calls to that function. This is called **generalization**.

It may be useful to look at the original design to recall what the original intention of the code that needs refactoring. In this case, I was trying to model the rolling of some dice. The interesting part of the problem is that the number of dice and the number of sides that the dice have will need to vary according to the range of values that need to be returned. This gives me a clue what the input parameters should be, and I decided to call them sides and dice. In return, I want to get a random integer back that falls within the specified range. Now, I can construct my new function.

```
def roll(sides, dice = 1):
    """Dice rolling simulator

    sides: Number of sides the die has

    dice: number of dice to be rolled (defaults to 1)
```

```
Returns a random number between dice and dice * sides
weighted towards the average.
"""
result = 0
for rolls in range(1,dice):
    result += random.randint(1,sides)
return result
```

Remember that this code will not get executed by the program yet, so the next thing to do is to go through the script and replace all the calls to random.randint() with calls to the new roll() function.

■ **Tip** The Find or "Search and Replace" functions in your text editor can be very useful in helping to make sure you don't miss any lines and keeping your changes consistent.

Once you have made the changes, they need to be tested before anything else happens. In fact, it's a good idea to test each case before you move on to the next. Otherwise, you could give yourself headaches trying to trace any problems that arise from the changes. In order for the new function to pass, the output must be exactly the same as before. Whatever the new function does should be invisible to the user.

Cutting Out the Waffle

This round of testing may bring new issues to light. In order to help you keep track of what's going on with your code, do the minimum necessary to get the new code to pass its tests. If the new code fails, you should roll back the changes to the point where the code passes again. Also, if using the function doesn't work, don't sweat it: reverse the changes and move on. There is no rule that says you have to abstract everything into a function.

The processes of placing code into functions (**abstraction**) and turning code that deals with specifics into general-purpose code (generalization) can also be applied to your testing procedures, and this is a good thing to do. All these test procedures will eventually get moved outside the program into a separate module, so abstraction and generalization are also good preparation. The rule to remember is to write your tests first and then make sure your existing code still passes before attempting to refactor it. Although this might seem like a laborious approach, in fact, it speeds up the development of new code and provides a mechanism for flagging up which part of the code needs fixing next, rather than having to keep all the details in your head. This has to be a *good thing*.

Next, I decided to abstract some of the larger repetitive sections of the program. Moving the character-generation code into its own function was straightforward. This section doesn't require any information to work on as it generates it all from scratch, so I could copy the whole section as it stood and added return profile to the end:

```
def generate_rpc():
    """Role-Playing Character generator

    Takes no arguments
    Returns a new character profile dictionary
    """
    print()
    print("New Character")
    print()
```

```
    # Create empty profile dictionary
    profile = {'Name':"", 'Desc':"", 'Gender':"", 'Race':"", 'Muscle':0,
            'Brainz':0, 'Speed':0, 'Charm':0, 'life':0,
            'magic':0, 'prot':0, 'gold':0, 'inventory':[]}
    ...
    return profile
```

I then replaced the copied section of code from the main section with profile = generate_rpc().

```
# The main body of the program starts here,
# So this is where the flow of execution begins.
# Generate characters
while len(players) < max_players:
    # Call character generation function.
    profile = generate_rpc()
    ...
```

The equipment buying section was trickier. Because I'd put a break statement inside the original while loop, the interpreter complained once I had moved it into a separate function, because the break statement was now outside the loop. Oops. The fix for this was to turn the break statement into a return statement that returns the value False. It could just as well return any value that evaluates to False, so None would also work. This forces the flow of execution to break out of the while loop that contains the call for this function. The return at the end of the function has to return *something*; it doesn't really matter what it returns, so long as it evaluates to True. I'm only using the return values to control the loop as the buy_equipment() function is actually a dictionary modification procedure, so it doesn't need to receive or return any values for any other reason.

Then, I had a small stroke of inspiration: over the course of testing, I had started to get annoyed by the unnecessary 'Would you like to buy some equipment? ' prompt. So I replaced it with profile['inventory'] == [], which would evaluate to True if the inventory was empty and False if it contained anything. The while loop wrapping the function call now looked like this:

```
        shopping = profile['inventory'] == []
        while shopping:
                shopping = buy_equipment()
    print "You own a", " ".join(profile['inventory'])
```

This change had the desired effect, except that it made it possible to exit the loop without having bought anything. I replaced the return False statement in the buy_equipment() function to return profile['inventory'] == [], which did the trick.

Next, I started to wonder what would happen if the generated character didn't have enough money to buy anything. I made one further alteration to the breakout return: profile['inventory'] == [] and profile['gold'] > 10. This answers the (theoretical) question of whether to continue shopping with True if the inventory is empty and enough money is left to buy something; otherwise, it returns False.

```
def buy_equipment():
    """Purchase an item of equipment

    ...

    # Prompt user to make a purchase.
    purchase = input('Please choose an item or type "done" to quit. ')
```

```
# If the item is in stock and the player has enough gold, buy it.
if purchase in stock:
    ...
elif purchase == 'done' or purchase == "":
    return profile['inventory'] == [] and profile['gold'] > 10
else:
    print("We don't have", purchase, "in stock.")
return purchase
```

That passed its initial testing, so I decided to move on immediately.

I was also getting fed up with having to choose a weapon when the character obviously had only one weapon in inventory. First, I needed to retrieve a list of what weapons the character has obtained. This was relatively easy to work out because everything in the inventory apart from the armor can be used as a weapon, so I constructed a list comprehension to return the members of profile['inventory'] not in the armour_types set. I made the following actions conditional on the length of the list. If the resultant list only contained one entry, that item is automatically chosen. If there are fewer, the character wields a fist by default. Otherwise, the user is prompted to choose a weapon as before.

I wondered whether I could use the same list comprehension technique to set up the armor statistics. So I replaced the following code

```
for armour_type in armour_types:
        if armour_type in profile['inventory']:
                profile['armour'] = stock[armour_type]
```

with this

```
armour_stats = [stock[item] for item in profile['inventory']
                            if item in armour_types]

if armour_stats:
        profile['armour'] = armour_stats[0]
else:
        profile['armour'] = (0,0,50)
```

This worked fine, but I don't know if it really constitutes much of an improvement. It doesn't fix any particular problem, but it does reduce one level of indentation. Sections that have lots of nested indented blocks are always likely to be good candidates for refactoring, and one of the aims of this exercise is to reduce the levels of indentation in the code. This must, however, be balanced with an attitude of "if it ain't broke, don't fix it." You can make the coding process much more fun if you stay focused on making the changes that give the most gratifying results and then move on as soon as those changes satisfy the design requirements. So again, I won't dwell on this section.

Keeping Your Code Readable

I also wanted to improve a couple of output messages. I wanted the inventory list to have an *and* separating the last two entries rather than a comma, and I wanted to be gender specific when reporting self inflicted actions.

I started by creating an empty structure:

```
def join_with_and(sequence):
    """Join up a list with commas and 'and' between last two items
    """
```

```
print "join_with_and(sequence) was called"
return
```

Next, I inserted a dummy call in the main body:

```
handbag = join_with_and(profile['inventory'])
```

Having an empty structure in place allows me to test that the basic call works first and then proceed to design the new function. The design for this one is fairly simple:

1. Pop off the last item of the list.

2. Join the rest of the list with commas.

3. Add the word *and* followed by the popped-off item.

I don't want to use list.pop() here for two reasons: if the function was sent a list, this method would modify it in place and I would lose the last entry as a side-effect of this function. Also, I want this function to be generalized enough that I could send it a tuple instead, so I used slice notation:

```
last_item = sequence[-1]
sentence = ", ".join(sequence[:-1])
sentence = sentence + " and " + last_item
```

This solution worked fine with lists that had more than one item, but it still added *and* to single item lists. So I added an if...else clause so that single item lists would pass through.

Implementing the gender fix looked slightly more complex. Again, I began with an empty function definition:

```
def fix_gender(gender, phrase):
    """Replace the word 'them' with gender-specific pronoun
    """
    print("fix_gender() called with arguments:", gender, phrase)
    return
```

As the chances of the actual phrase coming up naturally were rather small, I inserted a dummy call into the buy_equipment() function to test my new function:

```
test_phrase = profile['Name'] + " buys themself some equipment"
print(fix_gender(profile['Gender'],test_phrase))
```

Having worked out the details of how to call the function, filling in the actual code became really straightforward:

```
if gender == 'female':
    sentence = phrase.replace('themself','herself')
elif gender == 'male':
    sentence = phrase.replace('themself','himself')
else:
    sentence = phrase.replace('themself','itself')
return sentence
```

Having ascertained that the function call worked as expected, it was now time to put a call in place to fix the bothersome output of the missed-shot handler, which follows the velocity calculation in the combat section. I simply needed to wrap a reference to `misses[miss_type]` up in a call to the new function:

```
fix_gender(players[attacker]['Gender'],misses[miss_type])
```

The best way to test this function was to choose a weak weapon, like a club for both combatants, to increase the chance of a miss. The results were satisfactory. It would be easy enough to expand the range of replacements if I needed to at any point in the future, but it wouldn't tick any boxes to spend any more time on it at this stage.

The Matrix Refactored

The last issue I wanted to look at was how to make it possible to have more than two combatants. I wanted to be able to create a list of matches and iterate through that for the combat section. Before making the big change in functionality, I made a couple of abstractions in the hope of increasing readability and ease of future development.

Again, I started with a couple of empty declarations.

```
def calc_velocity(attacker, target):
    """Calculate velocity of hit (or miss)
    """
    return velocity

def calc_damage(attacker, target, velocity):
    """Calculate the damage of the hit
    """
    return damage
```

Next, I moved the code into the functions, replacing each of the empty declarations with a call to the function and testing them one at a time. Once the program ran without errors again, I moved on to deal with the final alteration of adding more combatants.

For this slightly more complex change, the idea I had was to multiply the list of players by itself to produce a matrix of attacker and target matches, where the attacker and target are not the same character.

I started by creating a general function to create a tuple of matches out of more or less any sequence. Notice how I have used empty slice notation in order to copy the given sequence to opponents, this is to prevent the side-effect of accidentally modifying a global list, if one is sent to the function.

```
def ziply(sides=None):
    opponents = list(sides[:])
    opponents.reverse()
    matches = [(actor, target) for actor in sides
                 for target in opponents
                 if target != actor]
    return tuple(matches)
```

Again, the main work is done using a comprehensive list, and I made the function return the data in an immutable form, just to be sure the data can't be accidentally modified by any other process.

Next comes the implementation of my new function. I can replace this messy old code

```
for attacker, player in enumerate(players):
    target = int(not bool(attacker))
```

with

```
matches = ziply(range(0,len(players)))
for attacker, target in matches:
```

This retrieves a matrix of list indices from the ziply() function, which is then iterated through for each round of combat. Once this change has been tested and passed with the two-contestant setup, then and only then is it time to find out what happens if I increase the max_players count. In theory, that is all I should have to do now. I shouldn't have to go searching through the code to replace random variables, because I sensibly put this declaration clearly in the preferences section at the beginning of the code page. Of course, it may not be quite that simple. I have already been staring at one line that is clearly expecting only two players. I increased the value to three and continued with the testing.

The new method worked surprisingly well, but there was an issue with the conflict resolution, as I expected. The combat ends when the first character dies, with that character's attacker declared as the winner. I now need to rewrite the code so that the combat continues until there is only one player left standing.

The most logical and robust way of doing this seemed to be to remove the dead character from the player list using del players[target] and make the while loop dependent on that list having more than one entry using while len(players) > 1:. This is much cleaner.

The program isn't perfect by any means, but all I am going to do to finish off this stage of development is add a prompt right at the start to set the number of players. The program satisfies the design requirements and runs cleanly, without errors, so I'm going to push version 0.2 out of the door.

Before releasing version 0.2 into the wild, some matters of administration must be attended to. Quite a few of changes have been made since the last version, so I need to go through all the docstrings and comments and make sure they reflect the current state of affairs. I could also create a CHANGELOG file to contain a brief explanation of the changes along with a note of the version number that the changes apply to and a date for the changes (a **date stamp**). Once the programming project starts generating additional files, it may be sensible to put them all in a separate directory named after the program, or you may find it useful to group all your projects together in a common Projects directory in your home folder.

The full code for rpcombat-0.2.py now is shown in Listing 6-4.

Listing 6-4. *rpcombat.py Refactored*

```
#! /usr/bin/env python

"""

rpcombat.py
Purpose: Simple Role-Playing Combat Game.
Target System: GNU/Linux
Interface: Command-line
Functional Requirements: The user must be able to generate more than one
  character profile, equip those characters with suitable weapons,
  and model hand-to-hand combat between characters.
Testing methods: trace table and play testing.
Test values: (Ez, Tall, Pixie, female), (Inkon, Small, Troll, male)
Expected results: All statistics should be integers in the (1-99) range.
```

```
    Apart from that, this script needs play-testing.
Limitations: Too many to mention.
"""

__version__ = 0.2
__maintainer__ = "maintainer@website.com"
__status__ = "Prototype"

# Import modules

import random

# set up constant data.

stock = {'shield':(15,25,50),
         'sword':(60,60,50),
         'dagger':(25,40,60),
         'halberd':(80,75,40),
         'club':(15,40,40),
         'flail':(50,60,55),
         'hammer':(99,100,40),
         'cuirass':(30,50,20),
         'armour':(101,100,0),
         'lantern':(10,5,30),
         'pole':(10,5,50),
         'rope':(10,5,70)}
armour_types = set(['shield','cuirass','armour'])
hits = ('hits','bashes','smites','whacks',
        'shreds','mutilates','lacerates','annihilates')
misses = ('misses', 'nearly hits', 'fails to connect with',
          'swipes wildly at', 'flails ineffectually at',
          'gets nowhere near', 'nearly decapitates themself instead of',
          'hits themself on the foot, to the amusement of')
damage_report = ('small insult','flesh wound','deep slash','ragged gash',
                 'savage laceration','fractured rib-cage',
                 'smashed-up face','split skull')
life_changing = ('a scar.','bruising.','serious blood-loss.',
                 'total debilitation.', 'chronic concussion.','a severed limb.',
                 'multiple fractures.','an amputated head.')

# Preferences
# Set to 'True' to trace variables.
trace = False
reply = input('How many players?: ') or 2
max_players = int(reply)

# This is a global variable.
players = []

def roll(sides, dice = 1):
    """Dice rolling simulator

    sides: Number of sides the die has
```

```
    dice: number of dice to be rolled (defaults to 1)
    Returns a random number between dice and dice * sides
    weighted towards the average.
    """
    result = 0
    for rolls in range(1,dice):
        result += random.randint(1,sides)
    return result

def ziply(seq=None):
    """Create a matrix of matches from a sequence

    Takes one argument seq, which should be a sequence of length > 1
    Returns a tuple of tuples - matches.
    """
    opponents = list(seq[:])
    opponents.reverse()
    matches = [(actor, target) for actor in seq
                for target in opponents
                if target != actor]
    return tuple(matches)
def join_with_and(sequence):
    """Join up a list with commas and 'and' between last two items

    Takes a sequence and returns a sentence.
    """
    if len(sequence) > 1:
        last_item = sequence[-1]
        sentence = ", ".join(sequence[:-1])
        sentence = sentence + " and " + last_item
    elif sequence < 1:
        sentence = "whole lot of nothing"
    else:
        sentence = sequence[0]
    return sentence

def fix_gender(gender, phrase):
    """Replace the word 'them' with gender-specific pronoun

    Takes two arguments:
    gender - a string which can be 'male', 'female' or something else.
    phrase - the string to be modified.
    Returns a string with non-gender specific pronouns replaced by
    gender specific ones.
    """
    if gender == 'female':
        sentence = phrase.replace('themself','herself')
    elif gender == 'male':
        sentence = phrase.replace('themself','himself')
    else:
        sentence = phrase.replace('themself','itself')
```

```
    return sentence

def generate_rpc():
    """Role-Playing Character generator

    Takes no arguments
    Returns a new character profile dictionary
    """
    print()
    print("New Character")
    print()
    # Create empty profile dictionary
    profile = {'Name':"", 'Desc':"", 'Gender':"", 'Race':"", 'Muscle':0,
               'Brainz':0, 'Speed':0, 'Charm':0, 'life':0,
               'magic':0, 'prot':0, 'gold':0, 'inventory':[]}

    # Prompt user for user-defined information (Name, Desc, Gender, Race)
    name = input('What is your name? ')
    desc = input('Describe yourself: ')
    gender = input('What Gender are you? (male/female/unsure): ')
    race = input('What Race are you? - (Pixie/Vulcan/Gelfling/Troll): ')
    # Validate user input
    profile['Name'] = name.capitalize()
    profile['Desc'] = desc.capitalize()
    gender = gender.lower()
    if gender.startswith('f'):
        profile['Gender'] = 'female'
    elif gender.startswith('m'):
        profile['Gender'] = 'male'
    else:
        profile['Gender'] = 'neuter'
    race = race.capitalize()
    if race.startswith('P'):
        profile['Race'] = 'Pixie'
    elif race.startswith('V'):
        profile['Race'] = 'Vulcan'
    elif race.startswith('G'):
        profile['Race'] = 'Gelfling'
    elif race.startswith('T'):
        profile['Race'] = 'Troll'
    else:
        profile['Race'] = 'Goblin'

    # Generate stats ('Muscle', 'Brainz', 'Speed', 'Charm')
    profile['Muscle'] = roll(33,3)
    profile['Brainz'] = roll(33,3)
    profile['Speed'] = roll(33,3)
    profile['Charm'] = roll(33,3)

    # Work out combat stats (life, magic, prot, gold)
    life = (profile['Muscle'] + (profile['Speed']/2) + roll(49,1))/2
    magic = (profile['Brainz'] + (profile['Charm']/2) + roll(49,1))/2
```

117

```
    prot = (profile['Speed'] + (profile['Brainz']/2) + roll(49,1))/2
    gold = roll(40,4)

    # Validate stats
    if 0 < life < 100:
        profile['life'] = life
    else:
        profile['life'] = roll(33,3)
    if 0 < magic < 100:
        profile['magic'] = magic
    else:
        profile['magic'] = roll(33,3)
    if 0 < prot < 100:
        profile['prot'] = prot
    else:
        profile['prot'] = roll(33,3)
    profile['gold'] = gold

    # Output the character sheet
    fancy_line = "<~~==|#|==~~++**\@/**++~~==|#|==~~>"
    print()
    print(fancy_line)
    print("\t", profile['Name'])
    print("\t", profile['Race'], profile['Gender'])
    print("\t", profile['Desc'])
    print(fancy_line)
    print()
    print("\tMuscle: ", profile['Muscle'], "\tlife: ", profile['life'])
    print("\tBrainz: ", profile['Brainz'], "\tmagic: ", profile['magic'])
    print("\tSpeed: ", profile['Speed'], "\tprotection: ", profile['prot'])
    print("\tCharm: ", profile['Charm'], "\tgold: ", profile['gold'])
    print()
    return profile

def buy_equipment():
    """Purchase an item of equipment

    Takes no arguments.
    This function modifies the current character profile dictionary in place.
    It returns a value which evaluates as either True or False
    intended to control the shopping loop.
    """
    # Display shop stock list with prices.
    print()
    print("<==|#|==\SHOP/==|#|==>")
    for item in stock:
        print("\t", item, stock[item][0])
    print("<==|#|==\@@@@/==|#|==>")
    print()
    print("You have", profile['gold'], "gold.")
```

```
    # Prompt user to make a purchase.
    purchase = input('Please choose an item or type "done" to quit. ')
    # If the item is in stock and the player has enough gold, buy it.
    if purchase in stock:
        if stock[purchase][0] <= profile['gold']:
            test_phrase = profile['Name'] + " buys themself some equipment"
            print(fix_gender(profile['Gender'],test_phrase))
            print("You buy a", purchase, "for",stock[purchase][0], \
                    "gold pieces.")
            profile['gold'] -= stock[purchase][0]
            profile['inventory'].append(purchase)
            print("You have a", join_with_and(profile['inventory']), \
                    "in your bag.")
            print("You have", profile['gold'], "left.")
        else:
            print("You don't have enough gold to buy that.")
    elif purchase == 'done' or purchase == "":
        return profile['inventory'] == [] and profile['gold'] > 10
    else:
        print("We don't have", purchase, "in stock.")
    return purchase

def calc_velocity(attacker, target):
    """Calculate velocity of hit (or miss)

    Takes two arguments:
    attacker and target are integer pointers to the players list
    This function looks up values from the players list
    and returns a weighted semi-random integer
    representing the velocity of the strike.
    """
    attack_speed = players[attacker]['Speed']
    weapon_speed = players[attacker]['weapon'][2]
    attack_chance = roll(players[attacker]['Brainz'])
    attack_velocity = attack_speed + weapon_speed + attack_chance
    target_prot = players[target]['prot']
    armour_speed = players[target]['armour'][2]
    target_velocity = target_prot + armour_speed
    velocity = (attack_velocity - target_velocity) / 2
    return velocity

def calc_damage(attacker, target, velocity):
    """Calculate the damage of the hit

    Takes three arguments:
    attacker and target are integer pointers to the players list
    velocity is an integer representing the velocity of the strike.
    Returns a tuple of two integers - damage and potential damage
    """
    attack_strength = players[attacker]['Muscle']
    weapon_damage = players[attacker]['weapon'][1]
    attack_damage = attack_strength + weapon_damage + velocity
```

```
    target_strength = players[target]['Muscle']
    armour_strength = players[target]['armour'][1]
    target_chance = roll(players[target]['Brainz'])
    target_defence = target_strength + armour_strength + target_chance
    potential_damage = (attack_damage - target_defence)
    if potential_damage < 1:
        potential_damage = 2
    damage = random.randint(1,potential_damage)
    return damage, potential_damage


# The main body of the program starts here,
# So this is where the flow of execution begins.
# Generate characters
while len(players) < max_players:
    # Call character generation function.
    profile = generate_rpc()
    # Go shopping if the inventory is empty
    shopping = profile['inventory'] == []
    while shopping:
        shopping = buy_equipment()
    handbag = join_with_and(profile['inventory'])
    print("You own a", handbag)

    # Choose a weapon
    print(profile['Name'] + ", prepare for mortal combat!!!")
    # See if player has any weapons
    weapon_stats = [stock[item] for item in profile['inventory']
                    if item not in armour_types]
    if len(weapon_stats) == 1:
        profile['weapon'] = weapon_stats[0]
    elif len(weapon_stats) < 1:
        profile['weapon'] = (0,20,50)
    else:
        weapon = input("And choose your weapon: ")
        # The weapon must be in player's inventory.
        # Default to fist if weapon not available.
        weapon = weapon.lower()
        if weapon in profile['inventory']:
            profile['weapon'] = stock[weapon]
        else:
            profile['weapon'] = (0,20,50)
    # See if player has any armor
    armour_stats = [stock[item] for item in profile['inventory']
                    if item in armour_types]
    if armour_stats:
        profile['armour'] = armour_stats[0]
    else:
        profile['armour'] = (0,0,50)
```

```
        print(profile['Name'], "is now ready for battle. ")
        # Add new player to list of players
        players.append(profile)

# Combat

print()
print("Then let the combat begin!")
print()

vel_max = 23
vel_min = 1
dam_max = 23

# Loop while more than one player is still alive
while len(players) > 1:
    # create list of matches using ziply function
    matches = ziply(range(0,len(players)))
    if trace:
        print(matches)
    for attacker, target in matches:
        life_left = players[target]['life']

        # Calculate velocity of blow
        velocity = calc_velocity(attacker, target)
        if trace:
            print("\tvel\thit\tdam\tchange")
            print("\t", velocity)
        if velocity > 0:
            # Print sutable Hit message
            if velocity > vel_max:
                vel_max = velocity
            hit_type = int(7 * velocity / vel_max)
            if hit_type > 7:
                hit_type = 7
            if trace:
                print("\t\tHit#", hit_type)
            print(players[attacker]['Name'], hits[hit_type], \
                    players[target]['Name'], end="")
        else:
            # Print suitable Miss message
            if velocity < vel_min:
                vel_min = velocity
            miss_type = int(velocity / vel_max)
            if miss_type > 7:
                miss_type = 7
            if trace:
                print("\t\tMiss#", miss_type)
            print(players[attacker]['Name'], \
                    fix_gender(players[attacker]['Gender'],misses[miss_type]), \
                    players[target]['Name'])
            # End player turn
            continue
```

121

```
            # Calculate damage inflicted by blow
            damage, potential_damage = calc_damage(attacker, target, velocity)
            if trace:
                print()
                print("\t\tDamage:", damage, potential_damage)
            if damage > dam_max:
                dam_max = damage
            # Print damage report
            damage_type = int(7 * damage/dam_max)
            if damage_type > 7:
                    damage_type = 7
            if trace:
                print("\t\t\tDamage#", damage_type)
            change_type = int(5 * damage/life_left)
            if change_type > 7:
                    change_type = 7
            if trace:
                print("\t\t\tChange#", change_type)
            print("inflicting a", damage_report[damage_type], \
                    "and", life_changing[change_type])

            # Inflict damage on target.
            players[target]['life'] -= damage
            # Check whether target is still alive or not.
            if players[target]['life'] <= 0:
                # Print loser
                print()
                print(players[target]['Name'], "collapses in a pool of blood")
                # Remove loser from players list
                del players[target]
                print()
                # End this round of combat immediately.
                break

    if trace:
        print()
        print("\t\tmax damage | velocity", dam_max, vel_max, ":: min", vel_min)
        print()

# Print winner
print(players[0]['Name'], "wins the fight.")
```

Any further changes that I can think of right now get noted in a new TODO file in the Projects subdirectory. It's really sensible to keep sane hours and know when to stop.

It will probably be obvious from here that you could continue the process of abstraction until the only line left in the main body is something like game() and everything else is contained within a function.

There are some valid reasons why you might want to do reduce your code to only one line, and it could be said that the next level of evolution in programming style—object-oriented programming—takes it even further. Before expanding into those dizzy horizons, further refinements that can be made at this level. Function-oriented programming is a major change in approach, and there are many tips, tricks, and potential pitfalls to be aware of.

In the next chapter, I will pull together the threads of your existing knowledge with such diverse topics as formatting strings and pattern-matching, debugging, project organization, style guides, and dealing with version changes. I will also be showing you how to make your programs executable as stand-alone applications.

If you want to examine your code further, remember you can start Python in interactive mode from the project directory and import the program as a module:

```
>>> import rpcombat
```

You will have to play through the game once. Then you can use the following command

```
>>> help(rpcombat)
```

to check out what happens to all those docstrings. You could also use this command for a comprehensive overview of the program:

```
>>> vars(rpcombat)
```

Jargon Busting

This chapter's jargon is defined here:

- *Abstraction*: When you introduce abstraction, you move a number of program statements into a function, thereby reducing the level of detail and making the main program easier to read.

- *Calling procedure*: A block of code containing a function call is a calling procedure.

- *Class*: A class is a user-defined compound type.

- *Date stamp*: This string of numbers and digits represents the date of an action or the present moment.

- *Exceptions*: An exception is an error that occurs when a program is run.

- *Formal parameters*: These are the names used inside a function to refer to the values passed as arguments.

- *Function call*: This statement executes (calls) a function. (Recall from Chapter 2 that a function is a named block of code that performs a task; accepts zero, one, or more arguments; and returns a value to the calling procedure when it is complete.) A function call consists of the name of the function followed by a list of arguments enclosed in parentheses.

- *Function definition*: This statement creates a new function, specifying its name, its parameters, and the statements it executes.

- *Generalization*: When you generalize code, you replace a piece of code that is only useful in specific circumstances with something that can be used more generally.

- *Global*: These are the variables defined in the main program.

- *Keyword arguments*: These values are passed to a function by name.

- *Lambda expression*: A lambda expression is a disposable, one-line function without a name.

- *Local*: This variable is defined inside a function and can be used only inside its function.

- *Modification procedure*: This function changes its arguments inside the function body. Only mutable types can be changed by modifiers.

- *Modularization*: To modularize a program, you split it into several files or subprograms.

- *Object*: An object is a bundle of attributes (variables) and related methods (functions). Software objects are often used to model real-world objects you find in everyday life. Almost all entities in Python are objects or parts of objects, but the term usually refers specifically to an instance of a **class**.

- *Pointer*: This variable name doesn't hold any information itself but points to another variable.

- *Positional arguments*: These are values passed to a function in order.

- *Pure function*: A pure function has no side-effects and can make changes to the calling program only through its return values.

- *Refactoring*: When you refactor, you break a process down into smaller procedures.

- *Result*: This is the value that comes back after a function has run.

- *Scope*: A scope is the area where a variable is available to your code, such as global scope where a variable is available to all your code or function scope, where a variable is available to just the function.

- *Side-effects*: A side-effect is a change to a value caused during the execution of a function that isn't caused by reading the return value of the function.

- *Source data*: A function performs its operations on source data.

- *Symbol table*: The symbol table is a container for all the names created during the course of a procedure's execution.

- *Token*: This part of a program is treated as a separate unit by the compiler. It's analogous to a word in a human language, such as English.

Summary

In this chapter, I covered how to abstract and generalize your code into functions. Functions allow you to make your code more readable, maintainable, and efficient. And it's not just for your main application; your test code can also benefit from this.

During our discussion, we covered passing data to functions and working with variable scope. Variable scope allows us to keep information where it belongs, whether it belongs in the global scope of an application or in a function only.

All this means you can now refactor your early Python programs to make them easier to work with and more elegant. To prove this, we refactored one of our sample applications.

■ ■ ■

## CHAPTER 7

Working with Text

It's likely that you'll be working with text an awful lot in your Python programs, because that's mainly how your program will interact with its users, and a lot of the data it will work with will be in the form of text. There are numerous features of Python that help you work with text, and I'll cover many of them in this chapter.

Specifically, I'll cover splitting and joining strings, which are the most basic string operations you'll carry out. That'll lead me onto formatting, editing, and searching for strings—all vital for a lot of Python programs. Finding strings is often linked to regular expressions, and Python provides us with a wide array of regular expression functionality, much of which I'll cover. Finally, I'll explain how to work with the files on your file system, another common programming task.

Strings and Things

Most commands in Python 3 will work in exactly the same way as in Python 2. There are, however, some important changes. Probably the most fundamental change is the rationalization of the `string` data type. In previous versions of Python, strings were coded as a sequence of single **bytes**, using the limited **American Standard Code for Information Interchange (ASCII)** character set to represent text, this 7-bit encoding allows for up to 128 characters including uppercase and lowercase letters, numbers, punctuation, and 33 invisible control characters. While **ASCII** is OK for representing languages that use Latin script, such as English and most European languages, it is completely useless when it comes to representing the 2,000 basic ideograms of the Chinese language. To deal with these sorts of problems, the **Unicode** standard was created to cover all written languages, so Python 3 has brought itself up-to-date by switching to Unicode as its default text encoding. The `str` type is what used to be the `unicode` type, and a new type, `byte`, has been introduced to represent raw text strings and binary data. Previous versions of Python went through all sorts of contortions in order to deal with text encoding; fortunately, all you really need to know is that the `str` type in Python 3 supports international characters by default, so you don't have to do anything special if you want to write a string like this:

```
>>> s = "«a¹» Zøë, «a²» Déjà Vù, «a³» ½µ"
```

■ **Tip** You can use international characters in Python 2, but you would have to write this as u"«a¹» Zøë, «a²» Déjà Vù, «a³» ¼µ", prefacing the string with u to indicate that you wanted to force Unicode encoding. The main difference is in Python's internal representation of the string. In Python 3, the string stays the way you typed it; Python 2 has to turn everything into 7-bit ASCII representation to store it, which involves lots of backslashes: '\xc2\xaba\xc2\xb9\xc2\xbb Z\xc3\xb8\xc3\xab, \xc2\xaba\xc2\xb2\xc2\xbb D\xc3\xa9j\xc3\xa0 V\xc3\xb9, \xc2\xaba\xc2\xb3\xc2\xbb \xc2\xbd\xc2\xb5'. The unicode version looks like this: u'\xab\xb9\xbb Z\xf8\xeb, \xaba\xb2\xbb D\xe9j\xe0 V\xf9, \xaba\xb3\xbb \xbd\xb5'. Fortunately, both strings print correctly as "«a¹» Zøë, «a²» Déjà Vù, «a³» ¼µ".

To go along with the string type changes, the Python 2.x print statement has been replaced with a built-in print() function, which takes keyword arguments to replace most of the special syntax of the former print statement. To balance this, the old raw_input() is replaced by input(), and you have to use eval(input()) to get the old functionality of input(). I'll explain how eval() works in Chapter 8.

Splitting Strings

As strings are immutable, you will often want to split them up into lists in order to manipulate their contents; my_string.split([sep[, maxsplit]]) returns a list of the words in string, using sep as the separator or delimiter string. Quick reminder—a delimiter is a character or string of characters that are used to separate words or units of data. The list will be split up to maxsplit times, so you'll end up with a list that's maxsplit + 1 items long. If no separator is specified, the string will be split up by **whitespace** characters as if they are words.

```
>>> sent4 = "A much, much longer sentence"
>>> sent4.rstrip('sentence').split()
['A', 'much,', 'much', 'longer']
```

You can do this from the end of the string too using string.rsplit([sep[, maxsplit]]).

```
>>> sent4.rsplit(' ',2)
['A much, much', 'longer', 'sentence']
```

Python has an alternative string splitting method, string.partition(sep), which returns a tuple: (head, sep, tail). The method searches for the separator (sep) inside the string and returns the part before it, the separator itself, and the part after it as separate items. If the separator is not found, the method will return the original string and two empty strings.

```
>>> sent3 = "eXamPLe tEXt"
>>> sent3.partition(' ')
('eXamPLe', ' ', 'tEXt')
>>> sent3.partition('-')
('eXamPLe tEXt', '', '')
```

You can do the same thing starting from the end of the string with `string.rpartition(sep)`.

```
>>> s.rpartition("«a")
('«a¹» Zøë, «a²» Déjà Vù, ', '«a', '³» ½µ')
```

Joining Strings, or Avoiding Concatenation

As I mentioned when I first introduced the string data type, using the + operator to join strings together is very inefficient; combined with lots of calls to the `print()` function (or statement in Python 2), using the + operator can potentially slow your program's execution to a crawl. Python isn't *that* slow. Often, it works out better to manipulate a list of words and then use `string.join(sequence)` to return a string that is a concatenation of the strings in the sequence. This method is the opposite of `string.split()`: the data you want to manipulate is in the sequence of the argument, and the string that you call the method on is just the string of characters you want to use to *separate* the items. This could be a space or an empty string.

```
>>> s0 = "example"
>>> s1 = "text"
>>> sep = " "
>>> sep.join([s0, s1])
'example text'
```

Remember that `string.join()` is expecting a sequence of strings as an argument.

```
>>> sep = " - "
>>> sep.join('potrzebie')
'p - o - t - r - z - e - b - i - e'
```

You may need to convert other data types into strings and join up any sublists first, so that you present the outermost `join()` with a list of strings.

```
>>> a = 1
>>> b = 2.37
>>> sep.join(('skidoo',['a','b']))
Traceback (most recent call last):
  File "<stdin>", line 1, in <module>
TypeError: sequence item 1: expected str instance, list found
This problem is easily fixable with a little ingenuity.
>>> sep.join(('skidoo', sep.join([str(a),str(b)])))
'skidoo - 1 - 2.37'
```

This is where you need to start keeping an eye out for nested parentheses. The preceding code has an awful lot of brackets in it. You could always evaluate each nested expression separately to make the code easier to read. Readable code is a *good thing*.

```
>>> ab = sep.join([str(a),str(b)])
>>> sep.join(['skidoo', ab])
'skidoo - 1 - 2.37'
```

You still need to make sure that each opening bracket is matched by a closing bracket and that the closing brackets for the inner nested expressions come before the outermost closing brackets. Leaving out closing brackets can lead to a syntax error being reported on the next line, because the interpreter is still waiting for closure of the previous statement.

Changing Case

User input often contains unexpected capital letters. Python has a variety of ways that you can neaten up the use of capital letters: string.capitalize() returns a string with the first character capitalized and all the rest in lower case.

```
>>> s3 = "eXamPLe tEXt"
>>> s3.capitalize()
'Example text'
```

If you want to capitalize every single word in the string, leaving everything else as lowercase, use string.title().

```
>>> s3.title()
'Example Text'
```

The one little gotcha with this is that every letter following some space or punctuation gets capitalized.

```
>>> s5 = "it's thirteen o'clock"
>>> s5.title()
"It'S Thirteen O'Clock"
```

You can convert the whole string to uppercase using string.upper().

```
>>> s3.upper()
'EXAMPLE TEXT'
```
Or lowercase using string.lower().
```
>>> s3.lower()
'example text'
```

It is very useful to convert strings to lowercase for many internal operations like storing and searching. I'd recommend lowercasing most user input as soon as it is received, unless the use of capital letters conveys important information. You can always put the capitals back using string.capitalize() or string.title() when you want to print out the string.

You can also get funky with string.swapcase(). This returns a copy of string with the uppercase characters converted to lowercase and vice versa.

```
>>> s3.swapcase()
'ExAMplE TexT'
```

I'm not quite sure why you'd want to do this, but it sure is great to know you have the power should you choose to wield it!

Simple Methods of Formatting

You have various choices for controlling the way strings are printed out. Basic formatting is provided through methods such as `mystring.center(width[, fillchar])`, which returns a string centered in a string of `width` characters long. Padding is done using the specified fill character (the default is a space). So, the following returns a 37-character string, with `mystring` in the middle and * as padding:

```
>>> x = s3.lower()
>>> x.center(37,'*')
'*************example text************'
```

There are related methods to align text within a string. To align text on the left, use `string.ljust(width[, fillchar])`.

```
>>> x.ljust(37, '=')
'example text========================='
```

And to align text on the right, use `string.rjust(width[, fillchar])`.

```
>>> x.rjust(37, '+')
'+++++++++++++++++++++++++example text'
```

Or you can pad the string out with zeros to the left to fill a field of the specified width using `string.zfill(width)`.

```
>>> s3.zfill(37)
'00000000000000000000000000eXamPLe tEXt'
```

Finally, `string.expandtabs([tabsize])` can be used to expand all the tab characters in a string using spaces. If `tabsize` is not given, a tab size of 8 characters will be used by default.

```
>>> s2 = "one\ttwo\tthree"
>>> s2.expandtabs()
'one     two     three'
```

Advanced Formatting

One of the nice new features of Python 3 is that strings have a new method `string.format(*args, **kwargs)` that allows you to drop the variables given as an argument into a specially prepared string, rather than having to go through the complicated process of joining lots of individual strings up. The string is prepared by putting references to the format arguments in curly braces at the point they are to be inserted in the string. These replacement **field names** can be numbers (positional arguments, i.e., *args) or names (keyword arguments, i.e., **kwargs). The format is similar to the one you would use to pass variables into a function.

```
>>> mystring = "value {0} equals {1}: {message}"
>>> mystring.format('x','23', message = '[ok]')
'value x equals 23: [ok]'
```

The replacement field names inside the curly braces can also include attributes and element indexes such as {someClass.data} or {some_list[i]}. This field name may be followed by an optional **conversion field**, which is preceded by an exclamation point (!) and can be modified using **format specifiers**, which are preceded with a colon (:).

The **conversion field** is used to force an item to be represented as a particular type, regardless of its own type's formatting rules. This can either be !s, which forces a string representation through str() or !r, which calls repr() on the value.

```
>>> mystring = "value {0!s} equals {1!r}: {message!s}"
>>> mystring.format('z','37',message = '[well, you know ...]')
"value z equals '37': [well, you know ...]"
```

Format Specification

Format specification is done using its own built-in minilanguage. The format specification string is a sequence of characters, each with its own special meaning.

The format specifier field contains a specification of how the value should be presented, that is, padding, alignment, sign, field width, decimal precision, and type. All these items are optional and follow the colon.

The first two characters after the colon work together. The first character may be any character to be used as a fill character, so long as it is followed by one of the alignment operators shown in Table 7-1.

Table 7-1. *Alignment Format Specifiers*

Option	Description
<	Align left (default).
>	Align right.
^	Center.
=	Place the padding after the sign (if any) but before the digits. This alignment option is only valid for numeric types.

Here's an example that formats three strings. The first string (0!s) is aligned to the center (^), given a minimum field width of 3, and padded with *, which fill any whitespace. The second string (1!s) is aligned to the right (>), given a minimum field width of 4, and padded with 0. The third string (message!s) is aligned to the left (<), given a minimum field width of 42, and padded with !.

```
>>> astring = "Value {0!s:*^3} equals {1!s:0>4}: {message!s:!<42}"
>>> astring.format('y', 42, message = "[not bad ...]")
'Value *y* equals 0042: [not bad ...]!!!!!!!!!!!!!!!!!!!!!!!!!!!!!!!!!!'
```

▒ **Note** Unless a minimum field width is defined, the field width will always be the same size as the data to fill it, so the alignment option has no meaning in this case.

Next, the sign option is only valid for number types and can be one of the values in Table 7-2.

Table 7-2. Sign Format Specifiers

Option	Description
+	A sign should be used for both positive as well as negative numbers.
-	A sign should be used only for negative numbers (default).
Space	A leading space should be used on positive numbers and a minus sign on negative numbers.

Here's an example that formats a number and uses precision as well. The part we are interested in is {1:0>+4.3}. This right-aligns the second input with 0 as padding and states that we want to use a sign for all numbers. The field is to be a minimum of 4 wide, and we want to have three decimal places (.3):

```
>>> msgs = ['[soso ...]', '[ok]', '[you know ...]', '[terrible]',
'[do I know you?]']
>>> numbers = ['23.5', 42, '37', '-1.234567', -98754.320999999996]
>>> letters = ['v', 'w', 'x', 'y', 'z']
>>> string = "Value *{0!s: ^3}* equals {1:0>+4.3}\t{message!s::<20}"
>>> for i in range(0,5):
...     print(string.format(letters[i],float(numbers[i]),message = msgs[i]))
...
Value * v * equals +23.5    [ok]:::::::::::::::::
Value * w * equals +42.0    [well, you know ...]
Value * x * equals +37.0    [not bad ...]:::::::
Value * y * equals -1.23[actually, terrible]
Value * z * equals -9.88e+04    [do I know you?]:::::
```

The next optional character, which you have already seen in use in the preceding example, is a decimal integer to specify the minimum field width in characters. If this is not specified, the field width will be determined by the content. Zero padding can be enabled by starting the width value with a 0.

This number may be followed by another decimal integer after a period (.). This is the number of decimal places to which a floating point number should be rounded.

The final character determines how numerical data should be presented. These characters will work on integers. You should not specify a precision value if you expect an integer.

Table 7-3. Integer Format Specifiers

Option	Description
b	The binary option outputs the number in base 2.
c	The character option converts the integer to the corresponding Unicode character before printing.
d	The decimal integer option outputs the number in base 10.
o	The octal format option outputs the number in base 8.
x	This hexadecimal format option outputs the number in base 16 using *lowercase* letters for the digits above 9.
X	This hexadecimal format option outputs the number in base 16, using *uppercase* letters for the digits above 9.
n	The number option is the same as d, except that it uses the current locale setting to insert the appropriate number separator characters.
None	This option is the same as d.

Here's an example that formats the same number in different ways:

```
>>> "{0:>8b}".format(numbers[1])
'  101010'
>>> "{0:>8c}".format(numbers[1])
'       *'
>>> "{0:>8d}".format(numbers[1])
'      42'
```

There are some additional type characters to represent floating point numbers and exponents.

Table 7-4. Float Format Specifiers

Option	Description
e	This exponent notation specifier prints the number in scientific notation using the letter *e* to indicate the exponent.
E	This exponent notation specifier is the same as e except it uses an uppercase *E* as the separator character.
f	This fixed point specifier displays the number as a fixed-point number.
F	This specifier is the same as f.
g	This general format specifier prints the number as a fixed-point number unless the number is too large, in which case it switches to e exponent notation.
G	This general format specifier is the same as g, except it switches to E if the number gets too large.
n	The number specifier works the same as g, except that it uses the current locale setting to insert the appropriate number separator characters.
%	The percentage specifier multiplies the number by 100 and displays in fixed f format, followed by a percent sign.
None	This specifier is the same as g.

Here's an example that formats the same number as an exponent, a floating point, and a percentage:

```
>>> "{0:>8E}".format(numbers[4])
'-9.875432E+04'
>>> "{0:>8f}".format(numbers[4])
'-98754.321000'
>>> "{0:>8%}".format(numbers[4])
'-9875432.100000%'
```

A format specifier field can also include nested replacement fields within it. Each nested replacement field can contain only a field name; conversion flags and format specifications are not allowed. The replacement fields within the format specifier are substituted before the format specifier string is interpreted. This allows the formatting of a value to be dynamically specified.

Editing Strings

Strings, as you have probably gathered by now, can't be edited in place, but they do have some useful methods that will return a new edited version of the string.

You often need to clean up the beginning and end of the string to remove extraneous whitespace or punctuation, especially if you're trying to compare some user input with a stored value. This is done with the `string.strip([chars])` method. This returns a copy of the string with chars removed from the beginning and the end if the sequence is found. If no arguments are given, `string.strip()` will remove whitespace characters by default.

```
>>> sent4 = "A much, much longer sentence"
>>> sent4.strip('A')
' much, much longer sentence'
```

You can choose to only strip characters from the start of the string using `string.lstrip([chars])`:

```
>>> sent3.lstrip('e')
'XamPLe tEXt'
```

or from the end of the string with `string.rstrip([chars])`.

```
>>> sent4.rstrip('sentence')
'A much, much longer '
```

You can replace all occurrences of one substring with another using `string.replace(old, new[, count])`. The optional argument count determines how many occurrences of the substring are replaced.

```
>>> sent3.replace('EX', 'wis')
'eXamPLe twist'
```

This last method is extremely useful.

Finding Strings

Sometimes, you might want to know whether a string contains a word or sequence of characters within it, this is called a substring. You can test for simple membership using the `in` operator.

```
>>> "bop" in "bopshoowopshoowop"
True
```

However, it may be important to know where in the string this substring occurs. For this, you need `string.find(sub[, start[, end]])`. This returns an index number, which is the number of characters into the string where the substring is found (starting at zero, of course). Note that `find()` returns the position of the first substring it finds or -1 if it doesn't find anything. You can include further arguments to specify the start and end of the search; these arguments work the same way as slice notation, including `start` and up to but not including `end`.

```
>>> s.find("«a",8,16)
10
```

If you want to find the position of the last occurrence of sub, you could use string.rfind(sub[, start[, end]]) instead, which searches from the end of the string backward.

```
>>> s.rfind("«a")
24
```

If you specifically want an error to be raised if the string is not found (see Chapter 11), use string.index(sub[, start[, end]]) instead of find(). This returns an integer index just like string.find() but raises a ValueError if the substring is not found.

```
>>> s.index("a",12)
25
>>> s.index("a",26)
Traceback (most recent call last):
File "<stdin>", line 1, in <module>
ValueError: substring not found
```

You can search for strings from the end of the string as well using string.rindex(sub[, start[, end]]).

```
>>> s.rindex("«a", 0, 23)
10
```

You can also count the number of times a substring occurs in a string using string.count(sub[, start[, end]]). Start and end values work like slice notation again.

```
>>> s.count('a')
3
```

Strings have an enormous number of methods; this section provides just a selection of the most immediately useful ones. Using string methods alone, it is possible to pretty up the output of your programs considerably, be more flexible, and possibly even improve the grammar of your application's printout.

Matching Patterns Using Regular Expressions

Sometimes, the basic string methods just aren't enough. For example, you may need to retrieve values that appear within a regular pattern in a piece of text, but you don't know what those values are going to be or just have a rough idea of what they should not be. This is where regular expressions come in. A **regular expression** (**regex**, for short) is a pattern that can match a piece of text. In its simplest form, a regular expression could just be a plain string of ordinary characters that matches itself. Regular expression syntax uses additional special characters to recognize a range of possibilities that can be matched. These expressions can be used in search and replace operations and to split up text in different way than string.split().

Regular expressions are complex, powerful, and difficult to read. Most of the time, you can manage without them, but they are particularly useful when dealing with complex, structured pieces of text. It's best to take regular expressions slowly, learning a bit at a time. Trying to learn the whole regular expression syntax all in one go could be quite overwhelming.

Regular expression matching operations are provided by the re module. As re is not built in by default, it is necessary to import the module first before it is possible to use it.

```
>>> import re
```

The module supports both 8-bit and Unicode strings, so it should be possible to recognize any characters that you can type in from the keyboard or read from a file.

Next, you need to construct a regular expression string to represent the pattern you want to catch. Let's use the rather colorful string from earlier in the chapter again.

```
>>> string = "«a¹» Zøë, «a²» Déjà Vù, «a³» ½µ"
>>> pattern = "«a.»"
>>> re.split(pattern, string)
['', ' Zøë, ', ' Déjà Vù, ', ' ½µ']
```

Here, I have used the re.split() method instead of string.split() to isolate the data from its strange labels. This method takes a regular expression and a string as arguments. The string is split according to the substrings that match the pattern; these substrings are discarded, returning the strings that remain as a list. Obviously, you could make use of string.strip() to clean up the results, but you could also construct a smarter regular expression. The pattern string consists of the characters that I'm looking for plus a special character, the period. This period matches any single character except for newlines, no more and no less. Because it matches any character, the period is known as a **wildcard** character. The asterisk * matches 0 or more characters of the preceding expression. The plus sign (+) matches one or more characters, and the question mark (?) matches one or zero characters of the preceding expression.

```
>>> pattern = "«.+» "
>>> re.split(pattern, string)
['', '½µ']
```

The preceding **greedy** version of the pattern gobbles up everything up to the last chevrons, which is not the sort of behavior I want to see.

We can mark an expression as **nongreedy** and match as few as possible; this is indicated with an additional question mark: *?, +?, and ??.

```
>>> pattern = "«.+?» "
>>> re.split(pattern, string)
['', 'Zøë, ', 'Déjà Vù, ', '½µ']
```

Adding in the question mark makes a better match. It would also be possible to specify the number of repetitions to be matched following the pattern with a pair of numbers in curly braces {m,n}, which matches the pattern repeated between m and n times.

```
>>> pattern = "«.{2,2}» "
>>> re.split(pattern, string)
['', 'Zøë, ', 'Déjà Vù, ', '½µ']
```

This example is still not perfect. Somehow, I'd like the pattern to match potential commas and spaces, if they exist, before the opening chevron.

Matching Subpatterns

I don't want to match just any old character here; I'm looking for a specific pattern ", ", but the problem is that it may or may not be present. The solution is to enclose the subpattern in parentheses, followed by a question mark, which makes the subpattern optional.

```
>>> pattern = "(, )?«.+?» "
>>> re.split(pattern, string)
['', None, 'Zøë', ', ', 'Déjà Vù', ', ', '½µ']
```

This kind of works, but we've collected a lot of extraneous items. Putting ?: inside the parentheses at the beginning stops the subpattern from being returned, but it is still counted as part of the match.

```
>>> pattern = "(?:, )?«.+?» "
>>> re.split(pattern, string)
['', 'Zøë', 'Déjà Vù', '½µ']
```

Regular expressions are not easy on the eyes. As you can see, we've already built up a pattern that looks like a sentence in some alien language. I have to be honest; I'm afraid it gets worse. If you want to match an actual punctuation mark or special character (e.g., ., ^, $, *, +, or ?) or brackets, you'll have to escape each character with a backslash. For example, \. would match an actual period. Some ordinary characters also have a special meaning if preceded by a backslash. Table 7-5 shows these special characters.

Table 7-5. Escaped Characters with Special Meaning in Regular Expressions

Character	Meaning
\<number>	Match the contents of the group of the same number.
\A	Match only at the start of a string.
\Z	Match only at the end of a string.
\b	Match an empty string but only at the start or end of a word.
\B	Match an empty string but not at the start or end of a word.

Table 7-5. *Escaped Characters with Special Meaning in Regular Expressions (continued)*

Character	Meaning
\d	Match any decimal digit.
\D	Match any nondigit character.
\s	Match any whitespace character.
\S	Match any nonwhitespace character.
\w	Match any alphanumeric character.
\W	Match anything that isn't an alphanumeric character.
\\	Match a literal backslash.

The good news is that the application of backslashes can be automated, to a certain extent, using the re.escape(pattern) method. See the "Letting the Characters Escape" section.

Matching Character Sets and Alternatives

If you want to match a specific range of characters, you can put them in square brackets; [abc] will match any one of the characters (a, b, or c) but not all of them together. You can also specify ranges such as [a-zA-Z0-9], which would include all uppercase and lowercase letters and digits. Inserting a caret (^) as the first character negates the set, so [^a-zA-Z0-9] would match any single nonalphanumeric character. The characters in square brackets don't have to be escaped in the same way as other characters in a regular expression, unless you need to catch square brackets or dashes.

You can specify alternative patterns after the choice operator, which is also known as the pipe symbol (|).

```
>>> pattern = "\W?«a\S»\w|(?:, )?«.+?» "
>>> re.split(pattern, string)
['', 'Zøë', 'Déjà Vù', '½µ']
```

Finding Patterns at the Beginning or End of a String

Sometimes, you will be looking for a pattern to occur specifically at the beginning or end of a sequence of characters. The caret (^) can be used to specify the start of a sequence, and the dollar sign ($) can be used to indicate the end. Note that the caret ^ works as a negation operator inside square bracketed character sets, so it can't be used to indicate the start of a sequence.

```
>>> pattern = "^«a"
>>> re.split(pattern, string)
['', '¹» Zøë, «a²» Déjà Vù, «a³» ½µ']
```

```
>>> pattern = "µ$"
>>> re.split(pattern, string)
['«a¹» Zøë, «a²» Déjà Vù, «a³» ½', '']
```

Creating a Regular Expression Object

You can compile a regular expression pattern into a regular expression object using
re.compile(pattern[, flags]). This returns a pattern object on which you can call all the previous
methods, but you no longer need to provide the pattern as an argument. You might want to do this if you
need to use this pattern to perform lots of matches all at once; compiling the pattern into an object
speeds up the pattern comparison process, because the pattern does not have to then be compiled each
time it is used. You might also need to use this approach where a function specifically requires a regular
expression object to be passed to it rather than just a pattern string.

```
>>> pattern = "\W?«a\S»\w|(?:, )?«.+?» "
>>> regex_object = re.compile(pattern)
>>> regex_object.split(string)
['', 'Zøë', 'Déjà Vù', '½µ']
```

Doing this creates a chance to save and name your patterns for later use and may also help to make
your code more readable if you name your patterns appropriately.

■ **Note** The options for the flags argument are covered in the official Python documentation. They apply to more
advanced uses of re, which I shall let you explore at your leisure. This chapter provides just a brief introduction.

Letting the Characters Escape

If your users are particularly grammatically expressive, you may have to deal with sentences containing
all kinds of random punctuation. There will be circumstances when you couldn't possibly edit the
strings yourself to put backslashes in front of all the characters that are not ordinary letters or numbers.
Fortunately, re.escape(pattern) will escape all the nonalphanumeric characters in pattern for you.

```
>>> re.escape(string)
'\\«a\\¹\\»\\ Z\\ø\\ë\\,\\ \\«a\\²\\»\\ D\\éj\\à\\ V\\ù\\,\\ \\«a\\³\\»\\ \\½\\µ'
```

Manipulating Strings Using Regular Expressions

As you have already seen, it is possible to split up a string according to the occurrences of a pattern using
re.split(pattern, string[, maxsplit]). This method returns a list containing the matching substrings.
There is an optional argument maxsplit that allows you to specify the maximum number of splits
allowed.

The re module can also perform replacement operations with the re.sub(pattern, repl, string[,
count]) method. This will return the string obtained by substituting the leftmost nonoverlapping

139

occurrences of the pattern in string with the replacement repl. You can limit the number of substitutions made by setting the optional argument count. The replacement, repl, can be either a string or a callable (i.e., a method or function); if it's a callable, it must accept the match object as the only argument and must return a string.

```
>>> re.sub("«a.»", "data:", string)
'data: Zøë, data: Déjà Vù, data: ½μ'
>>> re.sub("«a.»", "data:", string, 2)
'data: Zøë, data: Déjà Vù, «a³» ½μ'
```

There is an alternative method re.subn(pattern, repl, string[, count]) that does the same thing as re.sub() but also returns the number of substitutions made in a tuple (new_string, number), where number is the number of substitutions that were made.

```
>>> re.subn("«a.»", "data:", string)
('data: Zøë, data: Déjà Vù, data: ½μ', 3)
```

The re module is primarily used for matching patterns, and this can be done in several ways. If you want to find all occurrences of a pattern in a string, re.findall(pattern, string[, flags]) will return a list of all nonoverlapping matches including empty matches.

```
>>> re.findall("«a.»", string)
['«a¹»', '«a²»', '«a³»']
```

Regular expressions have other useful methods available, which allow more fine-grained control over groups of matches. They have a powerful language all of their own, as shown in Table 7-6, which needs its own book to fully explain. The methods I have described here will get you started and offer you a lot of power to manipulate text.

Table 7-6. *Characters with Special Meaning in Regular Expressions*

Character	Meaning
.	Match any character except a newline.
^	Match the start of a string.
$	Match the character at the end of a string or the one just before the newline at the end of a string.
*	Match zero or more repetitions of the preceding regular expression. This character creates a greedy expression.
+	Match one or more repetitions of the preceding regular expression. This character creates a greedy expression.
?	Match zero or one of the characters in the preceding regular expression. This character creates a greedy expression.

Table 7-6. Characters with Special Meaning in Regular Expressions (continued)

Character	Meaning
*?, +?, and ??	Nongreedy versions of the previous three special characters.
{m,n}	Matches from m to n repetitions of the preceding regular expression.
{m,n}?	This is the nongreedy version of {m,n}.
\\	Use this to either escape special characters or signal a special sequence.
[]	Use this to indicate a set of characters. A caret as the first character indicates a complementing set.
|	This denotes "or". For example, A|B creates a regular expression that will match either A or B.
(. . .)	Match the regular expression inside the parentheses. The contents can be retrieved or matched later in the string, using the \<number>escape.
(?:. . .)	Ignore this group.

Using Files

So far, data has either been written into the program itself or received via the input() function and printed out using the print() function. Once the program has finished its execution, the data is lost. In order for an application to have any practical value, it is necessary to be able to store that information and retrieve it the next time the program is run. The vast majority of computer information is stored in files on a hard drive or similar storage medium or can be transmitted via some file-like object. File-like objects share some similar properties with files and can often be treated with the same methods; streams are an important kind of file-like object, which I will come to a little later.

Opening Files

File objects can be created with the built-in open(filename[, mode[, buffering]]) function. File objects are also returned by some other built-in functions and methods. I'll start by opening a plain text file in the same directory as I started the interpreter.

```
>>> open('story.txt')
<io.TextIOWrapper object at 0xb7ba990c>
```

Oh look—another Python object! This one says it's an io.TextIOWrapper; in plain language, that's a file object. If the file doesn't exist, you'll get an IOError. *IO* stands for *input/output*, in other words, reading and writing to files. The file object now holds the contents of story.txt, but in order to do anything with it, you need to learn some file methods.

I hope you're getting used to the concept that everything in Python is some type of object and that any type of object will usually have several methods that you can use to access its values or edit it. Before you can make use of the different file methods, it is important to understand the different ways that Python can open a file to create a file object.

Modes and Buffers

Opening the file by just passing the filename to open() creates a read-only file object. If you want to be able to write to that file as well, it is necessary to set the optional mode argument. This argument can be a single character: r (read), w (write), or a (append), any of which may be followed by b (binary) or + (read/write). If you don't provide a mode argument, Python will assume your file is a text file, and mode r will be assumed.

```
>>> open('story.txt', 'rb')
<io.BufferedReader object at 0xb7ba990c>
```

The b mode returns a different kind of object to the default file object—one that contains the same information in byte format. You might want to use this if you wanted to handle image or audio data. Write mode (w) lets you change the contents of the file completely. Append mode (a) only lets you add information to the end. This last option is useful for creating log files.

The buffering argument, used with w or a, can either be 0 or 1. If it's 0, your data is written straight to your hard-drive. If it's 1, Python creates a temporary file to store the text in before it gets written out. The data is not written to disk unless you explicitly call file.flush() or file.close(). You probably won't need this option immediately.

Reading from and Writing to Files

The most basic method you can use to access the file's contents is file.read([size]). This reads up to size bytes from the file (less if the read hits the end of the file before it gets to size bytes). If the size argument is negative or not given, the whole file will be read in as a single string. The bytes are returned as a string object, unless you opened the file as a binary object, in which case you'll get the raw bytes. If you are reading a plain text file containing ordinary characters, you might not notice a great deal of difference.

```
>>> text = open('story.txt')
>>> text.read()
'Once upon a time, it wasn\'t your time nor my time
[... pages more text here ...]
and if they live happy, so may you and me.\n'
```

If you are dealing with a large body of text like the following example, you may wish to deal with it in smaller pieces. file.readline([size]) reads a single line from the file (up to the next newline character, \n). The size argument is the maximum number of bytes to read (including the trailing newline), and an incomplete line may be returned. An empty string is returned only when the end of the file is encountered immediately.

```
>>>text = open('story.txt')
```

```
>>> text.readline()
```
"Once upon a time, it wasn't your time nor my time, but a very long time ago, there lived a gentleman and a lady in a very beautiful part of the country. They had only one daughter, who was very pretty and good, and both her parents were very fond of her. When the girl was about five years old, her mother died. The father was heartbroken over the loss of his wife and left the little girl pretty much to herself. She cried endlessly, because she did not understand where her mother had gone or why she did not come to her.\n"

Files are their own iterators, so you can also iterate through lines in a file using a for loop. Each iteration returns the same result as file.readline(), and the loop ends when the readline() method returns an empty string.

```
>>> for line in text:
...     print(line)
```

I'll let you try this one out yourself, as the output would fill up the rest of this chapter. Alternatively, you can read the lines of a file into a list for later consumption, using file.readlines([sizehint]). If the optional sizehint argument is present, instead of reading up to the end of the file, whole lines totaling approximately sizehint bytes are read. Some file-like objects may not implement file.readlines().

Writing to the file is simple. As long as you opened the file in w or a mode, file.write(str) writes a string to the file.

```
>>> out_file = open('story.html', 'w')
>>> out_file.write(content)
522
>>> out_file.close()
```

If you opened the file in write mode, the first write will overwrite the entire file, and any successive writes will follow on from where the last write left off. If you opened the file in append mode, the writes will begin at the end of the file.

```
>>> out_file = open('story.html', 'a')
>>> out_file.write(content)
522
>>> out_file.close()
```

You can also write a list of strings to the file using file.writelines(sequence). The sequence can be any iterable object producing strings, though typically it's a list of strings; writelines() does not add line separators, so you'll have to remember to put in the extra \n characters yourself.

Finding Your Way Around Files

The place in the file that the interpreter has read up to is represented by the number of bytes (characters) into the file it is. This will be referred to as the file's current position. It's equivalent to having your finger on the text or to keeping track of the position of the cursor in a text editor. The file.tell() method returns the file's current position.

```
>>> out_file = open('story.html', 'a')
>>> out_file.tell()
0
>>> out_file.write(content)
522
>>> out_file.tell()
1566
```

■ **Caution** On Windows, tell() can return illegal values when reading files with Unix-style line endings. Use binary mode 'rb' to circumvent this problem.

It is also possible to set the file's current position using file.seek(offset[, whence]).

```
>>> out_file.seek(223, 0)
223
```

The whence argument is optional and can be 0, 1, or 2: 0 gives a position relative to the start of the file; 1 gives a position relative to the current position; and 2 gives a position relative to the end of the file. The offset is in bytes again, just like the value returned by file.tell() For whence values of 1 and 2, the offset must be 0, so you can't perform seeks relative to the end or current position.

```
>>> out_file.seek(0, 2)
1566
```

■ **Note** Seeks can't be performed on all file objects.

Closing Files

It is a good idea to use file.close() to close a file after you are finished with it. Python will probably notice that you're not using the file anymore and free up the memory space eventually, but explicitly closing it is cleaner. Often, the data in a file.write() operation is stored in a buffer until the file is closed. You can make sure the data gets written out to the file without closing it by using file.flush(). A closed file cannot be read or written any more. Calling close() more than once is allowed.

Applications

One of the most common uses of string manipulation is to convert text into different formats. You may have a plain text file, for example that you want to display as a web page. Web pages often use Hypertext Markup Language (HTML), which encloses text between pairs of **tags** in angle brackets. These tags can indicate paragraphs, headings, bold and italic text, and so on.

Converting Text

The pseudocode for a script to convert a text file into a basic HTML page would be very simple, as shown in Listing 7-1.

Listing 7-1. *Pseudocode for a Text Conversion Script*

```
# Get filename from user input.
# Open file.
# Manipulate text.
# Write out web page.
```

I have used the `string.replace()`, `string.split()`, and `string.rstrip()` methods to create a suitable output filename and title for the page using the input filename and stripping the `.txt` ending. The manipulations in the body of the script are performed by `re.sub()`. The challenge here is to find suitable patterns in the source text that can be matched precisely enough to avoid unwanted parts of the text being matched but also general enough to match all instances of the text we do want. Listing 7-2 shows a particularly ungraceful way of doing it. With a little ingenuity, I'm sure you could improve the regular expressions I've used in Listing 7-2. The results are shown in Figure 7-1.

Listing 7-2. *txt2html.py*

```
"""
Convert text file to HTML page
"""

import re

input_filename = eval(input('Enter a filename:-> '))
output_filename = input_filename.replace('.txt', '.html')
title = input_filename.split('/')
title = title[-1].rstrip('.txt').title()
header = """<html>
<head>
<title>{0!s}</title>
</head>
<body>
<h1>{0!s}</h1>
<p>
```

```
""".format(title)
footer = """
</p>
</body>
</html>
"""


# Open file
input_file = open(input_filename)
text = input_file.read()
input_file.close()

# Manipulate text
# Change anything like 'Ashpetal' or 'Ashey Petl' to 'Cinderella'.
text = re.sub('[Aa]sh.*?[Pp](etl|etal)', '<b>Cinderella</b>', text)
# Add <p> tags to newlines after periods etc.
text = re.sub('([\]\".:?!-])\n', '\\1</p>\n<p>', text)
# Add <br> tags to newlines after letters and commas.
text = re.sub('([a-z,;])\n', '\\1<br />\n', text)
# Italicise everything between quotes.
text = re.sub('(".+?")', '<i>\\1</i>', text)
# Make everything bold between asterisks.
text = re.sub('(\W)\*([a-z A-Z]+?)\*(\W)', '\\1<b>\\2</b>\\3', text)
# Underline words between underscores.
text = re.sub('(_\w+?_)', '<u>\\1</u>', text)
# Join up Header, text and footer
text = ''.join([header, text, footer])

# Write out web page
output_file = open(output_filename, 'w')
output_file.write(text)
output_file.close()
print((output_filename, "written out."))
```

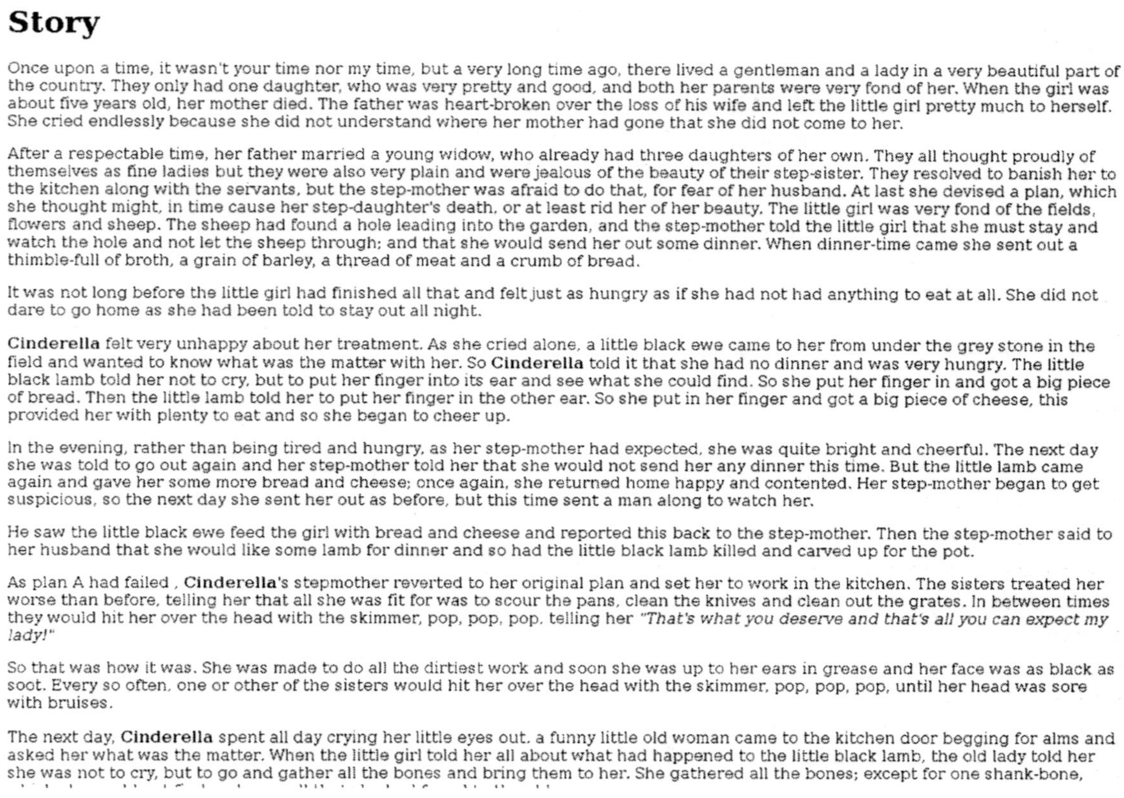

Story

Once upon a time, it wasn't your time nor my time, but a very long time ago, there lived a gentleman and a lady in a very beautiful part of the country. They only had one daughter, who was very pretty and good, and both her parents were very fond of her. When the girl was about five years old, her mother died. The father was heart-broken over the loss of his wife and left the little girl pretty much to herself. She cried endlessly because she did not understand where her mother had gone that she did not come to her.

After a respectable time, her father married a young widow, who already had three daughters of her own. They all thought proudly of themselves as fine ladies but they were also very plain and were jealous of the beauty of their step-sister. They resolved to banish her to the kitchen along with the servants, but the step-mother was afraid to do that, for fear of her husband. At last she devised a plan, which she thought might, in time cause her step-daughter's death, or at least rid her of her beauty. The little girl was very fond of the fields, flowers and sheep. The sheep had found a hole leading into the garden, and the step-mother told the little girl that she must stay and watch the hole and not let the sheep through; and that she would send her out some dinner. When dinner-time came she sent out a thimble-full of broth, a grain of barley, a thread of meat and a crumb of bread.

It was not long before the little girl had finished all that and felt just as hungry as if she had not had anything to eat at all. She did not dare to go home as she had been told to stay out all night.

Cinderella felt very unhappy about her treatment. As she cried alone, a little black ewe came to her from under the grey stone in the field and wanted to know what was the matter with her. So **Cinderella** told it that she had no dinner and was very hungry. The little black lamb told her not to cry, but to put her finger into its ear and see what she could find. So she put her finger in and got a big piece of bread. Then the little lamb told her to put her finger in the other ear. So she put in her finger and got a big piece of cheese, this provided her with plenty to eat and so she began to cheer up.

In the evening, rather than being tired and hungry, as her step-mother had expected, she was quite bright and cheerful. The next day she was told to go out again and her step-mother told her that she would not send her any dinner this time. But the little lamb came again and gave her some more bread and cheese; once again, she returned home happy and contented. Her step-mother began to get suspicious, so the next day she sent her out as before, but this time sent a man along to watch her.

He saw the little black ewe feed the girl with bread and cheese and reported this back to the step-mother. Then the step-mother said to her husband that she would like some lamb for dinner and so had the little black lamb killed and carved up for the pot.

As plan A had failed , **Cinderella's** stepmother reverted to her original plan and set her to work in the kitchen. The sisters treated her worse than before, telling her that all she was fit for was to scour the pans, clean the knives and clean out the grates. In between times they would hit her over the head with the skimmer, pop, pop, pop, telling her *"That's what you deserve and that's all you can expect my lady!"*

So that was how it was. She was made to do all the dirtiest work and soon she was up to her ears in grease and her face was as black as soot. Every so often, one or other of the sisters would hit her over the head with the skimmer, pop, pop, pop, until her head was sore with bruises.

The next day, **Cinderella** spent all day crying her little eyes out. a funny little old woman came to the kitchen door begging for alms and asked her what was the matter. When the little girl told her all about what had happened to the little black lamb, the old lady told her she was not to cry, but to go and gather all the bones and bring them to her. She gathered all the bones; except for one shank-bone,

Figure 7-1. HTML output from my original text file displayed in a browser

Checking and Correcting Styles

In order to help upgrade my existing programs to Python 3, I wanted to be able to go through my Python scripts and pull out any comments that contained the words TODO or FIXME and the magic variables set at the beginning of the script, the _version_ and _maintainer_ variables. I wanted to be able to check that they were formatted consistently and then update or create the appropriate text documentation.

Identifying these items is to help me stick to the coding style I have set for myself; you might want to do things differently.

The initial pseudocode design in Listing 7-3 made this task look pretty simple.

***Listing 7-3.** Pseudocode for a Style Checker Script*

```
"""

Purpose:
        Python script style & version checker
Target System:
```

```
        GNU/Linux
Interface:
        Command-line
Functional Requirements:
        Automatically go through all lines in a Python file
        pulling out TODO comments and appending TODO file
        check & update AUTHORS file
        check for existence of README, [NEWS and ChangeLog]
        So all documentation can be auto-created from main python files.
        Print warnings and prompt before any changes are made.
"""

# Input: get Python filename from user.
# Open the file for reading.
# Test if file is valid python 3.0; if not, suggest running 2to3 on file.
# Iterate through lines in script.
        # Check that the script calls the correct version of the interpreter.
        # Check that the script declares Unicode encoding.
        # Turn comments into proper docstrings.
        # Check magic variables are correctly formatted if present.
        # Check for TODO & FIXME lines.
# Print out results.
# Check for existence of AUTHORS, ChangeLog, NEWS, README and TODO files in the
# same directory as file.
# If no AUTHORS file, write out author_s to AUTHORS.
# Check TODOs and Warnings: If fixed append Changelog, else append TODO.
```

■ **Note** As well as importing the re module, I imported the time module, using time.strftime(), to give me a timestamp. I passed it time-formatting code and no time, so it will use the current time by default. The time module is further discussed in Chapter 10.

The script (see Listing 7-4) sets up a bunch of regular expressions, so I can check the content of the script against them later. I have also set up a dictionary called spellbook to hold all the magic variables set in the script.

I used a while loop that will loop around if the filename given does not have a .py extension. The script iterates through the lines in the script being examined and compares the lines against the regular expression objects I set up at the start. Finally, another function format_info() gathers all the information from spellbook and formats it nicely for output.

Listing 7-4. fix_style.py

```
"""
fix_style.py
Purpose:
    Python script style & version checker
Target System:
    GNU/Linux
Interface:
    Command-line
Functional Requirements:
    Automatically go through all lines in a Python file
    pulling out TODO comments and appending TODO file
    check & update AUTHORS file
    check for existence of README, [NEWS and ChangeLog]
    So all documentation can be auto-created from main python files.
    Print warnings and prompt before any changes are made.
"""
__version__ = 0.1
__status__ = "Prototype"
__date__ = "16-10-2008"
__maintainer__ = "maintainer@website.com"
__credits__ = "Inspired by Duncan Parkes' remark about inline TODO comments."


import re
import time

# Datestamp
Now = time.strftime("%d-%m-%Y")


# Set up some regular expressions for later use
# Putting them all in one place makes editing and troubleshooting much easier.
filename_format = re.compile(".+?\.py")
version_format = re.compile("[\"']?(?:[0-9]+?\.)?[0-9]+?\.[0-9]+?[\"']?")
status_format = re.compile("[\"'](Prototype|Alpha|Beta|RC|Stable)[\"']")
date_format = re.compile("[\"'][0-3][0-9]-[01][0-9]-[0-9]{4}[\"']")
email_format = re.compile("[\"'].+?@.+\..+?[\"']")
todo_format = re.compile("^\s*?#\s*?(TODO|todo|FIXME|fixme):?\s*?(.+)")


# Dictionary to hold namespace variables of file
spellbook = {'version':0.0,
             'status':"",
             'date':"33-13-2023",
```

```
                    'maintainer':"",
                    'author':"",
                    'credits':""}

    def get_file():
        filename = input('Python script to be checked:-> ')
        if filename_format.match(filename):
            print("Looks like a Python file. [OK]")
        else:
            print("This file does not have a .py extension.")
            filename = ''
        return filename

    def format_info(app):
        author_s = """
        Author: {0!s}
        Maintainer: {1!s}
        Credits: {2!s}
        """.format(app['author'], app['maintainer'], app['credits'])
        app_s = """
        File: {0!s}
        Version: {1!s} - {2!s}
        Last Modified: {3!s}
        """.format(app['file'], app['version'], app['status'], app['date'])
        out_str = """
#===(*)===# Application Details #===(*)===#
{0}
#===(*)===# AUTHORS #===(*)===#
{1}
#===(*)===#===(*)===#===(*)===#
        """.format(app_s, author_s)
        return out_str


###
# Main
###

# Input: get Python filename from user.
filename = ''
while not filename:
    filename = get_file()
# Store filename in spellbook.
spellbook['file'] = filename
```

```
# Open the file for reading.
script = open(filename)

# TODO: Test if file is valid python 3.0; if not, run 2to3 on file.

print("\n#===(*)===# TODO #===(*)===#\n")
#
# Iterate through lines in script.
for line_no, line in enumerate(script):
    # Check that the script calls the correct version of the interpreter.
    if line_no == 0 and line != "#! /usr/bin/env python\n":
        print("Warning: wrong interpreter invoked")
    # Check that the script declares Unicode encoding.
    if line_no == 1 and line != "# -*- coding: UTF8 -*-\n":
        print("Warning: no text encoding declaration")

    # Next should be a docstring
     # TODO: Turn comments into proper docstring.

    # Check for magic variables.
    if line.startswith('__'):
        label, value = line.split(' = ')
        # store magic variables in spellbook
        spellbook[label.strip('__')] = value.strip().strip('"')
        # Check magic vars are correctly formatted if present.
        # __version__ = "(?:[0-9]+?\.)[0-9]+?\.[0-9]+?"
        if label == '__version__' and not version_format.match(value):
            print("Warning: dodgy", label)
        # __status__ = "Prototype|Alpha|Beta|Release Candidate|Stable"
        if label == '__status__' and not status_format.match(value):
            print("Warning: dodgy", label)
        # __date__ = "[0-3][0-9]-[01][0-9]-[0-9]{4}"
        if label == '__date__' and not date_format.match(value):
            print("Warning: dodgy", label)
        # __maintainer__ = "\W+?@\W+\.\W+?"
        if label == '__maintainer__' and not email_format.match(value):
            print("Warning: dodgy", label)

    # Check rest of lines for "#\s*?TODO|todo|FIXME|fixme(.*)"
    # This should be a 'try' statement
    # ... but they aren't covered until Chapter 11.
    if todo_format.match(line):
        #
```

```
            task = todo_format.match(line)
            label, desc = task.groups(1)
            todo_text = """
{4!s} {2!s}: {0!s} line {1!s}
    *** {3} ***
            """.format(filename, line_no, label, desc, Now)
            print(todo_text)

# We won't be needing this anymore.
script.close()

# Fill in some empty variables.
if not date_format.match(spellbook['date']):
    spellbook['date'] = Now
if spellbook['author'] == '':
    spellbook['author'] = spellbook['maintainer']

# Print out results.
print(format_info(spellbook))

# TODO: Check for existence of AUTHORS, ChangeLog, NEWS,
# README and TODO files in the same directory as file.
# TODO: if no AUTHORS file, write out author_s to AUTHORS.
# TODO: Check TODOs and Warnings: If fixed append Changelog, else append TODO.
```

This is what happened when I ran the script on itself:

```
$ ./fix_style.py
```

```
Python script to be checked:-> fix_style.py
Looks like a Python file. [OK]

#===(*)===# TODO #===(*)===#


16-10-2008 TODO: fix_style.py line 90
    ***  Test if file is valid python 3.0; if not, run 2to3 on file. ***


16-10-2008 TODO: fix_style.py line 103
    ***  Turn comments into proper docstring. ***


16-10-2008 TODO: fix_style.py line 148
    ***  Check for existence of AUTHORS, ChangeLog, NEWS, README and
TODO files in the same directory as file. ***
```

```
16-10-2008 TODO: fix_style.py line 149
    ***  if no AUTHORS file, write out author_s to AUTHORS. ***


16-10-2008 TODO: fix_style.py line 150
    ***  Check TODOs and Warnings: If fixed append Changelog, else append TODO. ***


#===(*)===# Application Details #===(*)===#

    File: fix_style.py
    Version: 0.1 - Prototype
    Last Modified: 16-10-2008

#===(*)===# AUTHORS #===(*)===#

    Author: maintainer@website.com
    Maintainer: maintainer@website.com
    Credits: Inspired by Duncan Parkes' remark about inline TODO comments.

#===(*)===#===(*)===#===(*)===#
```

And to compare, I ran it on another script, which I had prepared with a few little TODOs of its own:

```
$ ./fix_style.py
```

```
Python script to be checked:-> rpcombat.py
Looks like a Python file. [OK]

#===(*)===# TODO #===(*)===#

Warning: wrong interpreter invoked
Warning: no text encoding declaration

16-10-2008 TODO: rpcombat.py line 17
    ***  Fix up interpreter call and file encoding ***


16-10-2008 TODO: rpcombat.py line 192
    ***  rewrite the character sheet output using string.format() ***


16-10-2008 TODO: rpcombat.py line 217
    ***  shop stock list .format() ***


16-10-2008 TODO: rpcombat.py line 291
    ***  Alternate option to read characters from file. ***
```

```
16-10-2008 TODO: rpcombat.py line 332
   ***  save rpcharacters to file ***


#===(*)===# Application Details #===(*)===#

    File: rpcombat.py
    Version: 0.2 - Prototype
    Last Modified: 16-10-2008

#===(*)===# AUTHORS #===(*)===#

    Author: maintainer@website.com
    Maintainer: maintainer@website.com
    Credits:

#===(*)===#===(*)===#===(*)===#
```

Having a list of TODOs like this is rather useful; I can now work through my TODO list item by item. This saves constantly trawling through the file to remind myself of what I intended to fix next. I'm going to ignore the first item for now, as that involves explaining how to make scripts executable on their own, which I'll get into in the next chapter, but we could take care of some other items now.

Formatting Data

On line 192 of rpcombat.py, I have a note that says "rewrite the character sheet output using string.format()". This task is fairly straightforward, except this time, I have a lot of values to pass to the method, which are all contained in the profile dictionary. What I'd like to do is pass the entire dictionary to string.format() and reference its keys by name. No problem—Listing 7-5 shows the code to do just that.

Listing 7-5. *Character Sheet Formatter*

```
# Output the character sheet
### Deleted section
# TODO: rewrite the character sheet output using string.format()
#fancy_line = "<~~==|#|==~~++**\@/**++~~==|#|==~~>"
#print()
#print(fancy_line)
#print("\t", profile['Name'])
#print("\t", profile['Race'], profile['Gender'])
#print("\t", profile['Desc'])
#print(fancy_line)
#print()
#print("\tMuscle: ", profile['Muscle'], "\tlife: ", profile['life'])
#print("\tBrainz: ", profile['Brainz'], "\tmagic: ", profile['magic'])
```

```
        #print("\tSpeed: ", profile['Speed'], "\tprotection: ", profile['prot'])
        #print("\tCharm: ", profile['Charm'], "\tgold: ", profile['gold'])
        #print()
        ###
        rpcharacter_sheet = """
<~~==|#|==~~++**\@/**++~~==|#|==~~>
        {Name!s}
        {Race!s}, {Gender!s}
        {Desc!s}
<~~==|#|==~~++**\@/**++~~==|#|==~~>
        Muscle: {Muscle: <2}    life:        {life: <3}
        Brainz: {Brainz: <2}    magic:       {magic: <3}
        Speed:  {Speed: <2}     protection: {prot: <3}
        Charm:  {Charm: <2}     gold:  {gold: >7}
        """.format(**profile)
        print(rpcharacter_sheet)
        return profile
```

The profile dictionary is unpacked into string.format() using the keyword argument gathering operator (**), and the items are referenced by their respective keywords rather than positional indexes. I have reduced twelve calls to the print() function down to one, and now, I only have to deal with a single format string to edit it further. As you can see, this code is much easier to read and understand. Once I'd tested it out, I then removed the old code that is marked out in comments in Listing 7-5.

I want to do something similar to the code block starting at line 217, as shown in Listing 7-6.

Listing 7-6. *Stock List Formatter*

```
        # Display shop stock list with prices.
        ### Deleted code
        # TODO: shop stock list .format()
        #print()
        #print("<==|#|==\SHOP/==|#|==>")
        #for item in stock:
        #     print("\t", item, stock[item][0])
        #print("<==|#|==\@@@@/==|#|==>")
        #print()
        #print("You have", profile['gold'], "gold.")
        ###
        stock_list = ["    {0!s:10}{1: >3}".format(item, stock[item][0])
                        for item in stock]
        shop = """
<==|#|==\SHOP/==|#|==>
{0}
<==|#|==\@@@@/==|#|==>
```

```
You have {1} gold
""".format('\n'.join(stock_list), profile['gold'])
    print(shop)
```

I made this in two parts: First the stock list is formatted separately using a list comprehension. Second, I drop this comprehension into a shop format. Now, I can be much more precise about how everything lines up, as shown in the following printout of the character sheet and shop listing:

```
<~~==|#|==~~++**\@/**++~~==|#|==~~>
    Ez
    Pixie, female
    Tall and wild
<~~==|#|==~~++**\@/**++~~==|#|==~~>
    Muscle: 46    life:        30
    Brainz: 37    magic:       30
    Speed:  28    protection:  23
    Charm:  46    gold:        67


<==|#|==\SHOP/==|#|==>
    dagger     25
    shield     15
    club       15
    armour     101
    pole       10
    halberd    80
    hammer     99
    cuirass    30
    flail      50
    rope       10
    sword      60
    lantern    10
<==|#|==\@@@@/==|#|==>

You have 67 gold
```

Storing Data

The last two TODOs, on lines 291 and 332, go together. I want an "Alternate option to read characters from file." and to "save rpcharacters to file". "How hard can that be?" I wondered.

I'll spare you the statistics of how many brain cells I fried over the years trying to figure out these tasks and cut to the chase. There is a major gotcha involved in retrieving data from text files: whatever format your data was originally in, as soon as you write it to a text file, *it becomes a text string*. Got that? I'll run it by you again.

In this example, I want to save the list of player profile dictionaries to a file. The dictionaries contain a variety of data types: two tuples, a list, several strings, and lots of integers. Once saved to a text file, *these all become string values* with no special meaning to the Python interpreter. In fact, all this data becomes one big string. I could write a really complicated function that isolates the different types of data, performs int(), list(), and tuple() conversions on some of the data types, and assigns them all to their correct variable names individually. But life would be much simpler if I could just load the entire dictionary back into place. That would also cut down on potential errors, as I would know that my data is exactly the same as the data the program used last time it was run.

The simplest answer to this conundrum is to use two built-in functions: repr() and eval(). In some ways, repr() is to eval() what str() is to print(). In other words, repr() outputs variables in the format that eval() expects to find, and eval() then turns those strings back into a legal Python expression and evaluates them. It is not a perfect solution, but it is simple, workable, and fixes this TODO item.

I created two new functions in rpcombat.py: write_out() and read_in(). The first function, write_out(players), is shown in Listing 7-7. It opens data_file in write mode and iterates through the players list, writing out the repr() form of each dictionary to a separate line in the file rpcharacters.rpg. I could have given it a .txt extension, but there is nothing to stop you creating your own file extensions if you want to. The file will still be a plain text file, but it is a way of indicating that the data contained within it is of a specific format.

Listing 7-7. *Function to Write Data Out to File*

```
def write_out(players):
    print("Saving character sheets")
    data_file = open('rpcharacters.rpg', 'w')
    lines = []
    for player in players:
        lines.append(repr(player) + '\n')
    data_file.writelines(lines)
    data_file.close
    return
```

And here's the data file itself (rpcharacters.rpg):

```
{'life': 30, 'Name': 'Ez', 'gold': 7, 'Gender': 'female', 'armour': (0, 0, 50),
 'Race': 'Pixie', 'Muscle': 46, 'Brainz': 37, 'magic': 30, 'weapon':
(60, 60, 50), 'prot': 23, 'Charm': 46, 'inventory': ['sword'], 'Speed': 28,
'Desc': 'Tall and wild'}
{'life': 20, 'Name': 'Inkon', 'gold': 9, 'Gender': 'male', 'armour': (0, 0, 50),
'Race': 'Troll', 'Muscle': 35, 'Brainz': 45, 'magic': 31, 'weapon': (50, 60, 55),
'prot': 16, 'Charm': 34, 'inventory': ['flail'], 'Speed': 11, 'Desc': 'Small and
clever'}
```

The second function I created, read_in() is shown in Listing 7-8. It simply has to iterate through the lines in the file (which is opened in read-only mode) and assign the evaluated line to player, which is then packed back into the players list. Don't forget to close() the file each time to prevent accidental corruption of the data.

Listing 7-8. *Function to Read in Data from a File*

```
def read_in():
    print("Reading in data")
    data_file = open('rpcharacters.rpg')
    for line in data_file:
        player = eval(line)
        players.append(player)
    data_file.close()
    print(players)
    return
```

Just to complete things for this chapter, I'll run fix_style.py on rpcombat.py again to check I got rid of all those TODO comments.

```
$ python fix_style.py
```

```
Python script to be checked:-> rpcombat.py
Looks like a Python file. [OK]

#===(*)===# TODO #===(*)===#


17-10-2008 TODO: rpcombat.py line 18
      ***  Fix up interpreter call and file encoding ***


#===(*)===# Application Details #===(*)===#

      File: rpcombat.py
      Version: 0.3 - Prototype
      Last Modified: 17-10-2008

#===(*)===# AUTHORS #===(*)===#

      Author: maintainer@website.com
      Maintainer: maintainer@website.com
      Credits:

#===(*)===#===(*)===#===(*)===#
```

In fact, there is still one TODO left, which I will deal with in the next chapter.

Jargon Busting

Let's look at the new terms introduced in this chapter:

- *Alphanumeric*: This refers to letter or number character and is equivalent to the regular expression [a-zA-Z0-9_].

- *American Standard Code for Information Interchange (ASCII)*: This method of encoding characters on computers uses just 7 bits of information. There are 128 values ranging from 0 to 127, of which 95 are printable characters and 33 are invisible control characters. ASCII encoding only covers the characters usually found in the English language and a few others that are specifically used by computers.

- *Conversion field*: This is the part of a replacement field after the exclamation point (!) used to force an item to be represented as a particular type, regardless of its own type's formatting rules.

- *Field names*: A replacement field is a placeholder for a variable value in a formatted piece of text. The field name is replaced by the value of the variable it refers to.

- *Format specifier*: The format specifier field contains a specification of how a value in a replacement field should be presented.

- *Greedy*: This type of regular expression will match as many characters as possible.

- *Nongreedy*: This type of regular expression will match as few characters as possible.

- *Regular expression*: This refers to a pattern that can match a piece of text.

- *Tags*: These additional marks are added to a text file to specify the manner of formatting. Tags are used by markup languages to indicate paragraphs, headings, bold and italic text, and so on.

- *Tarball*: This refers to an archived group of one or more files. The files need not be compressed however. An archived and compressed file might end in .tar.gz.

- *Unicode*: This method of defining characters is suitable for languages throughout the world. It allows for the representation of the many different characters required to make up international character sets (i.e., alphabets).

- *Whitespace*: This refers to any character that prints out as space in text, including tabs (\t), newlines (\n), and so on, as well as the actual space character. This is equivalent to the regular expression [\t\n\r\f\v].

- *Wildcard*: The * character can match any other character in a pattern match.

Summary

As you've seen, text is integral to most Python programs, and you saw how often of our examples use it. We take text input from users, manipulate that text, and display messages in response. This is why Python comes with so many text-related features.

In this chapter, you learned how to split and join strings; format, edit, and search for strings; use regular expressions to search for patterns within strings; and work with the files on your file system. We then applied much of this in our example application.

■ ■ ■

## CHAPTER 8

Executable Files, Organization, and Python on the Web

Up to this point, you've been running your scripts via the python interpreter.

This is all well and good, but it would be nice if we could get the scripts to run by themselves, just like real programs, so that's just what we'll look at first. I'll then cover how to organize and spruce up your code, because clean, organized code makes you more efficient and gives you time to write even more lovely Python code.

This leads us onto some of the dynamic features of Python: modules and the exec() and eval() functions. These features give you more flexibility and choice when writing Python applications.

The final topic in this chapter, and another whole world of choice, is Python on the Web. I'll go over a simple CGI form to show you how to process data on a web form.

Making Programs Executable as Stand-Alone Applications

Assuming you are using a Unix-compatible computer, a couple of things need to be added to your script to be able to run it directly (you will still need to have the correct version of Python installed in order for it to work). If you wish to create a stand-alone Python application for a Windows-compatible computer, you will need to obtain the py2exe compiler. The instructions in this section apply to Unix-compatible computers only.

First, you need to add either of the following two lines to the very beginning of your script, if you haven't already (choose the one where your Python distribution is located):

```
#! /usr/bin/env python
```

or

```
#! /usr/bin/python
```

This tells the operating system where to look for the Python **executable**. The first version leaves it up to your operating system to decide which Python version to use; the others directly point to the Python executable you want. You can check the location of the executable with which. For these examples, I will assume you have access to a **Bash** prompt via the terminal. There are some important variations in the way different operating systems (or platforms) are set up to run Python programs, so you will probably need to read up on the specific details for your system.

```
$ which python
/usr/bin/python
```

If you have an alternative version of Python installed, you might want to use the following instead:

```
#! /usr/bin/python3.0
```

This way, you can keep scripts around on your system that use different versions of Python without having to keep checking which version of the interpreter you are using when you want to run them.

```
# -*- coding: UTF8 -*-
```

This tells the interpreter what encoding you are using. UTF8 is Unicode, and you want to use this for Python 3 scripts. In fact, Python 3 defaults to UTF8, so adding this line is just extra insurance.

Next, you must set the file permissions on the script. This allows you to execute it by itself without having to call it as an argument to python:

```
$ chmod 751 myscript.py
```

or

```
$ chmod u+x myscript.py
```

In the first version of this command, chmod is given a numeric mode. This is made up of up to four **octal** integers (any omitted digits are assumed to be leading zeros, so I have omitted the first digit in this example). The second digit sets permissions for the user who owns the file; the third sets permissions for users in the file's group; and the fourth sets permissions for all other users. The octal permissions value can be calculated by adding up the following values:

```
read += 4
write += 2
execute += 1
```

The 7 in the first place of chmod's argument means that you, the owner of the file, can run and edit the file. The 5 in the next place allows members of the same group as the file to read and run the program, and the final 1 allows other users of the system to run the file but not read or write.

The alternative version of the command simply gives executable privileges to the owner of the file. You may be able to set the executable bit using your file browser—look for an option to set the permissions or properties of the file.

▪ **Caution** Some tutorials may suggest setting the permissions to 777 or a+rwx; this is a bad habit to get into, because it allows other users to edit and execute your files and, therefore, creates a potential security problem. You may find it useful to open up the permissions of a file in this way to troubleshoot permissions-related problems during development, but it is wise to close permissions down to a minimum before the application goes live in any public situation. You should read your system's documentation to find out how it controls permissions.

Now, you can run your program from the command line like this:

```
$ ./myscript.py
```

This works so long as you are in the same directory as the script. You can also run the script by clicking or double-clicking its icon in your file browser (depending on your operating system).

If you want this script to be accessible to anyone, anywhere on the system, you need to create a link to the script in one of the directories in the system's PATH. To find out which directories are in your PATH.

```
$ echo $PATH
```

You can add directories to your PATH if you need to create a location that you have permission to write to.

```
$ PATH=$HOME/bin:$PATH
$ export PATH
$ echo $PATH
/home/tim/bin:/usr/local/bin:/usr/bin:/bin:/usr/games
```

This adds a directory called bin to the PATH that is searched for executable files by the system.

Note Other users will also need to add this directory to their PATH, and the appropriate permissions need to be set in order for them to be able to make use of programs located in custom directories. Also, note that altering the PATH is temporary, for the current session only! You will need to edit the .bash_profile file to make changes reappear after logging in again. If you're not familiar with Linux or Unix, you should refer to an introductory text on this and related subjects. You might want to take a look at *Beginning Ubuntu Linux, Fourth Edition* by Keir Thomas, Andy Channelle, and Jaime Sicam (Apress, 2009).

The next step is to create a link to the script from the bin directory.

```
$ ln -s /full/path/to/myscript.py bin/myscript
```

Now, I can call my new script from anywhere without giving an explicit path.

```
$ myscript
```

Nice. Rather than making a link, you could write a short Bash script that calls the Python file and save that in ~/bin. The beauty of calling myscript.py indirectly like this, though, is that it gives a lot more room if you want to rename or reorganize your code. It doesn't make any difference to your users if myscript points to ~/bin/myscript.py or /usr/local/lib/python3.0/myscript_1.0_stable.py, so long as the program still accepts the same arguments.

Sooner or later, you will encounter the major gotcha, which is that any references to files using relative path names won't work. Now is a great chance to test whether any parts of your code were dependent on being called from a specific directory. The most likely fix will be to replace any relative paths with full paths that go right back to the root directory of your filesystem or that are relative to a path stored as a variable.

Organizing Your Project

At the start of this book, I suggested creating a separate folder for your programs. It's up to you to organize your code how you want it, but having some kind of plan is a really sensible idea. I like to keep the programs that I am developing in a folder called ~/Projects/. Once the application is stable and I want to make it available for use, I copy a cleaned-up version of the folder and its contents into ~/lib/python3.0/ following my system's conventions:

> ${prefix}/bin/python: This is the recommended location of the interpreter.
>
> ${prefix}/lib/python<version>: This is the recommended location of the directories containing the standard modules. Note that these modules are reusable; individual application code might be in other directories.
>
> ${prefix}/include/python<version>: This is the recommended location of the directories containing the include files needed for developing Python extensions and embedding the interpreter.

I have replaced ${prefix} with my **home directory** (shown in Figure 8-1). If I want to make an application available to the whole system, I prefer to make a link in ~/bin/, as I did in the myscript.py example. Also, I could add ~/lib/python3.0/ to my PYTHONPATH, which is a list of directories that are searched for modules to be imported by the import statement.

```
$ PYTHONPATH=$HOME/lib/python3.0:$PYTHONPATH
$ export PYTHONPATH
```

Putting my private directory first means it will be searched before the others.

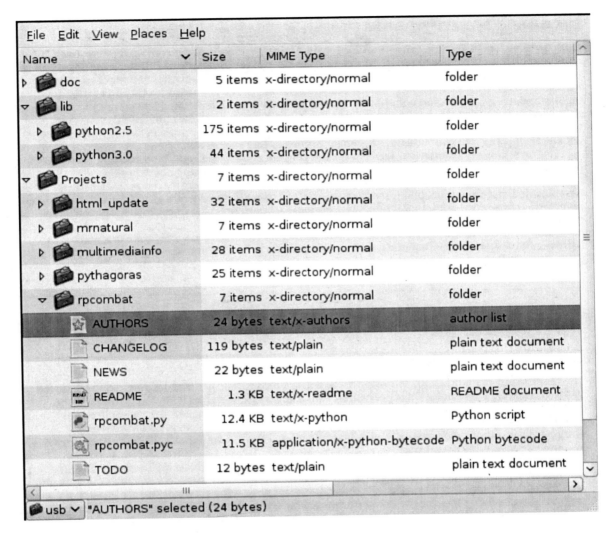

Figure 8-1. My home directory

Writing Stylish Code

Python was designed to be readable, on the grounds that code is read more often than it is written. Python does not dictate how you should name things or use comments and docstrings. These matters are considered to be part of your coding style, so it is worth putting some thought towards the style you use. You can create your own unique style if you want, but it does pay to be consistent. Consistency prevents you from getting confused yourself, and when you want to share your work with other coders, you will either need to be able to explain the conventions you have used or adopt a common style.

Becoming More Pythonic

Every so often, you will come across the word *Pythonic* in discussions about coding. It refers to a combination of approaches to programming that are considered idiomatic to Python, as opposed to the way you might approach programming in other languages; there are a growing number of conventions involving methods and code constructions that are generally agreed to be more efficient or mutually understandable by the Python community. These approaches are not dictated by Python; you won't get an error message if you don't follow these guidelines, so it is up to you how much of this you want to take on board. However, I would recommend following the generally accepted Pythonic style to start with and adjusting it to your taste when you have more coding experience.

Listing 8-1 shows a somewhat formal way of laying out code. It is a legal Python script, although the program itself doesn't actually do very much. Up till now, I have been using docstrings in a slightly haphazard way to keep a record of the initial specification of requirements for the program. Once you have decided that the application is ready to release into the wild, the docstrings will need to be updated to provide some information that is more appropriate for your users. The docstrings should all be self-explanatory.

Also, in the example script in Listing 8-1, each statement should be on a separate line with consistent indentation. The first line tells the system where to find Python; the second tells it to use Unicode encoding.

■ **Tip** Older versions of Python don't require the encoding to be declared. You should use ASCII or Latin-1 instead of UTF-8 if you include this line.

The first line of Python code following these declarations should be the docstring. This is followed by the version information for this application. I am using magic variables with double underscores before and after the name to record this information, so that it can be used by helper applications like pydoc. The pydoc module imports a Python module and uses the contents to generate help text at runtime; pydoc outputs docstrings for any objects that have them. Additionally, all of the documentable contents of the module are output.

Next, any modules you might need are imported. Each import should be on a separate line, and modules should be grouped according to where they come from. Only then does the real coding begin.

One of the reasons for this ordering is that some items need to be set up before other parts of the program can use them: modules have to be imported before they are called on to perform their duties; variables need to be assigned before they can be referenced; and functions must be declared before they are called. Additionally, before you use anything, it must be in scope. An import, an assignment of a variable, and a function definition are all just ways of getting a variable in the current namespace.

It follows that the next things to be set are constants and global variables, that is, data that won't change its value or need to be available to several different parts of the program. This is followed by the definition of any classes or functions that you are going to need. The main body of the program comes last of all and in this example is very short and slightly cryptic.

Listing 8-1. *style_guide.py*

```
#! /usr/bin/env python
# -*- coding: UTF8 -*-
```

```python
"""Docstring: Short title and summary on first line followed by a new line

style_guide.py
A Docstring should be usable as a 'Usage:' message. It should contain:
A description of the script's function;
command-line syntax and parameters;
notes about the algorithm used
and a decent usage example.
This script takes no arguments and prints out a useless message.

The closing triple quote should be on a line by itself.
"""

# Version information goes immediately after the docstring
# with a blank line before and after.
# These variables with double leading and trailing underscores
# are 'magic' objects, which should only be used as documented.
__version__ = 0.1
__status__ = "Prototype"
__date__ = "31-10-2008"
__maintainer__ = "maintainer@website.com"
__credits__ = "Thanks to everyone."

# Import any modules we might need.
# Standard library imports
import os
import re

# Related third party imports

# local application / library specific imports

# Globals and constants
# Set variables whose values won't change before any others.
Global = ""
_private_global = "This variable is only used inside the program"

# Class declarations would normally happen about here
# Classes are covered in the next chapter.

def code_layout():
    """Indentation
```

```
    Use 4 spaces per indentation level
        Never mix tabs and spaces
            In fact, just use spaces.
    """
    line_length = "Limit all lines to a maximum of 79 characters, for \
        big blocks of text 72 chars is recommended. You can use the \
        implied line continuation inside () [] and {} or a backslash \
        to wrap long lines of text."

    # Always keep comments up to date when the code changes,
    # delete old and irrelevant comments.
    # Comments should be complete grammatical statements.

    ###
    ## Stub of code or development note
    ## to be removed before the program is released.
    ## This function doesn't do anything. (note:…there may be a def function here one day.
    ###

    return

def naming_conventions(functions = "lower case with underscores"):
    """Variable naming

    Choose names that people might be likely to guess, whole words are
    good, but don't make it too long. Use singular names to describe
    individual things, use plurals for collections. Single letters are
    only useful for throw-away variables.
    """
    variable_names = "lower case with underscores"
    a, b, c = 0, 1, 2
    int_variables = [a, b, c]
    x, y ,z = 0.5, 1.65, 2.42
    float_variables = [x, y, z]
    result = [i + j for i in int_variables for j in float_variables]
    if result is not None:
        return result

def main_func():
    """Docstring: The title should make sense by itself.

    A function's docstring should:
    Summarize the function's behaviour;
```

```python
        Document its arguments;
        Return values;
        Side-effects;
        Exceptions raised;
        and restrictions on when the function can & cannot be called.
        Optional arguments and keywords should also be explained if they are
        part of the interface.
        """
        result = naming_conventions()
        return result

if __name__ == '__main__':
    results = main_func()
    print("\nPoints awarded for style: ")
    for result in reversed(sorted(results)):
        print('\t', result)
    print()
```

You may guess from the use of double underscores that there is magic afoot. If the program has been run directly, rather than being imported as a module, the magic variable __name__ will contain the value '__main__'. In this case, the main_func() is called, and results are output. If the script was imported as a module, none of the code would actually be directly available, but the functions would all be available, if declared public, to the calling procedure.

```python
>>> import style_guide
>>> help(style_guide)
```

If you actually want the program's output, you would have to explicitly call the style_guide's main_func().

```python
>>> style_guide.main_func()
[0.5, 1.6499999999999999, 2.4199999999999999, 1.5, 2.6499999999999999, 3.4199999999999999,
 2.5, 3.6499999999999999, 4.4199999999999999]
```

You will have noticed that it is standard practice to separate function definitions with blank lines, the same is true for classes and their methods, as you will see in the next chapter. It is acceptable to use extra blank lines to group related functions and logical sections of code together.

You should avoid putting extra whitespace characters immediately inside parentheses; before commas, colons, and semicolons; and inside expressions—the main exception being that you *should* put a space either side of operators. You should also try to avoid double and triple nested loops; try to refactor the nested blocks as functions to reduce the amount of indentation.

Importing Modules

Modules are imported using the import statement either via the interactive command line or at the start of a script. An example would be import foo_module.

```
>>> import sys
```

This will import everything from the module named sys. The sys module contains some very useful dynamic objects:

- sys.argv: A list of command line arguments, argv[0] contains the path to the script itself
- sys.stdin: The standard input file object as used by input()
- sys.stdout: The standard output file object as used by print()
- sys.stderr: The standard error object that is used for error messages

These objects allow you to pass data in and out of the program via command-line arguments, as in sys.argv, or piped in via sys.stdin. I'll show you how to do this in a moment.

The objects, function and attributes of a module are usually accessed using dot notation, so you would write module.object to use the object from module in your script, for example. If you wanted to read in data from stdin, you would write sys.stdin.read(), which calls the read() method on the stdin file-like object in module sys.

The import statement can take a couple of other forms. The first is this:

```
>>> from sys import argv
```

This will only import the argv object, so it can now be accessed without putting the module name and dot in front of it, like so:

```
>>> argv
['']
```

The list is empty, because I'm looking at it from the command line.

As I mentioned, the import statement provides an alternative version in case importing something like this would cause a clash with a name that you are already using in the script.

```
>>> from sys import argv as arguments
>>> arguments
['']
```

This gives you a lot of choice in the way you import functions and objects into your programs. Python has a lot of specialized and extended functionality that can be imported from modules, which have been prewritten and tested by other programmers. You have already seen the re and time modules in action and have imported your own scripts to view their help() output. In Chapter 11, I'll give you an overview of some of the most commonly used modules. Listing 8-2 shows a simple example of how to use command-line arguments and how to read information from stdin and write it to stdout.

Listing 8-2. sysargs.py

```
#! /usr/bin/env python
# -*- coding: UTF8 -*-

"""Using command-line arguments
This script can receive command line arguments
and data from stdin.
The output of any command can be fed into the script via | the pipe command.

$ echo "Foo" | ./sysargs.py bar baz
Datestamp:
2008-11-12

Command-line arguments:
0      ./sysargs.py
1      bar
2      baz

Stdin:
Foo
"""

import sys
import time

now = time.strftime("%Y-%m-%d") # the time function yields system time, date, etc.

def get_args():
    result = ['\t'.join([str(i), str(arg)]) for i, arg in enumerate(sys.argv)]
    return result

def get_input():
    result = sys.stdin.read()
    return result

def output(args, data):
    arguments = "\n".join(args)
    output_string = '\n'.join(["Datestamp: ", now,
                    "\nCommand-line arguments: ", arguments, "\nStdin: ",data])
    sys.stdout.write(output_string)
    return

if __name__ == '__main__':
```

```
arguments = get_args()
data = get_input()
output(arguments, data)
```

In Listing 8-2, the first function, get_args(), performs a list comprehension on sys.argv. The second function, get_input(), reads data in from stdin. Their results are bundled together and printed prettily by the output() function. Listing 8-2 does much the same job as the original hello_world.py, but this time using the sys module to perform input and output instead of the built-in input() and print() functions.

■ **Tip** Some modules are better documented than others. You can get a very brief overview of the available methods and attributes of any Python object using dir(object) or help(object).

Using exec() and eval()

While we're on the subject of dynamic applications, I'd like to look at two rather useful, but dangerous, built-in functions: exec(string) and eval(string).

The exec() function was a keyword and statement in Python 2.x but is now a function. It allows you to execute arbitrary strings as if they were Python statements. Similar to print, the exec statement has been replaced in Python 3 with an exec() function.

```
>>> list_numbers=[1,2,3,4]
>>>exec("for number in list_numbers: print(number)")
```

If you type the preceding code into an interactive prompt, you can see that are actually executing a command string from within the exec() function: you made a list and then merely iterated over the items in the list with a for loop. The exec() function is a powerful feature, as you can imagine, but should be used with care.

One of the things you should never do is apply exec() to the results of the input() function, or indeed allow your user any direct access to this function or the main namespace of the program. The exec() function allows you to build code strings on the fly, so you can never be entirely sure what the final string will contain; that will depend on where the code string gets its constituent parts from. For example, if the input string was built by the user at runtime, issues could arise if the user entered code that wouldn't run or violated security measures. A variation of the previous code is shown here:

```
>>>
>>> list_numbers=[1,2,3,4]
>>>mycode="for number in list_numbers: print(number)"
>>>exec(mycode)
```

In this case, all we did was create a text string to execute. Certainly, it could have been created on the fly via an input statement—just consider the security issue first!

Using eval() is just as easy and allows you to evaluate a statement. Examine the following:

```
>>>t=3
>>>result=eval("t > 5") # 3 is not greater than 5

>>>print (result)
```

Note that we are evaluating a code string, in this case "t > 5", which, of course, results in False.

Both of these functions provide the possibility of an alternative method of making choices and controlling the flow of program execution. This approach is an interesting avenue to explore briefly and may be of some use before you come to building your own classes in the next chapter.

■ **Caution** Using exec() and eval() opens up whole new areas of security risks. Take care to strictly control the content of any strings you send to either of these functions.

Putting Python on the Web

If you run your own web site or have access to a server, you may be interested in using Python to run web-based services. You will need FTP access to try this example.

■ **Tip** If you're running Linux and have root privileges (or you're running another operating system that supports Apache), you could install Apache and configure it to run as your own private local server to use as a web testing zone. Refer to the official Apache documentation for information on how to set things up to run Python **Common Gateway Interface (CGI)** scripts.

The simplest way to find out if your server supports Python is to upload a Python script to your cgi directory and see if it works. In the top-level directory of your web site (shown in Figure 8-2), you will probably have an html folder, where the pages of your web site reside along with a cgi folder, which may well still be empty. If the directory isn't this easy to spot, you will need to ask your hosting provider for the location of your cgi directory.

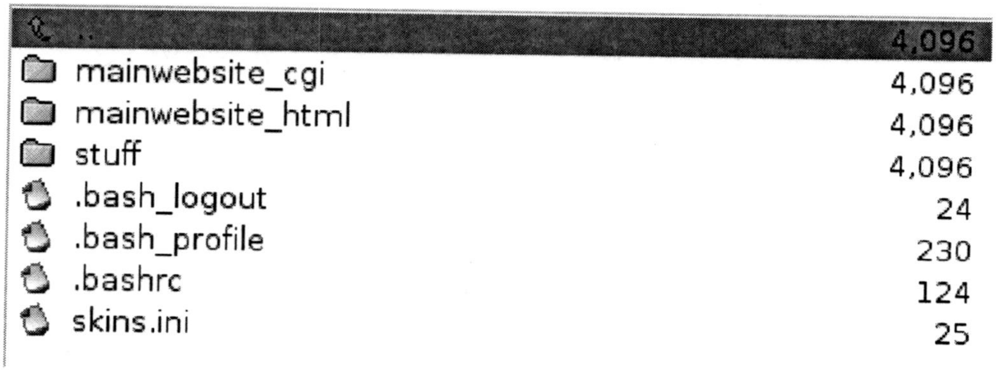

📁 mainwebsite_cgi	4,096
📁 mainwebsite_html	4,096
📁 stuff	4,096
🔧 .bash_logout	24
🔧 .bash_profile	230
🔧 .bashrc	124
🔧 skins.ini	25

Figure 8-2. Web site top-level folder

Copy Listing 8-3 into a text file, and save it as `hello.cgi`. Upload this file to your web site's `cgi` directory. Make sure the web site copy of `hello.cgi` has the correct permissions set, as I showed you in the `myscript.py` example. All users probably need to be able to read and execute the file, but only you should be able to write to it. It may be possible to limit permissions further, as often the web-server has a dummy user set up who is used to run programs. You will need to check all these details independently, as they will vary from situation to situation.

Listing 8-3. hello.cgi

```
#! /usr/bin/env python
# -*- coding: UTF8 -*-

"""Simple CGI script

"""

import time

now = time.strftime("%A %d %B %Y")

def print_content():
    print("Content-type: text/html")
    print()

def print_header():
    print("""<html>
    <head>
    <title>Simple CGI script</title>
    </head>
    <body>""")
```

```
def print_footer():
    print("</body></html>")

print_content()
print_header()
print("""<h1>It's {0!s}!</h1>
<p>Your server is correctly set up to run Python programs.</p>""".format(now))
print_footer()
```

Once the file is uploaded, you should be able to test it out by pointing your browser to an address like http://www.mywebsite.com/cgi-bin/hello.cgi. If your server has already been set up correctly to run Python scripts, you will see a rather plain web page bearing today's date and a positive message, like the one shown in Figure 8-3.

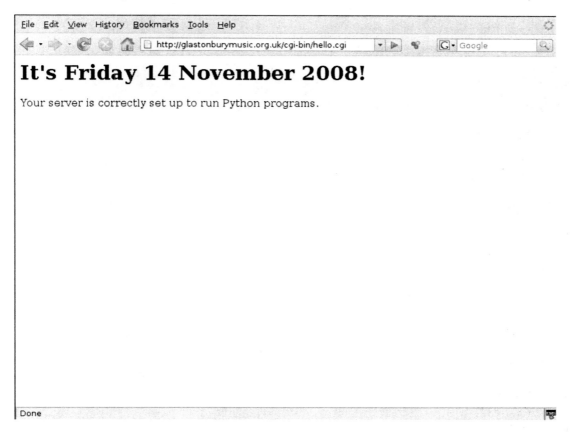

Figure 8-3. Confirmation that we can run Python on our web server

If you see some other message displayed, you may not have been so lucky as to have a correctly configured web server. You will probably need to ask your Internet service provider (ISP) or your system administrator or consult log files to decide what to do next in order to get Python to run properly on your web server.

You will notice that the error messages you receive from the web server really aren't that informative. The situation can be improved by using the `cgitb` module, which will display some familiar-looking traceback information in the browser window if an error is encountered. This can be enabled by adding the following two lines to the start of your script:

```
import cgitb
cgitb.enable()
```

If this provides you with a useful Python error message (see Figure 8-4), you're in luck—the error was with your code, which means you can do something about it.

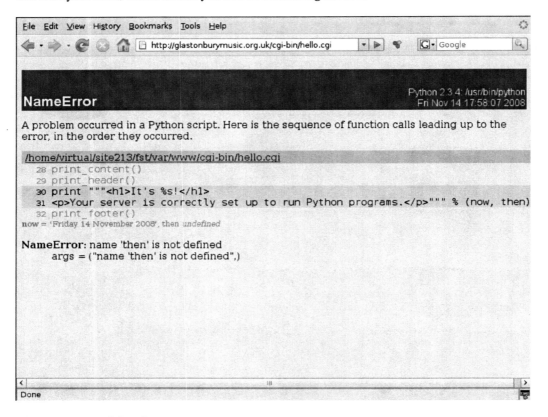

Figure 8-4. A useful Python error message

Creating a Quick CGI Form

Once you've got your web server working correctly, you can move on to getting user input, as shown in Listing 8-4. Input is supplied to the CGI script by an HTML form. You can retrieve the data from the form's fields using the FieldStorage class from the cgi module. I'll explain how classes work fully in the next chapter. For now, all you need to know is that cgi.FieldStorage returns a dictionary-like interface, which allows you to access the form fields by name. The items in the FieldStorage dictionary contain more than just the value, so you have to explicitly ask for the value. There are several ways you could do this: the best is to use the getvalue(key, default_value) method, which is provided by the FieldStorage object.

Listing 8-4. form.cgi

```
#! /usr/bin/env python
# -*- coding: UTF8 -*-

"""CGI form example

"""

import cgi
import cgitb
import time

# Enable CGI traceback
cgitb.enable()

# Create datestamp
now = time.strftime("%A %d %B %Y")

# Get the contents of the form
form = cgi.FieldStorage()
name = form.getvalue('name', 'new user')

def print_content():
    print("Content-type: text/html")
    print()

def print_header():
    print("""<html>
      <head>
      <title>Simple CGI form</title>
      </head>
      <body>""")

def print_form():
    print("""
      <form action='form.cgi'>
```

```
        Enter your name: <input type='text' name='name' />
        <input type='submit' />
        </form>
        """)

def print_footer():
    print("</body></html>")


print_content()
print_header()
print("""<h1>It's {0!s}!</h1>
<p>Hello {1!s}, your server is correctly set up to run Python programs.</p>""".format(now,
name))
print_form()
print_footer()
```

Figure 8-5 shows the first run of this script.

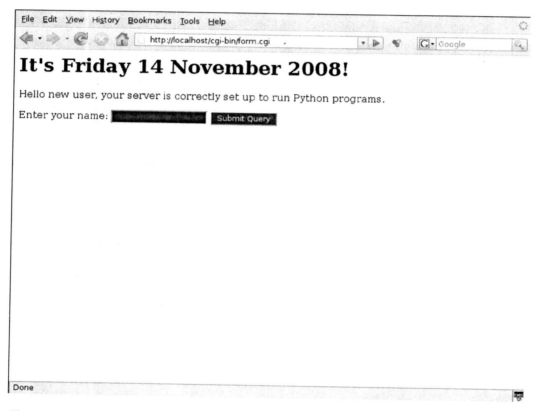

Figure 8-5. *The results of running this script for the first time*

Jargon Busting

These are the new terms from this chapter:

- *Bourne-Again Shell (Bash)*: Bash is a layer on top of Unix and Linux operating systems that interprets commands for the operating system and allows you to run commands at the command line.
- *Common Gateway Interface (CGI)*: This is a technique for processing data and generating dynamic content on the Web.
- *Executable*: An executable file contains a stand-alone application executed by an operating system. All applications, such as Microsoft Word and Emacs, are run using an executable.
- *Home directory*: On a multiuser operating system, this is the directory where an individual user's personal files are kept. This keeps them separate from operating system files and the files of other users.

Summary

A lot of information has been covered in the short space of this chapter. You have learned how to create stand-alone applications, organize your projects, lay out your code, use modules to accept command-line arguments and input from stdin, execute and evaluate arbitrary strings, and create a custom namespace. Finally, you have learned how to write a simple CGI script that can receive input from a web-based form.

You can now create proper programs that will work in the same way as any other application you have installed on your system. Your end users don't need to know anything about what language you wrote it in or the details of the code; they only need to know what commands are available via the interface you have created for them. It's up to you whether the program is self-explanatory or in what form you provide help files. If in doubt, there is nothing wrong with plain text.

Caution You now have the power to mess up really badly. Of course, you will probably get away with many minor errors and indiscretions, but now is a really good time to start considering security issues during the testing phase.

You are now ready for the next coding paradigm shift—full object-oriented programming. Nearly everything in Python is an object of some type or another, and in the next chapter, you will learn about classes and see how to create and implement your own.

CHAPTER 9

■ ■ ■

Classes

Python is an object-oriented language. You have already seen what can be achieved using the methods provided by the basic data types. Central to the concept of object orientation is the **class**—a template for creating your own data types. A data type may be a person, for example, each of whom has unique aspects that might be specified by data such as LastName, FirstName, Age, Sex, and EyeColor. You might think of a class as a noun, representing objects that are described by unique aspects. These aspects are technically referred to in OOP as attributes.

Class definitions are sometimes referred to as *templates*, as their entire purpose is to serve as a blueprint or model of class objects for you to use in your programs. **Classes** form the basis of a whole new style of programming. You have already moved the focus of your programs from simple top-down scripts to function-driven applications. Classes enable you to move the action into custom-built objects, which can contain both data (**attributes**) and commands (**methods**). Creating objects involves a further stage of abstraction from function-driven programming and provides a means of modeling real-world constructs as single entities in your code.

Object orientation can help to reduce complexity, particularly in long programs. It also encourages programmers to re-use existing, tested code because it is possible to create objects that inherit the majority of their attributes and methods from an existing class, leaving the programmer to add or override the pieces that specifically need to be different. Using the principle known as inheritance, specific objects can be created out of general ones, producing a family tree of objects similar to the classification of natural species.

Imagine you have three base classes, Animal, Vegetable, and Mineral; these classes would contain general attributes that could be applied to any object of the same class. You could then derive further subclasses from these base classes, so Animal could become the parent to several child classes, such as Mammal, Reptile, Fish, Bird, Insect, and so on. Each of these children would contain new attributes specific to their type, but they'd also inherit the general attributes of an Animal. You could further subclass Mammals into Dog, Cat, Pig, and so forth. When you want to use an Animal in your program, you could, for example, create an instance of Dog called rover, which inherits the bark() method that all Dogs have. In your code, issuing the command rover.bark() could then result in something like "Woof!" being printed to the screen.

■ **Note** This is just an example. I don't recommend creating such a large family of subclasses in actual practice; you should create only the classes you need to use.

As in the real world, you don't need to know all the details about Animals and Mammals to get your Dog to bark(), you just need to know what commands your Dog understands. Organizing your data into self-contained units makes it easier to figure out problems using the same sort of logic that you are used to using in real-world situations. Many programmers find that object orientation allows their code to grow in a more natural way than constantly having to create new functions from scratch.

Empowering objects

Objects are the primary means of representing data in Python. All data in a Python program is represented by some type of object or by the relationship between objects. A class is a template for an object that bundles up several related pieces of data and defines a bunch of functions for accessing and manipulating that data. A class definition is similar to a function definition in that nothing happens until you tell Python to make an object based on the class template; this is called creating an **instance** of that class. Even then, any methods that are part of the class won't do anything until they are specifically called, just like functions.

Defining Classes

The simplest way to understand how classes work is to create one. Based on the first definition, here is a simple version of a class in Python:

```
class Person:
    def setName(self, name):
        self.name  = name.title()

    def getName(self):
        return self.name
# end of class definition

#start of program
person1 = Person() #create instance of class
person1.setName('Mr. Smith')  #set name
print(person1.getName()) # get name
```

Now, that program doesn't do too much, but it does explain, via program code, what we outlined at the start of the chapter. To move along, try the next example of a Player class, which does a bit more. (If you are curious about "self," hang on as that will be explained shortly.)

```
class Player:

    def setName(self, name):
        self.name = name.title()

    def getName(self):
        return self.name

    def setDesc(self, desc):
        self.desc = desc.capitalize()

    def getDesc(self):
        return self.desc
```

This code just creates the possibility of a type of object called Player. You need to create a Player object and assign some values to it in order to use it.

```
player1 = Player()
player1.setName('inkon')
player1.setDesc('short, stocky and mean')
character_sheet = """
Name: {0!s}
Desc: {1!s}
""".format(player1.getName(), player1.getDesc())
print(character_sheet)
```

■ **Tip** I recommend using short, singular, capitalized nouns to name your classes.

This code produces the following results:

```
Name: Inkon
Desc: Short, stocky and mean
```

First, player1 is created as an instance of Player. Notice the empty parentheses following the word Player. This causes the class definition to produce an object that you can use. I have given player1 a name using the setName() method I defined earlier, and created a description string using the setDesc() method. The values can be retrieved using the **accessor** methods getName() and getDesc(). Accessor methods are a means of accessing attributes and are named after the attribute, by convention, with get, set, or del prepended to the method name. So far, my Player type seems to work a bit like a dictionary, except that the values become automatically capitalized when they are created. Later on in this chapter, I'll show you how you can make your new type behave exactly like a dictionary if you so wish.

Who Is self?

The main difference between methods and functions is this additional parameter called **self**; self refers back to the object upon which the operation is taking place, so in this instance self refers to player1. The name of the object is passed to any methods called on it, along with any additional arguments. It is also used in the class definition where values are assigned to attributes. Attributes are like variables contained within the object, such as self.name. These attributes can be accessed from outside the object as (in this instance) player1.name. In most cases, however, you don't want to access them like this because you will usually want to process or format the data using a class method like setName() or getDesc(). It is good practice to always use methods to access attributes (see the Properties section later in this chapter). The idea is that an object should be like a black box—you don't need to know what the box contains, as long as you know (or can find out) what methods it supports. This black box approach is known as **encapsulation**.

■ **Tip** You can get an idea of what methods and attributes an instance of an object supports using the built-in function `dir()`. In this instance `dir(player1)` will return a list of names available within the **namespace** of that object.

Identity

An object's identity never changes once it has been created; you can find out an object's identity using the built-in id() function and compare the identity of two objects using the is operator.

```
>>> player1 = Player()
>>> player2 = Player()
>>> player1 is player2
False
>>> id(player1)
136928972
>>> id(player2)
136930284
```

The id() function returns an integer representing its identity, which you can think of as its location in memory. Every object has a different id().

Determining an Object's Type

An object's type determines the operations and methods the object supports and can be discovered using the built-in type() function.

```
>>> type(player1)
<class 'Player'>
```

The type() and id() functions should really be used only for investigation and debugging. Inside a program, the recommended approach is to try the method you want and see if it works. This is known as *duck typing*. The premise is that if it looks like a duck and quacks like a duck, you can assume it is a duck for programming purposes. This approach makes working with objects mercifully simple; you really need to consider only the methods you want the object to support. When using your own custom classes, you can create the necessary methods as you need them.

It is also possible to create special **magic methods**, which allow you to use standard operators like +, /, < and == with your custom classes, and you can replicate the behavior of other existing types, such as lists and dictionaries, allowing slice notation, indexing and iteration. So, it is possible to get your custom objects to behave in similar ways to the built-in objects you have already encountered. This overloading of operators to work with many different forms of objects is known as **polymorphism**.

▓ **Note** Obviously, if the method you want to use is not present, you will get an error. In Chapter 10 I will show you how to catch and handle exceptions while the program is running.

Namespaces and Why We Need Them

Each object has its own **namespace**, which is implemented by a dictionary object. This is important to prevent name collisions. You may already have variables called name and desc in the body of the program, for example, but they won't conflict with player1.name or player1.desc. Methods and attributes can be accessed by following the name of the object with a dot followed by the name of the item you wish to access.

Each name refers to an object. Names are added to the namespace by an operation called **name binding**. This is what happens when you first assign a value to a variable using the = operator, or when you import a module. The value is said to be **bound** to a particular name and each name can only refer to one object, although it is perfectly legal to bind several different names to an object.

Scope defines the visibility of a name within a code block. Each block has its own namespace. Namespaces are organized like a family tree or directory structure; a name will be valid in any code blocks contained within the defining one, but not in any outer ones. Like rooms within a room, when you enter into a space, you can see everything inside it but you are no longer aware of anything outside.

The outermost scope is therefore global; names defined in the outermost scope will be recognized anywhere in the program's world, as long as those names don't become *masked* by being assigned to different values within any of the subroutines. The exception to this rule is that names defined inside a class definition don't extend to any of the methods contained in the class; you have to refer to them via self inside the class definition. The set of all scopes visible to a code block is called the block's **environment**.

Class attribute references are first looked up within the immediate scope of the class. When the attribute name is not found there, the attribute search continues in the base classes. If a name is not found at all, a NameError exception is raised. If the name refers to a local variable that has not been bound, an UnboundLocalError exception is raised.

When Should Classes Be Used?

You may frequently find yourself writing several functions to manipulate similar sets of global variables. If the function is not used for any other data structures and the variables could be grouped together as aspects of a single object, then creating a class is probably the way to go. In the original version of rpcombat.py (first shown in Chapter 5), most of the action involved manipulating a dictionary containing a set of variables specific to each character. It might simplify things to create a new type of object called Player, which manages its own **state**: that is, it manipulates its own attributes and provides means for other objects to interact with its attributes as well.

The combination of attributes and methods that are available for use are known as the object's **interface**. Many of the functions in rpcombat.py could be further abstracted so they are encapsulated within the Player class. This means the rest of the program only needs to worry about the methods available in the object's interface while the inner workings of the Player object remain invisible.

Another way of working out what classes you need is to read through the original statement of requirements for your application. The nouns may suggest potential classes; the verbs may suggest methods; and the adjectives in the specification may suggest attributes. The original specification for rpcombat.py was *"The user must be able to generate more than one character profile, equip those characters with suitable weapons, and model hand-to-hand combat between characters."* Table 9-1 breaks down the rpcombat.py specification, though note there are no pertinent adjectives in this case.

Table 9-1. *Breakdown of rpcombat.py Specification*

Nouns	Verbs	Adjectives
User	generate	
Character	profile	
	equip	
	combat	
Weapon		

This analysis makes it very clear what needs to be done. I'm going to merge User and Character into Player, so each Player needs a generate() method and an equip() method, plus it needs to be able to fight (see Listing 9-1). In the specification, combat occurs between players, so each player will need something like attack() and defend() methods. Our original profile from Chapter 5 was a dictionary containing: {'Name':"", 'Desc':"", 'Gender':"", 'Race':"", 'Muscle':0, 'Brainz':0, 'Speed':0, 'Charm':0, 'life':0, 'magic':0, 'prot':0, 'gold':0, 'inventory':[]} so these will become the Player attributes. User stories or use cases can also be helpful for refining your design. Go through each case step by step and make sure all the requirements are covered in your new class specification.

Listing 9-1. *Creating the Player Class*

```
class Player:

    def setName(self, name):
        self.name = name.title()

    def getName(self):
        return self.name

    def setDesc(self, desc):
        self.desc = desc.capitalize()

    def getDesc(self):
        return self.desc

    def setGender(self, gender):
        gender = gender.lower()
        if gender.startswith('f'):
            self.gender = 'female'
        elif gender.startswith('m'):
```

```
            self.gender = 'male'
        else:
            self.gender = 'neuter'

def getGender(self):
    return self.gender

def setRace(self, race):
    race = race.capitalize()
    if race.startswith('P'):
        self.race = 'Pixie'
    elif race.startswith('V'):
        self.race = 'Vulcan'
    elif race.startswith('G'):
        self.race = 'Gelfling'
    elif race.startswith('T'):
        self.race = 'Troll'
    else:
        self.race = 'Goblin'

def getRace(self):
    return self.race

def setMuscle(self):
    self.muscle = roll(33,3)

def getMuscle(self):
    return self.muscle

def setBrainz(self):
    self.brainz = roll(33,3)

def getBrainz(self):
    return self.brainz

def setSpeed(self):
    self.speed = roll(33,3)

def getSpeed(self):
    return self.speed

def setCharm(self):
    self.charm = roll(33,3)

def getCharm(self):
    return self.charm

def setLife(self):
    self.life = int((self.getMuscle() + (self.getSpeed()/2) + roll(49,1))/2)
    if 0 < self.life < 100:
        pass
    else:
        self.life = int(roll(33,3))
```

```
def getLife(self):
    return self.life

def setMagic(self):
    self.magic = int((self.getBrainz() + (self.getCharm()/2) + roll(49,1))/2)
    if 0 < self.magic < 100:
        pass
    else:
        self.magic = int(roll(33,3))

def getMagic(self):
    return self.magic

def setProt(self):
    self.prot = int((self.getSpeed() + (self.getBrainz()/2) + roll(49,1))/2)
    if 0 < self.prot < 100:
        pass
    else:
        self.prot = int(roll(33,3))

def getProt(self):
    return self.prot

def setGold(self):
    self.gold = int(roll(40,4))

def getGold(self):
    return self.gold

def setInv(self):
    self.inv = []

def getInv(self):
    return ", ".join(self.inv)

def generate(self):
    """Role-Playing Character generator

    Takes no arguments
    Returns a new Player object
    """
    print()
    print("New [Test] Character")
    print()

    # Prompt user for user-defined information (Name, Desc, Gender, Race)
    name = input('What is your name? ')
    desc = input('Describe yourself: ')
    gender = input('What Gender are you? (male/female/unsure): ')
    race = input('What Race are you? - (Pixie/Vulcan/Gelfling/Troll): ')
```

```
        self.setName(name)
        self.setDesc(desc)
        self.setGender(gender)
        self.setRace(race)
        self.setMuscle()
        self.setBrainz()
        self.setSpeed()
        self.setCharm()
        self.setLife()
        self.setMagic()
        self.setProt()
        self.setGold()
```

This may look complex, but consider that I have moved the functionality of the old generate_rpc() function entirely into the Player type. Now new players can be generated in just two lines in the main body.

```
player1 = Player()
player1.generate()
```

Parents and Children—Inheritance

In a simple sense, children inherit features from their parents. So, in a similar sense, you might have a class object that inherits attributes from the parent class it is based on. Using the preceding examples, let's take a look at how this unfolds.

I need to create a Weapon class and, come to think of it, I'll probably need an Armour class as well. And there are some other things that the Player can interact with that don't fall into the category of either Weapon or Armour. I could create three separate classes of Weapon, Armour, and general Things, but now that I think about it, Weapons and Armour are specific instances of Things, so I will create a base class called Thing. Each Thing needs three basic attributes: price, strength, and speed. These attributes need to be assigned (possibly from a table of predefined values) when the object is created. For now I will give them default values.

```
>>> class Thing:
...     price = 0
...     strength = 0
...     speed = 0
...
>>> box = Thing()
>>> box.price
0
>>> box.lid
Traceback (most recent call last):
  File "<stdin>", line 1, in <module>
AttributeError: 'Thing' object has no attribute 'lid'
```

I have created a box, which is an instance of Thing. It has a price, strength, and speed, but no lid. Now I can create a subclass of Weapon like so:

```
>>> class Weapon(Thing):
...        print("Weapon made.")
...
Weapon made.
>>> axe = Weapon()
>>> axe.price
0
```

I could assign values to the Weapon laboriously one by one.

```
>>> axe.price = 75
>>> axe.strength = 60
>>> axe.speed = 50
```

But in practice I'd like to be able to assign them all in one go.

Using Methods

The way to do this is to create a method that will take the three values as arguments and assign them to the correct attributes for you. Here is a good example of encapsulation. In the original version, these values were expressed rather cryptically as a tuple, with no explanation of what the values meant. A suitable method could deal with this tuple automatically.

```
>>> class Thing:
...        def setValues(self, price, strength, speed):
...            self.price = price
...            self.strength = strength
...            self.speed = speed
...        def printValues(self):
...                print("""Price: {0!s}
... Strength: {1!s}
... Speed: {2!s}
... """.format(self.price, self.strength, self.speed))
...
>>> class Weapon(Thing):
...        print("new weapon made")
...
new weapon made
>>> axe = Weapon()
>>> axe.setValues(75, 60, 50)
>>> axe.printValues()
Price: 75
Strength: 60
Speed: 50
```

The subclass Weapon inherits its methods and attributes from the superclass Thing. If you want your Weapon class to behave differently from an ordinary Thing, it is possible to override the methods of Thing by defining the methods within the Weapon class definition.

```
>>> class Weapon(Thing):
...     def setValues(self, price, strength, speed):
...         self.price = price
...         self.strength = strength
...         self.damage = strength
...         self.speed = speed
...     def printValues(self):
...         print("""Price: {0!s}
... Damage: {1!s}
... Speed: {2!s}
... """.format(self.price, self.damage, self.speed))
...
>>> axe = Weapon()
>>> axe.setValues(75, 60, 50)
>>> axe.printValues()
Price: 75
Damage: 60
Speed: 50

>>> box = Thing()
>>> box.setValues(0, 0, 0)
>>> box.printValues()
Price: 0
Strength: 0
Speed: 0
```

This is a very rough example. The principle is that all Things have setValues() and printValues() methods. It doesn't matter what subclass of Thing it is, but if we want to know if a Thing is some kind of weapon, we have a simple test—does it have a damage attribute?

```
>>> box.damage
Traceback (most recent call last):
  File "<stdin>", line 1, in <module>
AttributeError: 'Thing' object has no attribute 'damage'
>>> axe.damage
60
```

Clearly the axe can be used as a weapon and the box cannot. This is similar to the way strings, lists, and dictionaries share some common methods, but not others. If you want to know if you're dealing with a list or not, for example, try to append() something to it. I could subclass Player in a similar way to allow for different professions, such as Warrior, Magician, Priest, or Hoodie; they might share some methods but vary in their methods of combat and the weapons they can use.

Customizing Classes

Classes also support some special methods known as *magic* methods, which are similar to the magic variables you encountered throughout the book. These are predefined names that allow you to override your custom type's behavior in respect to the various standard code constructs in Python. The names used for these special methods are part of the programming language, so you can't use arbitrary names.

Magic methods are easy to recognize, having double underscores before and after the name. Each magic method has a specific purpose and needs to be defined in an object's class definition in order for it to work. For example, you could manipulate your type with mathematical and comparison operators or make it imitate the behavior of an integer or list. This is Python's approach to a technique called operator **overloading**, which plays a major role in polymorphism.

If you want to emulate the methods of a built-in type, it is important that the methods make sense for the object being modeled. For example, some sequences might work well with retrieval of individual elements, but extracting a slice might be meaningless.

Constructors

The first special method to be used in most class definitions will be the object.__init__(self[, ...]) method. This method is called immediately after the object has been created. The one special constraint on **constructors** is that no value may be returned; doing so will result in a TypeError. The entire function of a constructor is to set up the new object, so a return value would be meaningless anyway. My base class Thing has a method called setValues(), which sets up a bunch of internal attributes and returns no value. This process is known as **initialization**, and it can be easily converted into a constructor method.

```
class Thing:
    def __init__(self, price, strength, speed):
        self.price = price
        self.strength = strength
        self.speed = speed
```

Now, new objects of type Thing can be created with a single instruction that passes it the three required arguments.

```
box = Thing(0, 0, 0)
```

How cool is that?

Now, I want my Weapon subclass to be set up slightly differently so I need to create an __init__() method for that as well. In the previous example, Weapon had its own setValues() method that overrides the method set on its parent object, but this involves rather a lot of repetitive code. It would be much better if I could call the __init__() method of the superclass Thing and then add the one line that needs to be different.

```
class Weapon(Thing):
    def __init__(self, price, strength, speed):
        Thing.__init__(self, price, strength, speed)
        self.damage = strength
```

Notice that I need to pass the same arguments to Thing.__init__(). Calling a special method like this, directly referencing its name with double underscores, is called referencing an *unbound* method. There is an alternative method super(), which is preferred. The super() function is smarter than calling an unbound method and usually does the right thing when dealing with unusual situations such as inheritance from multiple superclasses. Note that self is not included in the arguments to __init__().

```
class Weapon(Thing):
    def __init__(self, price, strength, speed):
        super().__init__(price, strength, speed)
        self.damage = strength
```

Now I can make Weapons with a single instruction too.

```
axe = Weapon(75, 60, 50)
```

Customizing Output

In a similar way, it is possible to automate a class's output format. The str(object) and print(object) functions both look for a special method called object.__str__(self) to compute the *informal* string representation of an object. This method must return a string object. Thing.printValues(self) could easily be converted for this purpose.

```
def __str__(self):
    stats = """\tPrice\tDamage\tSpeed
{price!s}\t{damage!s}\t{speed!s}\t""".format(**vars(self))
    return stats
```

I am using the vars() function to send the Thing object's internal dictionary of values to the string.format() method.

The *official* string representation of an object is created by object.__repr__(self), which is called by the built-in repr() function. This should look like a valid Python expression that could be used to re-create an object with the same value; if this is not possible a string containing some useful value should be returned. The return value in either case must be a string object. If no __str__() method is provided by the class, __repr__() may also be used for the *informal* representation.

```
def __repr__(self):
    stats = 'Weapon({price!s}, {strength!s}\
, {speed!s})'.format(**vars(self))
    return stats
```

Once I have the Thing class set up nicely, the code in the body of the program becomes very simple. I can create instances of the objects I need at the same time as I create an inventory dictionary.

```
inventory = {"box":Thing(0, 1, 0),
             "axe":Weapon(75, 60, 50),
             "shield":Armour(60, 50, 23)}
```

Then I can print out the entire inventory using only a few lines.

```
print("\n::Inventory::\n------------")
for key, item in inventory.items():
    print(key, item, repr(item))
print()
```

Which gives this nicely formatted result:

193

```
::Inventory::
-------------
box       Price     Str     Speed
       0    1      0     Thing(0, 1, 0)
shield       Price      Str     Speed
      60       50      23      Armour(60, 50, 23)
axe       Price     Damage     Speed
      75       60      50      Weapon(75, 60, 50)
```

Now we're cooking with gas!

Emulating Existing Types

Python provides a whole host of other magic methods that allow you to emulate existing types. In rpcombat.py, I had originally implemented the Player type as a dictionary; in order to facilitate the changeover, I wanted my new Player class to refer to its attributes via index notation, like dictionaries do, so I wouldn't need to rewrite the whole program in order to get it to work with this new class.

In order to emulate a container type such as a list or dictionary, you need to include certain recognizable methods, depending on how closely you want to emulate the type.

Tip If you want to create a type that differs only slightly from one of the standard types, it is better to subclass that type and override the methods that you need to work differently.

In order to implement basic container-like behavior, you need to include two specific methods.

- object.__len__(self): This method should return the length of the object, that is the number of items contained within the object expressed as an integer >= 0. This integer is returned by the built-in len() function. If you don't define a __bool__() method or __nonzero__() method, the object will return False in a Boolean context.
- object.__getitem__(self, key): This method should return the value corresponding to the given key as in self[key]. For sequence types, the accepted keys should be integers and slice objects. For a mapping you can use any type of key.

Note The special interpretation of negative indexes is up to the __getitem__() method.

I implemented both of these methods for my Thing type, as I want to be able to access items as if using a dictionary. However, I need my Things to be immutable; once set, the values can't be changed. My Weapon and Armour types will also inherit this behavior but it only needs to be specified once in the parent (Thing) class.

```
def __len__(self):
    return len(vars(self))

def __getitem__(self, key):
    names = vars(self)
    try:
        item = names[key]
    except:
        item = 0
    return item
```

If I wanted to make a mutable type, I would need to implement another two methods:

- object.__setitem__(self, key, value): This method allows assignment to self[key], so that the value can be retrieved by object.__getitem__().

- object.__delitem__(self, key): This method allows deletion of self[key]. This is brought into play when the del statement is used on part of an object and should delete the element associated with that key.

Obviously, you only need to include these methods if it is appropriate to allow values to be modified using index notation. It may be more appropriate to use accessor methods—get*() and set*()—or use the properties() function (I'll come to that later).

My Player type needs to allow the setting of values using indexes, so I implemented __setitem__() like this.

```
def __setitem__(self, key, value):
    self.__dict__[key] = value
    return
```

There are a few additional methods that are recommended for types that are supposed to emulate containers. Both mappings and sequences should implement the object.__iter__(self) method to allow efficient iteration through the container. This method is called when an iterator is required for a container. It should return a new iterator object that can iterate over all the objects in the container. For mappings, it should iterate over the keys of the container, and should also be made available as the method keys(); for sequences, it should iterate through the values.

You should also include the object.__reversed__(self) method to complement it. This is called by the built-in function reversed() to implement reverse iteration. It should return a new iterator object that iterates over all the objects in the container in reverse order.

The membership test operators (in and not in) are normally implemented as an iteration through a sequence. However, container objects can supply the following special method with a more efficient implementation, which also does not require the object be a sequence.

The object.__contains__(self, item) method is called to implement membership test operators. It should return True if the item is in self, False otherwise. For mapping objects, it should consider the keys of the mapping rather than the values or the key-item pairs; for sequences, it should search through the values.

If you want to create a fully dictionary-like object, you also need to include the standard mapping methods: keys(), values(), items(), get(), clear(), setdefault(), pop(), popitem(), copy(), and update(). These methods should behave in a similar manner to the methods included in Python's standard dictionary objects. Mutable sequences should provide methods append(), count(), index(), extend(), insert(), pop(), remove(), reverse() and sort(), like Python's standard list objects.

Finally, sequence types should implement concatenation (using the addition operator +) and repetition (using the multiplication operator *) by defining the methods __add__(), __radd__(), __iadd__(), __mul__(), __rmul__() and __imul__(); they should not define other numerical operators. I will explain these special numerical methods later in the chapter.

Properties

There are several different ways of accessing an object's attributes; you have already seen accessor methods get*() and set*() being used. It is often the case that you will want to make sure additional actions are taken, such as validation, when getting and setting values rather than assigning and retrieving arbitrary raw data. However, the code that uses this object shouldn't need to know about the details. This is where the property([fget][, fset][, fdel][, doc]) function comes in.

▪ **Note** Actually it's not a function but a class, but let's not split hairs at this stage.

```
class Player:

    def setName(self, name):
        self.__name = name.capitalize() #double underscores in front

    def getName(self):
        return self.__name # double underscores in front

    name = property(getName, setName)
```
This allows you to use the name property as follows:
```
>>> player1 = Player()
>>> player1.name = 'inkon'
>>> player1.name
Inkon
```

The property() function automatically wraps the attribute access, so you can be sure the additional actions (in this case capitalization) take place every time. The property function takes four optional arguments. You can include none of these, which will make the attribute inaccessible. If you want the attribute to be read-only, use just one argument—the get method. If you want read/write access, you must define two arguments—get and set. The third argument is used to delete the attribute and the fourth argument (also optional) is used to provide a docstring for the property. You can provide these as keyword arguments if, say, you want to include a docstring in a read-only property.

Customizing Attribute Access

There may be times when it is not appropriate to use properties (if you are using old-style classes, for instance). In such cases, the following methods can be defined to customize the meaning of attribute access:

- object.__getattr__(self, name): This method is called when an attribute lookup has not found the attribute in the usual places, where name is the attribute name. This method should return the (computed) attribute value or raise an AttributeError exception.
- object.__getattribute__(self, name): This method is automatically called when the attribute name is accessed. It does not work with older version of Python.
- object.__setattr__(self, name, value): This method is called when an attribute assignment is attempted, where name is the attribute name and value is the value to be assigned to it.
- object.__delattr__(self, name): This method is called when an attempt is made to delete the attribute name.

Emulating Numeric Types

The methods listed in Table 9-2 can be defined to emulate numeric objects. I'll just give you a brief overview here because it's a lot of information to take in all in one go. There are many more methods available, but this is enough to get you started. Methods corresponding to operations that are not supported by the particular kind of number implemented should be left undefined.

Table 9-2. *Overloading Rich Comparison Operators*

Magic Method	Operation
object.__lt__(self, other)	self < other
object.__le__(self, other)	self <= other
object.__eq__(self, other)	self == other
object.__ne__(self, other)	self != other
object.__gt__(self, other)	self > other
object.__ge__(self, other)	self >= other

These are called *rich comparison* methods, and are called for comparison operators in preference to __cmp__(). A rich comparison method may return the singleton NotImplemented if the method does not implement the operation for a given pair of arguments. By convention, False and True are returned for a successful comparison. However, these methods can return any value, so if the comparison operator is used in a Boolean context (for example, in the condition of an if statement), Python will call bool() on the value to determine if the result is true or false.

■ **Note** There are no implied relationships among the comparison operators. The truth of x==y does not imply that x!=y is False. Therefore, you need to define all of these methods so that all forms of comparison work correctly.

- object.__cmp__(self, other): This method is called by comparison operations if rich comparison is not defined. It should return a negative integer if self < other, zero if self == other, and a positive integer if self > other.
- object.__bool__(self): This is called to implement truth value testing and the built-in operation bool(); it should return False or True. When this method is not defined, __len__() is called if it is defined, and True is returned when the length is not zero. If a class doesn't define either __len__() or __bool__(), all its instances are considered true.

Table 9-3 shows methods that implement numerical operators.

Table 9-3. *Methods Implementing Numerical Operators*

Magic Method	Operation
object.__add__(self, other)	self + other
object.__sub__(self, other)	self _ other
object.__mul__(self, other)	self * other
object.__div__(self, other)	self / other
object.__floordiv__(self, other)	self // other
object.__mod__(self, other)	self % other
object.__divmod__(self, other) self other	divmod(self, other)
object.__pow__(self, other[, modulo]) self ** other	pow(self, other[, modulo])
object.__lshift__(self, other)	self << other
object.__rshift__(self, other)	self >> other
object.__and__(self, other)	self & other
object.__xor__(self, other)	self ^ other
object.__or__(self, other)	self	other

If one of those methods does not support the operation with the supplied arguments, it should return `NotImplemented`.

Table 9-4 shows methods that overload inclusive numerical operators.

Table 9-4. *Overloading Inclusive Numerical Operators*

Magic Method	Operation
object.__iadd__(self, other)	self += other
object.__isub__(self, other)	self -= other
object.__imul__(self, other)	self *= other
object.__idiv__(self, other)	self /= other
object.__itruediv__(self, other)	self /= other
object.__ifloordiv__(self, other)	self //= other
object.__imod__(self, other)	self %= other
object.__ipow__(self, other[, modulo])	self **= other
object.__ilshift__(self, other)	self <<= other
object.__irshift__(self, other)	self >>= other
object.__iand__(self, other)	self &= other
object.__ixor__(self, other)	self ^= other
object.__ior__(self, other)	self |= other

These methods should attempt to do the operation in place (modifying `self`) and return the result (which could be, but does not have to be, `self`). If a specific method is not defined, the augmented operation falls back to the normal methods. Table 9-5 shows methods that overload some built-in functions.

Table 9-5. *Overloading Some Built-in Functions*

Magic Method	Operation
object.__neg__(self)	-self
object.__pos__(self)	+self
object.__abs__(self)	abs(self)
object.__invert__(self)	~self
object.__complex__(self)	complex(self)
object.__int__(self)	int(self)
object.__float__(self)	float(self)
object.__index__(self)	operator.index() Must return an integer.

Application

As I started looking through the code of my little role-playing program to see what else needed abstracting, I noticed some interesting anomalies. I had to set up the stock dictionary after the class definitions, because it contained objects of some of those classes. It struck me that a shop could be a kind of object, one that the players could inhabit rather than something they'd pick up and use. Taking this thought process to its logical extreme, I figured that all my custom objects could benefit from sharing a few attributes, so I set about designing "one class to rule them all." I called this class GameObject and used it to set up all the properties that a game object might need. Next, I subclassed GameObject into Player, Thing, and Location types. Most of the code that was previously in a function was moved. For example, generate_rpc() was moved into Player.__init__(), allowing me to either generate a Player from scratch or load stored details by providing a dictionary of suitable values as an argument. The old buy_equipment() function was largely moved into the Player object as Player.buy(item), with some of the functionality moved into the Shop object. Similarly, calc_velocity() became Player.strike(target). This final stage of abstraction moves as much of the action into self-contained objects as is practical. Where an outcome is the result of the interaction of two objects, you must decide which object runs the code, which object will be the actor, and which will be the recipient. If you have designed your objects well, the flow of events may be obvious. In this instance, the Player must be able to buy, but the Shop must also be willing to sell.

Suddenly the whole dynamic of the program changes. If you study Listing 9-2, it will be apparent that the code on the page merely sets up lots of objects and prepares them for action. The game itself doesn't start until four lines from the end.

I standardized the Thing object to fit in with the names used on other GameObjects. Now the only difference between Things, Weapons and Armour is that they are technically of a different type—a feature that I made use of to filter inventory lists using the built-in issubclass() function.

Next, I filled in the details of the Location object. A game location only really needs a name, a description, and, importantly, an inventory, which I am using to represent the location's physical

contents. In order to be able to use the in operator with my new object, I defined
Location.__contains__(item) so that it looks in Location.inventory to find matches; the inventory will
be treated as the object's contents for all intents and purposes. It has one additional attribute—
Location.commands, which is a dictionary of command words mapped to executable strings. I have also
included a mechanism for retrieving Locations from stored values, in case I need it in the future.

   I decided that most of the in-game commands should be a function of the Location. In order to
facilitate this, I defined a few methods for the Location type. First, the Player must be able to get into the
object, so Location.enter(player) adds the Player to Location.inventory and starts up a mini
command-line. The command-line is dealt with by Location.interpret(command, player), which finds
the relevant command in Location.commands, formats it with any additional arguments, and the sends
the whole thing to exec(). (The try: ... except: statement wrapping will be covered in Chapter 10.)

   It follows that all the combat commands should go in the Location too, so I moved most of the
combat section in the main body into Location.combat(), which controls the main loop, and into
Location.resolve_conflict(attacker, target), which deals with the individual strokes. The
calc_damage() function became Location.damage(attacker, target, velocity). Using properties
considerably simplifies item access, what was players[target]['Name'] in the previous version becomes
target.life in this one. Finally Location.exit(player) removes the Player from Location.inventory.

   I created a subclass called Shop to implement some different game commands and provide a
contents list with prices. In most of its details, a shop is just like any other Location, with the sole
difference that trading may take place (and combat cannot).

   The program now has only seven global functions, some of which could be further abstracted. I
added the trace(text) function as a wrapper to the print() function to provide verbose debugging
output when trace_on is set to True.

   The main body of the program is now wrapped up in a if __name__ == '__main__': condition to
prevent the main body being executed when rpcombat is imported as a module. The main body only
deals with an overview of events. First, the user is prompted for a number of players and then the
locations are set up by creating two Location objects, arena and shop, which are then stocked with
values. Next the role-playing characters are generated and last of all the game begins with
arena.enter(players[0]). At this point all the code loaded into memory comes into play, and because
you are no longer limited by the order statements come in the script, the action of the game can proceed
in any order (well, in theory at least). The limitation now is simply the commands that are recognized by
the game Location's mini command-line.

Listing 9-2. *rpcombat-0.6.py*

```
#! /usr/bin/env python
# -*- coding: UTF8 -*-

"""RPCombat: Simple Role-Playing Combat Game.

Usage: rpcombat.py
First you are prompted to enter the number of players you want and then you
are taken through character generation where you get the chance to equip your
character with a suitable weapon at our fabulous Emporium.
Available commands: *look*, *buy <item>*
The characters then engage in hand-to-hand combat in the arena until one is
victorious!
Available commands: *look*, *attack*, *say*
Target System: GNU/Linux
Interface: Command-line
```

```python
Functional Requirements: The user must be able to generate more than one
 character profile, equip those characters with suitable weapons,
 and model hand-to-hand combat between characters.
Testing methods: trace table and play testing.
Expected results: All statistics should be integers in the (1-99) range.
        Apart from that, this script needs play-testing.
Limitations: Too many to mention.
"""

__version__ = 0.6
__maintainer__ = "maintainer@website.com"
__status__ = "Prototype"
__date__ = "16-12-2008"

# Import modules

import random
import time

# Preferences
###
Boilerplate = """
<==|#|==\@@@@/==|#|==>
   Cloud Cuckoo Land
   A simple role-playing game
   version: {0!s}
<==|#|==\@@@@/==|#|==>
""".format(__version__)

# Set to 'True' to trace variables.
trace_on = False

# Set amount of delay between combat strikes
# Higher numbers make combat slower
drag = 23

# Create players list
players = []

# Constants
armour_types = set(['shield','cuirass','armour'])
hits = ('hits','bashes','smites','whacks',
        'shreds','stabs','mutilates','lunges at','slashes', 'lacerates',
        'carves up','wipes the floor using')
misses = ('misses', 'nearly hits', 'tickles', 'fumbles', 'fails to connect with',
        'swipes wildly at', 'flails ineffectually at', 'gets nowhere near',
        'hurts themself badly as a result of gross stupidity',
        'nearly decapitates themself instead of',
        'hits themself on the foot, to the amusement of')
damage_report = ('a small insult', 'a flesh wound', 'a deep gouge',
        'ragged tearing of skin', 'blood to spurt everywhere',
```

```
                     'massive head injuries','savage laceration',
                     'a fractured rib-cage','facial mutilation','the skull to split in two')
life_changing = ('a scar.','internal bruising.','serious blood-loss.',
                     'other debilitating injuries.', 'chronic concussion.',
                     'leaving a severed limb dangling at a horrible angle.',
                     'multiple fractures.','a broken neck.',
                     'the rupturing of internal organs.','a decisive mortal blow.')

class GameObject:
    """Generic Game Object

    One class to rule them all.
    The class sets up the properties which are available to all GameObject
    sub-classes. It has no methods of its own. The idea is that the other
    game objects, Players, Things and Locations are all sub-classes of
    GameObject; features shared by all GameObjects should go here.
    Text properties: name, desc, gender and race.
    Base stats: strength, brainz, speed and charm.
    Derived stats: life, magic, prot and gold.
    Plus an inventory list.
    """

    def setName(self, name):
        self._name = name.title()

    def getName(self):
        return self._name

    name = property(getName, setName)

    def setDesc(self, desc):
        self._desc = desc.capitalize()

    def getDesc(self):
        return self._desc

    desc = property(getDesc, setDesc)

    def setGender(self, gender):
        gender = gender.lower()
        if gender.startswith('f'):
            self._gender = 'female'
        elif gender.startswith('m'):
            self._gender = 'male'
        else:
            self._gender = 'neuter'

    def getGender(self):
        return self._gender

    gender = property(getGender, setGender)
```

```python
def setRace(self, race):
    race = race.capitalize()
    if race.startswith('P'):
        self._race = 'Pixie'
    elif race.startswith('V'):
        self._race = 'Vulcan'
    elif race.startswith('G'):
        self._race = 'Gelfling'
    elif race.startswith('T'):
    self._race = 'Troll'
    else:
        self._race = 'Goblin'

def getRace(self):
    return self._race

race = property(getRace, setRace)

def setStrength(self):
    self._strength = roll(33,3)

def getStrength(self):
    return self._strength

strength = property(getStrength)

def setBrainz(self):
    self._brainz = roll(33,3)

def getBrainz(self):
    return self._brainz

brainz = property(getBrainz)

def setSpeed(self):
    self._speed = roll(33,3)

def getSpeed(self):
    return self._speed

speed = property(getSpeed)

def setCharm(self):
    self._charm = roll(33,3)

def getCharm(self):
    return self._charm

charm = property(getCharm)

def setLife(self, value):
```

```
        self._life = int(value)

    def getLife(self):
        return self._life

    life = property(getLife, setLife)

    def setMagic(self, value):
        self._magic = int(value)

    def getMagic(self):
        return self._magic

    magic = property(getMagic, setMagic)

    def setProt(self, value):
        self._prot = int(value)

    def getProt(self):
        return self._prot

    prot = property(getProt, setProt)

    def setGold(self, value):
        self._gold = int(value)

    def getGold(self):
        return self._gold

    gold = property(getGold, setGold)

    def setInv(self, contents):
        self.inv = contents

    def getInv(self):
        return self.inv

    def strInv(self):
        flatlist = [str(item) for item in self.inv]
        text = join_with_and(flatlist)
        return text

    inventory = property(getInv, setInv)

class Player(GameObject):
    """Role-Playing Character
```

```
    Takes an optional dictionary as an argument.
    The dictionary must contain the output of repr(Player)
    Player([dict]), if dict is not provided, the Player will self-generate,
    prompting for name, desc, gender and race.
    Player has two methods:
    Player.buy(purchase)
    Player.strike(target)
    """

    def __init__(self, store = {}):
        if store == {}:
            print("\nNew Character\n")

            # Prompt user for user-defined information (Name, Desc,
            # Gender, Race)
            name = input('What is your name? ')
            desc = input('Describe yourself: ')
            gender = input('What Gender are you? (male/female/unsure): ')
            race = input('Race? (Pixie/Vulcan/Gelfling/Troll): ')

            # Set game statistics
            self.setName(name)
            self.setDesc(desc)
            self.setGender(gender)
            self.setRace(race)
            self.setStrength()
            self.setBrainz()
            self.setSpeed()
            self.setCharm()

            # Calculate derived statistics
            self._life = int((self.strength + (self.speed / 2) + \
roll(49,1))/2)
            if 0 < self._life < 100:
                pass
            else:
                self._life = int(roll(33,3))
            self._magic = int((self.brainz + (self.charm / 2) + roll(49,1))/2)
            if 0 < self._magic < 100:
                pass
            else:
                self._magic = int(roll(33,3))
            self._prot = int((self.speed + (self.brainz / 2) + roll(49,1))/2)
            if 0 < self._prot < 100:
            pass
            else:
                self._prot = int(roll(33,3))
            self._gold = int(roll(40,4))
            self.setInv([])
```

```
            # Equip player if the inventory is empty
            shopping = self.inventory == []                if shopping:
                # Display shop stock list with prices in gold.
                print("You have", self.gold, "gold.")
                shop.enter(self)
            handbag = join_with_and(self.inventory)
            print("You own a", handbag)

            # Choose a weapon
            print(self.name + ", prepare for mortal combat!!!")
            # See if player has any weapons
            available_weapons = [item for item in self.inventory
                            if \
                            issubclass(type(item), Weapon)]
            available_weapons.append(Weapon('Fist', 0, 20, 50))
            self.weapon = available_weapons[0]

            # See if player has any armor
            available_armour = [item for item in self.inventory
                        if \
                            issubclass(type(item), Armour)]
            available_armour.append(Armour('None', 0, 0, 50))
            self.armour = available_armour[0]

        else:
            # Load character from stored value.
            self.__dict__ = store

        print(self.name, "is now ready for battle. ")

    def __repr__(self):
        # Output class constructor string.
        stats = 'Player({0!s})'.format(vars(self))
        return stats

    def __str__(self):
        # Output the character sheet.
        rpcharacter_sheet = """
<~~==|#|==~~++**\@/**++~~==|#|==~~>
    {_name!s}
    {_race!s}, {_gender!s}
    {_desc!s}
<~~==|#|==~~++**\@/**++~~==|#|==~~>
    Strength: {_strength: <2}    life:        {_life: <3}
    Brainz:   {_brainz: <2}    magic:       {_magic: <3}
    Speed:    {_speed: <2}    protection: {_prot: <3}
    Charm:    {_charm: <2}    gold: {_gold: >7}
<~~==|#|==~~++**\@/**++~~==|#|==~~>
    ::Equipment::
    {0!s}
    """.format(self.strInv(), **vars(self))
        return rpcharacter_sheet
```

```python
    def __len__(self):
        # Return the number of attributes
        return len(vars(self))

    def __getitem__(self, key):
        # Retrieve values by index
        names = vars(self)
        item = names[key]
        return item

    def __setitem__(self, key, value):
        # Set values by index
        self.__dict__[key] = value
        return

    def buy(self, purchase):
        """ Buy item

        If the item is in the shop and the player has enough gold, buy it.
        Takes one argument, purchase, which is the name of the item you want
        to buy.
        """
        items = [item for item in shop.inventory
                    if issubclass(type(item), Thing) and \
                        item.name == purchase.capitalize()]
        if items == []:
            print("We don't have a", purchase, "for sale.")
        elif 0 < items[0].gold <= self.gold:
            item = items[0]
            msg = fix_gender(self.gender, self.name + " buys themself \
                    some equipment")
            print(msg)
            print("You buy a", purchase, "for",item.gold, "gold pieces.")
            self.gold -= item.gold
            self.inventory.append(item)
            print("You have a", self.strInv(), "in your bag.")
            print("You have", self.gold, "gold left.")
        else:
            print("You don't have enough gold to buy that.")
        return purchase

    def strike(self, target):
        """Calculate velocity of hit (or miss)

        Takes one argument:
        target is another Player object
        This method looks up values from the players
        and returns a weighted semi-random integer
        representing the velocity of the strike.
        """

        weapon = self.weapon
```

208

```
            armour = target.armour
            attack_chance = roll(99)
            attack_velocity = self.speed + weapon.speed + attack_chance
            target_velocity = target.prot + armour.speed + roll(target.brainz)
            velocity = (attack_velocity - target_velocity)
            return int(velocity)

class Thing(GameObject):
    """Tools and Treasure

    Takes four mandatory arguments:
    Thing(name, gold, strength, speed)
    where name is a string and gold, strength speed are integers between 0-99.
    Things are largely immutable and have no public methods.
    Attributes may be retrieved using index notation.
    """

    def setStrength(self, value):
        self._strength  = value

    def getStrength(self):
        return self._strength

    strength = property(getStrength)

    def setSpeed(self, value):
        self._speed = value

    def getSpeed(self):
        return self._speed

    speed = property(getSpeed)

    def __init__(self, name, gold, strength, speed):
        self.setGold(gold)
        self.setStrength(strength)
        self.setSpeed(speed)
        self.setName(name)
        self.setDesc('')

    def __str__(self):
        return str(self.name)

    def __repr__(self):
        stats = 'Thing({_name!r}, {_gold!s}, {_strength!s} \
            , {_speed!s})'.format(**vars(self))
        return stats

    def __len__(self):
        return len(vars(self))
```

```
        def __getitem__(self, key):
            names = vars(self)
            try:
                    item = names[key]
            except:
                    item = 0
            return item

class Weapon(Thing):
    """Weapon - subclass of Thing"""

    def __repr__(self):
        stats = 'Weapon({_name!r}, {_gold!s}, {_strength!s} \
            , {_speed!s})'.format(**vars(self))
        return stats

class Armour(Thing):
    """Armour - subclass of Thing"""

    def __repr__(self):
        stats = 'Armour({_name!r}, {_gold!s}, {_strength!s} \
            , {_speed!s})'.format(**vars(self))
        return stats

class Location(GameObject):
    """Game Location

    Takes two optional arguments, either:
    Location([name]) - which creates a new location called *name*.
    Location([dict]) - which loads a stored location from a dictionary
    Locations provide the environment in which game-play can occur.
    Locations have several public methods:
    Location.enter(player) - adds player to location and provides prommpt.
    Location.interpret(command, player) - executes in-game commands.
    Location.combat() - initializes comabt sequence.
    Location.resolve_conflict(attacker, target) - resolves comabt rounds.
    Location.exit(player) - removes player from location.
    """

    def __init__(self, name = 'Somewhere', store = {}):
        if store == {}:
            self._name = name.capitalize()
            self._desc = "It looks like a building site, nothing to see."
        self.setInv([])
            self.commands = {'look':'print({0!s})',
                             'attack':'self.combat()',
                             'say':'print(me.name, \
                                "says", {0!r})'}
        else:
            self.__dict__ = store
```

210

```
    def __str__(self):
        rpcs = [item.name for item in self.inv if issubclass(type(item), \
            Player)]
        stuff = [str(item) for item in self.inv if issubclass(type(item), Thing)]
        view = """
<==|#|==\{_name!s}/==|#|==>
 {_desc!s}
Contents:
 {0!s}
Players:
 {1!s}
<==|#|==\@@@@/==|#|==>
 """.format(join_with_and(stuff), join_with_and(rpcs), **vars(self))
        return view

    def __repr__(self):
        # Output class constructor string.
        stats = 'Location({0!s})'.format(vars(self))
        return stats

    def __contains__(self, item):
        # *in* checks contents of inventory
        # Can match against strings or Things (ie. GameObjects)
        objects = [str(i) for i in self.inv]
        if item in self.inv:
            return True
        elif item in objects:
        return True
        else:
            return False

    def interpret(self, command, player):
        """Game Command interpreter

        Takes two arguments:
        command - the command string
        player - a player object
        Executes the command string by retrieving string from
        self.commands, formatting it and sending to exec().
        It returns no value.
        Note: There are probably more secure ways of doing this. ;-)
        """
        here = self
        me = player
        command_list = command.split()
        if command != '' and command_list[0] in self.commands:
            command = self.commands[command_list[0]]
            if len(command_list) > 1:
                command = command.format(' '.\
                    join(command_list[1:]),target = player)
            else:
```

```
                command = command.format('self', \
                        target = player)
            trace("Command:", command)
            try:
                exec(command)
            except:
                print("No can do.")
        return

    def enter(self, player):
        """Commands run when the player enters a location

        Takes a player object as an argument.
        Adds Player to the location's inventory
        Provides a command-line prompt until 'exit' is called.
        No return value.
        """
        command = 'enter'
        self.inventory.append(player.name)
        print(self)
        print("You enter the", self.name)
        while command != 'exit':
            command = input(":-> ")
            self.interpret(command, player)
        self.exit(player)
        return

    def damage(self, attacker, target, velocity):
        """Calculate the damage of the hit

        Takes three arguments:
        attacker and target are Player objects
        velocity is an integer representing the velocity of the strike.
        Returns a tuple of two integers - damage and potential damage
        """
        attack_strength = int(attacker.strength)
        weapon_damage = int(attacker['weapon'].strength)
        attack_damage = attack_strength + weapon_damage + int(velocity) - roll(172)
        target_strength = int(target.strength)
        armour_strength = int(target['armour'].strength)
        target_chance = roll(int(target.brainz) * 3)
        target_defence = target_strength + armour_strength + target_chance
        potential_damage = int((attack_damage - target_defence) * 0.3)
        if potential_damage < 1:
            potential_damage = 2
        damage = random.randint(1,potential_damage)
        return int(damage), int(potential_damage)

    def resolve_conflict(self, attacker, target):
        """Conflict Resolution
```

```
    Takes two Player objects as arguments, relating to the *attacker* and *target*.
    Calculates velocity, hit or miss, calculates and inflicts appropriate damage.
    Prints out a commentary on the action to the world.
    Returns True if the blow resulted in fatality, False if the blow misses.
    """
    life_left = target.life
    # Calculate velocity of blow
    velocity = attacker.strike(target)

    if velocity > 0:
        size = len(hits) - 1
        # Print sutable Hit message
        if velocity > self._vel_max:
        self._vel_max = velocity
        hit_type = int(size * velocity / self._vel_max)
        if hit_type > size:
            hit_type = size
        strike_msg = ''.join(['#', str(hit_type)])
        print(attacker.name, hits[hit_type], \
                target.name, end=' ')
    else:
        size = len(misses) - 1
        # Print suitable Miss message
        if velocity < self._vel_min:
            self._vel_min = velocity
        miss_type = int(size * velocity / self._vel_max)
        if miss_type > size:
            miss_type = roll(7)
        if miss_type < 0:
            miss_type = roll(7) - 1
        strike_msg = ''.join(['@', str(miss_type)])
        print(attacker.name, \
                fix_gender(attacker.gender,\
                 misses[miss_type]), \
                target.name)
        # End player turn
        return False

    # Calculate damage inflicted by blow
    damage, potential_damage = self.damage(attacker, target, velocity)

    if damage > self._dam_max:
        self._dam_max = damage
    elif damage < self._dam_min:
        self._dam_min = damage
    # Print damage report
    size = len(damage_report) - 1
    damage_type = int(size * damage / self._dam_max)
    if damage_type > size:
        damage_type = size
    elif damage_type < 0:
```

```
                    damage_type = 0
        size = len(life_changing) - 1
        change_type = int(size * damage / life_left)
        if change_type > size:
            change_type = size
        elif change_type < 0:
            change_type = 0
        outstring = ' '.join(["with their", attacker['weapon'].name.lower(), \
                                "causing", \
                                damage_report[damage_type], \
                                "and", \
                                life_changing[change_type]])
        output = fix_gender(attacker.gender, outstring)
        print(output)
        trace("""vel[{0}] :: hit[{1}] :: dam[{2}/{3}] :: type[#{4}] :: change[#{5}]
        """.format(velocity, strike_msg, damage, potential_damage, damage_type, \
            change_type))

        # Inflict damage on target.
        target.life -= damage
        # Pause slightly to stop this all scrolling past too fast.
        gap = +(drag / velocity)
        time.sleep(gap)
        # Check whether target is still alive or not.
        if target.life <= 0:
            # Print loser
            print('\n', target.name, "collapses in a pool of blood", '\n')
            # End this round of combat immediately.
            return True

    def combat(self):
        """Initialize combat sequence

        Takes no arguments. Creates a list of matches, iterating through them
        until one Player is victorious. Returns False if no victory is achieved.
        """
        print('\n', "Let the combat begin!", '\n')
        self._vel_max = self._dam_max = 23
        self._vel_min = self._dam_min = 1
        # Loop while more than one player is still alive
        players = [item for item in self.inventory
                    if issubclass(type(item), \
                        Player)]
        miss_counter = 0
        while len(players) > 1:
            # Seed random generator
            random.seed()
            random.shuffle(players)
            # create list of matches using ziply function
            matches = ziply(list(range(0,len(players))))
```

```
            trace("Matches:", matches)
            for attack, targ in matches:
                winner = self.resolve_conflict(players[attack],\
                    players[targ])
                if winner == False:
                    miss_counter += 1
                    if miss_counter > 6:
                        print("\n",\
                            players[attack].name, "and", players[targ].name, "declare
a truce.\n")

                        return False
                elif winner:
                    # Remove loser from players list
                    del players[targ]
                    self.inventory = players
                    break
                else:
                    miss_counter = 0
        # Print winner
        trace("Winner:", players[0])
        print(players[0].name, "is victorious!")
        trace("""max damage | velocity
{0} | {1}
 {2} | {3}
""".format(self._dam_max, self._vel_max, self._dam_min, self._vel_min))
        return

    def exit(self, player):
        """Commands run when a player exits a Location

        Takes one argument - a Player object.
        Removes Player from Location's inventory.
        If the player in question is Dead, gives 'Game Over' message.
        Doesn't return anything either.
        """
        if player.name in self.inventory:
            self.inventory.remove(player.name)
            print("You leave the", self.name)
        else:
            print("Game Over")
        return

class Shop(Location):
    """Sub-class of Location, which allows trading.

    Same as Location but Shop.commands allows different game commands.
    The str() output is different to allow a price-list to be displayed.
    """

    def __init__(self, name = 'Somewhere', store = {}):
        super().__init__(name, store)
```

```
        self.commands = {'look':'print({0!s})',
                            'buy':'player.buy("{0}")'}

    def __str__(self):
        stock_list = ["    {0!s:10}{1: >3}".format(item, item.gold)
                        for item in self.inventory
                        if issubclass(type(item),\
                            Thing)]
        view = """
<==|#|==\{_name!s}/==|#|==>
 {_desc!s}
     Stock List:
{0!s}
<==|#|==\@@@@/==|#|==>
 """.format('\n'.join(stock_list), **vars(self))
        return view

def trace(*text):
    """Verbose output for trouble-shooting purposes

    Takes same arguments as print()
    """
    if trace_on:
        print(" <<-::", *text)
    return

def join_with_and(sequence):
    """Join up a list with commas and 'and' between last two items

    Takes a sequence and returns a sentence.
    """
    # Make sure all the list items are in string format.
    sequence = [str(item) for item in sequence]
    if len(sequence) > 1:
        last_item = sequence[-1]
        sentence = ", ".join(sequence[:-1])
        sentence = sentence + " and " + last_item
    elif len(sequence) < 1:
        sentence = "whole lot of nothing"
    else:
        sentence = sequence[0]
    return sentence

def roll(sides, dice = 1):
    """Dice rolling simulator

    sides: Number of sides the die has
    dice: number of dice to be rolled (defaults to 1)
    Returns a random number between dice and dice * sides
    weighted towards the average.
    """
```

```
        result = 0
        for rolls in range(1,dice):
            result += random.randint(1,sides)
        return result

def ziply(seq=None):
    """Create a matrix of matches from a sequence

    Takes one argument seq, which should be a sequence of length > 1
    Returns a tuple of tuples - matches.
    """
    opponents = list(seq[:])
    opponents.reverse()
    matches = [(actor, target) for target in opponents
                    for actor in seq
                    if target != actor]
    random.shuffle(matches)
    return tuple(matches)

def fix_gender(gender, phrase):
    """Replace the word 'them' with gender-specific pronoun

    Takes two arguments:
    gender - a string which can be 'male', 'female' or something else.
    phrase - the string to be modified.
    Returns a string with non-gender specific pronouns replaced by
    gender specific ones.
    """
    if gender == 'female':
        phrase = phrase.replace('them','her')
        phrase = phrase.replace('their','her')
        phrase = phrase.replace('themself','herself')
    elif gender == 'male':
        phrase = phrase.replace('them','him')
        phrase = phrase.replace('their','his')
        phrase = phrase.replace('themself','himself')
    else:
        phrase = phrase.replace('them','it')
        phrase = phrase.replace('their','its')
        phrase = phrase.replace('themself','itself')
    return phrase

def write_out(players):
    """Save Players

    Write Player stats out to file."""
    print("Saving character sheets")
    data_file = open('rpcharacters.rpg', 'w')
    lines = []
    for player in players:
        lines.append(repr(player) + '\n')
```

```
            data_file.writelines(lines)
            data_file.close
            return

    def read_in():
        """Open Players

        Read in Player stats from file."""
        print("Reading in data")
        data_file = open('rpcharacters.rpg')
        for line in data_file:
            player = eval(line)
            players.append(player)
        data_file.close()
        trace("Data:", players)
        return

##
# The main body of the program starts here,
##

if __name__ == '__main__':
    print(Boilerplate)

    # Prompt to set number of players
    reply = input('How many players?: ') or 2
    max_players = int(reply)

    # Set up locations
    arena = Location('Main Arena')
    arena.desc = """Welcome to Cloud Cuckoo Land,
this is where all the action takes place. You can type
*look here* if you want to look around;
*say* stuff if you want or just type
*attack* if you want to fight and
*exit* when you want to quit.
"""
    arena.inventory = []
    shop = Shop('The Emporium')
    shop.desc = """Welcome to your friendly local equipment store!
You can *buy* something if you want or type
*look* to see the Stock List or
*look me* to check your stats and
*exit* when you want to quit.
"""
    shop.inventory = [Armour('shield',15,25,50),
                Weapon('sword',60,60,50),
                Weapon('dagger',25,40,60),
                Weapon('halberd',80,75,40),
                Weapon('club',15,40,40),
                Weapon('flail',50,60,55),
```

```
            Weapon('hammer',99,100,40),
            Armour('cuirass',30,50,20),
            Armour('armour',101,100,0),
            Thing('lantern',10,5,30),
            Thing('pole',10,5,50),
            Thing('rope',10,5,70),
            Thing('box',5,1,90)]

# Set up players
read_in()
if len(players) > max_players:
    players = players[:max_players]
while len(players) < max_players:
    profile = Player()
    # Add new player to list of players
    players.append(profile)
write_out(players)

# Start the game
# by placing the players in the combat arena
arena.inventory = players
arena.enter(players[0])
del reply

# That's all folks!!!
```

You may notice that the mini command-line has a few quirks. The way I have done it allows the execution of arbitrary strings, which is not good. The structure of the code means that you can easily add new Locations, Things, and Players, creating your own adventures. In fact, you could short-circuit the entire setup by putting import rpcombat at the beginning of a new file and designing your adventure from scratch. You'll find out more about modules in Chapter 11. Obviously, there is still room for improvement and plenty of scope for designing your own games. This has been a very condensed taste of what is possible using classes.

Jargon Busting

Here is some further explanation of the terms presented in this chapter:

- *accessor*: A method that allows the getting or setting of an attribute.

- *attribute*: A value associated with an object that is referenced by name using dotted expressions.

- *block*: A block is a section of the text of a Python program that is executed as a unit. Modules, function bodies, and class definitions are all considered to be blocks, as is each command you type in the interactive interpreter.

- *class*: A template for creating your own data types, which bundles up several related pieces of data and defines a bunch of methods for accessing and manipulating that data. An instance of a class is called an *object*.

- *encapsulation*: The grouping together of data and functionality, which allows the implementation details to be hidden behind an interface.

- *inheritance*: A way to form new classes using classes that have already been defined.

- *initialization*: The process of setting the initial value of an object. Initialization is done only once for each object when that object is created.

- *instance*: An object created from a (class) definition.

- *interface*: A set of instructions that an object provides to allow outside control of its contents.

- *method*: A function that is defined inside a class body. If called as an attribute of an instance of that class, the method will get the instance object as its first argument (which is usually called self).

- *namespace*: A container that provides a context for names, allowing the same name to be used in different subprocedures without causing confusion. In Python, modules, classes, functions, and methods all form namespaces.

- *parent*: A class (or node of a tree data structure) that passes on its attributes and methods to one or more child classes.

- *polymorphism*: A feature that allows values of different data types to be handled using a uniform interface.

- *state*: A unique configuration of information in an object.

Summary

You have covered most of Python's main coding constructs now and have started on the path of object-oriented programming. You have learned about concepts with brash new names like polymorphism, inheritance, and encapsulation. You have grasped the basic usage of attributes, methods, and their related properties. Now you are happily creating subclasses and overloading operators using magic methods. If I have done my work well, you will also understand the meanings of all these terms. The last remaining constructions you really need to know are the ones involved in handling Errors and Exceptions. You saw an example of a try: ... except: construction already in Listing 9-2. Chapter 10 will fill in the details.

Beyond that, the power of Python lies in its sprawling standard library. The remaining chapters of this book will give you insight into the functions and classes contained in some of the more commonly used modules.

CHAPTER 10

■ ■ ■

Exceptions

Things rarely go quite as expected, particularly in the realm of programming. An **exception** is what happens when Python encounters an error that would make it impossible or dangerous to continue executing the code. As you have already seen, dealing with errors is an integral part of the discipline of programming. In this chapter, you will be learning how to handle exceptions as and when they happen using `try...except` statements. I will introduce you to the different exception objects and the way they are organized and created and show you how to access the properties of the raised exception and then log the output. You will discover how to make proper use of tracebacks and how to create your own exception classes to cover the specific needs of your programs. Later in this chapter, you'll find out how to handle more complex errors and grok the art of exception chaining. Finally, I'll deal with cleaning up after the error, so the program can continue to run smoothly.

When Something Goes Wrong

Only the simplest programs are guaranteed to always behave exactly as expected. The `hello_world.py` script in Chapter 2, when run, will always echo the text that the user types in, and the programmer can tell just by looking at the script that, if it runs successfully once, it will do so every time.

As programs get bigger and more complex, their behavior becomes harder to predict. For example, a program might have a configuration file: what happens if that file contains settings that are unsuitable or if the file doesn't exist at all? Almost certainly, programs will use input data that will change over time: what if the data is corrupted or somehow unusable? And what if another system resource, for example, a network connection needed to contact a remote web service to obtain additional data, is unavailable? Worse, what if any number of these abnormal events occur in some method that you use many times throughout your code? Sometimes, you simply don't care about the error but other times you do: how can your program handle errors intelligently in this scenario?

While any specific abnormal or exceptional event can be catered for by tedious extra coding by the programmer, the ideas of exceptions and exception handling are implemented in many languages to make such procedures convenient, safe, and maintainable across all the programs you might care to write. Python's exception handling, which we explore in this chapter, is intended to be sufficiently simple, and fast, that you should rarely if ever need to handle errors in any other way.

Handling Simple Exceptions

Let's begin with one of the most basic errors that a program can encounter: trying to divide a number by zero. You'll see how Python's own exception handling deals with the problem and how it can be used in quite subtle ways to turn a simple error into intelligent reporting and management.

In interactive mode, type the following, and press Enter to see the result:

```
>>> 1 / 0
Traceback (most recent call last):
  File "<stdin>", line 1, in <module>
ZeroDivisionError: int division or modulo by zero
```

You've seen this sort of error report before while experimenting with Python. In fact, the report you're reading is the final stage in a procedure that Python has already gone through to try to **handle** the underlying problem. Let's look at that procedure in more detail.

As in written arithmetic, the division operator takes two arguments, a dividend to the left and a divisor to the right. The operation is quite simple, but the operator has a number of checks built into it; for example, both of its arguments must be numeric, and the divisor must be nonzero. Usually, these conditions are expected to be satisfied. However, the operator itself has no way of recovering when one of these checks fails. The operator instead falls back on Python's standard method of dealing with exceptional circumstances, exceptions.

If the divisor is zero, the operator causes an exception object of class ZeroDivisionError to be created. We then say that this exception is **raised** by the operator (or by the attempted operation). This can be taken to mean "raising" in the sense of discussing a problem at work with your boss and, more widely, in the sense of a problem passing up through a chain of command. When function A calls function B, and function B includes a division by zero, the division operator raises the exception within function B. And if function B doesn't know how to handle the exception, it raises the exception with function A.

Ultimately in our example, the exception is raised with the interactive mode, which doesn't know how to handle the circumstances and must therefore raise the exception with *you*, the programmer. This needs to be done in a human-readable way, which results in the error report. This is usually called a traceback, which we'll discuss in more detail later.

Some programming languages talk of throwing and catching exceptions rather than raising them: the division operator throws an exception up to function B; if function B doesn't catch that exception, it carries on to function A. This is just another metaphor for the same underlying process. In this book, we'll use Python's terminology instead.

Using the try Statement with an except Clause in Python

If the exception is created deep in a program (e.g., within a method), it can be caught and dealt with in between the original error and the program's output. Python's **try statement** is used to deal with exceptions, and in its most basic form, it can be used as shown in Listing 10-1.

Listing 10-1. The Basic Structure of the try Statement

```
try:
    # Something that might cause an exception!
    r = dangerous_method(a, b, c)
```

```
except SomeSpecificTypeOfError as e:
    # A particular class of errors we might expect
    r = something_else(a, b, c)

except:
    # Catch all other errors, regardless of their classes
    r = something_else_again(a, b, c)
```

To demonstrate this in action, let's create two methods to do division for us: one of these will be able to handle a ZeroDivisionError; the other will not. Run the code in Listing 10-2; you can paste it straight into the interactive prompt, or save it to a file called basic_handling.py and run it.

Listing 10-2. Testing Division Methods with Basic Exception Handling

```
# Method without exception handling
def divide_by(x, y):
    return x / y

# Method with exception handling
def divide_by_safe_inaccurate(x, y):
    try:
        return divide_by(x, y)
    except ZeroDivisionError:
        return 10000000000000000

print("Safe 3 / 2 = {0:g}".format(divide_by_safe_inaccurate(3, 2)))
print("Unsafe 3 / 2 = {0:g}".format(divide_by(3, 2)))
print("Safe 3 / 0 = {0:g}".format(divide_by_safe_inaccurate(3, 0)))


print("Unsafe 3 / 0 = {0:g}".format(divide_by(3, 0)))
```

Listing 10-2 will produce the following output:

```
Safe 3 / 2 = 1.5
Unsafe 3 / 2 = 1.5
Safe 3 / 0 = 1e16
Traceback (most recent call last):
  File "basic_handling.py", line 15, in <module>
    print("Unsafe 3 / 0 = {0:g}".format(divide_by(3, 0)))
  File "basic_handling.py", line 3, in divide_by
    return x / y
ZeroDivisionError: int division or modulo by zero
```

In Listing 10-2, we cause the unsafe method to raise an exception only at the very end: the program terminates at the first uncaught exception. If there were any code after the exception is raised, it wouldn't be run. It's important to remember that exceptions are created within *both* divide_by() and divide_by_safe(), when the division operator "notices" that its second argument is zero. But the try...except in `divide_by_safe_inaccurate()` tells the method how to handle the exception, so it is raised no further. The error in `divide_by()`, on the other hand, is raised by the division operator and then by the `divide_by()` method itself, rising into the main body of the program: then the program as a whole finally gives up and reports to the user.

It's also important to realize that discarding the exception and returning a result that doesn't reflect the inputs is not generally advisable: most programmers using your method would expect it *not* to return a standard big number when the divisor is zero; in fact, they would expect an *exception*! So we'll now expand on this simple exception handling to show you how it can help you while still letting your methods behave the way that they ought.

Classes of Exceptions

Python has many different built-in classes of exception. This means that when an exception is raised, you can tell a lot about what has gone wrong from the exception's class alone.

Exception objects and the hierarchy of classes

Although there are a lot of different exception classes, they're actually all ultimately subclasses (or subclasses of subclasses, etc.) of the BaseException class. In fact, all exceptions you might ever use in Python *must* be based on this class.

Let's raise some example exceptions and use the __bases__ attribute of their __class__ attribute to investigate what classes they inherit from. In Listing 10-3, we raise a number of exceptions and handle them by storing them in an array. We then look recursively at their superclasses until we reach the object class, which has no superclasses. Run the code in this listing and examine the output.

Listing 10-3. Provoking and Handling Different Exceptions and Investigating Their Class Hierarchies

```
store = []

# Create some exceptions and handle them
try: {}["foo"]
except KeyError as e: store.append(e)
try: 1 / 0
except ZeroDivisionError as e: store.append(e)
try: "".bar()
except AttributeError as e: store.append(e)

# Loop over the store of errors and print out their class hierarchy
for exception_object in store:
    ec = exception_object.__class__
    print(ec.__name__)
    indent = " +-"
    while ec.__bases__:
        # Assign ec's superclass to itself and increase
        ec = ec.__bases__[0]
        print(indent + ec.__name__)
        indent = "  " + indent
```

The script in Listing 10-3 will return results that look like this:

```
KeyError
 +-LookupError
   +-Exception
     +-BaseException
       +-object
ZeroDivisionError
 +-ArithmeticError
   +-Exception
     +-BaseException
       +-object
AttributeError
 +-Exception
   +-BaseException
     +-object
```

Here, we have traced each individual exception's class hierarchy to the shared root of BaseException (and object). The full hierarchy of all built-in exception classes is part of Python's online documentation at http://docs.python.org/3.0/library/exceptions.html, but typically, you won't ever need this exhaustive list of classes: either you will want to take care to catch a small number of classes, treating each one differently, or you will want to play safe and catch all exceptions with a nonspecific except clause.

All exception classes in Python must belong somewhere on this hierarchy. This includes any custom exception classes that you create yourself, as explained in the next section: new exception classes must inherit from an existing class. We'll discuss the consequences of this hierarchy later, in the "Handling Complex Errors" section.

Creating and Raising an Exception Object

Typically, you can rely on Python's internal methods to raise exceptions whenever something goes wrong in their own internals. But in order to make full use of exceptions, you will sometimes want to raise them yourself in the depths of your program, so that the higher levels of the program will have more detail about what has just gone wrong and will know how to deal with it.

For this, we use the raise statement. This keyword can be followed by either an exception class, for example, TypeError, or an instance of that class, for example, TypeError('this is an error message'). It can also be invoked with no arguments inside an except clause, to reraise the exception currently being handled. Examples of the three main syntaxes of the raise statement follow:

```
>>> raise KeyError
Traceback (most recent call last):
  File "<stdin>", line 1, in <module>
KeyError
>>> raise KeyError('foo')
Traceback (most recent call last):
  File "<stdin>", line 1, in <module>
KeyError: 'foo'
>>> try: {}['foo']
```

```
... except KeyError as e: raise
...
Traceback (most recent call last):
  File "<stdin>", line 1, in <module>
KeyError: 'foo'
```

Imagine you're thinking of placing bets on the chances of some events happening. But you're a busy person, so you want to write a program that takes all the bets for a given day, and a minimum likelihood above which you're happy to bet, and gives you your total expected winnings if you place all of those bets. You already have two existing bits of code for keeping track of how likely it is that things might happen: you might be controlling a complicated scientific experiment or predicting the behavior of financial markets. However, one set uses percentages and the other uses probabilities, and you'd now like to use them together.

You could either rewrite one or other set of the existing bits of code, or you could write two conversion methods to go from percentage to fractional probability and back. But although generally speaking percentages can be greater than 100 percent, fractional probabilities can't be greater than 1. So you might want to receive a warning if your combined program tries to convert a percentage over 100 percent into a probability.

Listing 10-4 shows a script that brings together your two lots of code and tells you how much you will win by placing all of the odds-on bets. Save this to a file called expected_gains.py—you will need to edit it shortly—and run it.

Listing 10-4. *Raising an Exception During Conversion, Where the Input Cannot Be Converted*

```python
# Cut and pasted from a statistics program
def is_odds_on(percentage):
    """Determine whether a percentage probability is 'likely' or not"""
    return (percentage > 50)

# Cut and pasted from a financial program
def expected_gains(amount_bet = 10, amount_to_win = 10, frac = 0.5):
    """For a given fractional chance of winning, and an amount bet, return
    the most likely gains"""
    return (amount_to_win * frac) - amount_bet

# Conversion methods - in both directions
def prob_to_perc(pr):
    """Convert a probability to a percentage"""
    return pr * 100
def perc_to_prob(pc):
    """Convert a percentage to a probability, but raise exception if too big"""
    if pc > 100:
        raise ValueError("Percentage {0:g}% does not give a valid
                         probability".format(pc))
    return pc / 100

# Execute this if the program is run directly - see Chapter 8
if __name__ == "__main__":
    # Some input data
    data = (
```

```
    # Percentage chance of winning, amount required to bet, amount you'll win
    (23,52,274,),
    (75,43,60,),
    (48,118,71,),
    (111,144,159,), # Misprint in the percentage data!
)

# Work out how much we'd win if we only placed likely bets
total = 0
for bet in data:
    if is_odds_on(bet[0]):
        total += expected_gains(bet[1], bet[2], perc_to_prob(bet[0]))

print("Total gains: {0:g}".format(total))
```

You should find that the program raises a ValueError. This is caused by what looks like a misprint in the data: a typographical error has added an extra one to the final percentage. Luckily, the program spotted it, because otherwise, the program would overestimate the amount of gains to be made if you betted on this data set.

Correct the error, and save and run the program again. You should find that, if you place just that one odds-on bet, you're likely to make a modest win, far less than if a 111 percent probability had been able to sneak through!

Creating Your Own Exception Classes

You can create exception classes of your own to match the internal details of your application. This might be because you want to subclass existing exceptions to provide your surrounding program with more precise information. Alternatively, you might want exceptions that more closely match situations in which your program will be used.

For an example of using very specific exceptions for a particular task, look at Listing 10-5. This program checks your house's security: not literally, of course, but you can inform it whether or not you've left the door open and it will judge your home security accordingly, as you'll see.

Save this to a file called home_security.py: you can run it right away, but you should see a SecurityError if you do so.

Listing 10-5. Defining and Raising Your Own Exception Classes

```
# We need to parse a report file, so import a module to help us
import re

# Our custom exceptions
class SecurityError(Exception):
    """Standard error for house security"""
    pass
class SecurityNotCertain(SecurityError):
    """Exception raised when security can't be guaranteed"""
    pass
class BuildingIntegrityError(SecurityError):
    """Exception raised when a door is open"""
```

```
        pass
class MotionDetectedError(SecurityError):
    """Exception raised when motion detected"""
    pass

def get_report(file = 'report.txt'):
    """Get a report on the security status of the house"""
    # Attempt to open the report file and read in the lines
    try:
        f = open(file)
        lines = f.readlines()
        f.close()
    except IOError:
        raise SecurityError("Cannot open status file {0}".format(file))
    # For each line, trim whitespace, split it at the colon and make a dict
    return dict([re.split(":\s*", l.strip(), 1) for l in lines ])

def check_report(report):
    """Check a house report dict, that everything is secure"""

    to_check = ("door_open_front", "door_open_rear",
        "motion_in_living_room", "motion_in_kitchen", "motion_in_attic")

    for check in to_check:
        # See if the value is what we expect for security
        try:
            if report[check] != "no":
                if check[0:9] == "door_open":
                    raise BuildingIntegrityError("Door open: {0}".format(check))
                elif check[0:9] == "motion_in":
                    raise MotionDetectedError("Motion detected: {0}".format(check))
        # If we can't find the item to check, security isn't certain!
        except (KeyError, SecurityNotCertain):
            raise SecurityNotCertain("Can't check security for {0}".format(check))

# Main program - in real life this would be scheduled to run e.g. every minute
report = get_report()
check_report(report)
```

The program begins by checking for a security report in the file report.txt, and when it can't find this file, it raises the SecurityError you may have already seen. This file is where you can tell the program whether or not the front or back door is open, and whether there's any movement in any of the rooms. Listing 10-6 is a complete report.txt, indicating a secure house: save it to the current directory and run the program.

Listing 10-6. *A Complete Security Report for Listing 10-5 to Parse*

```
door_open_front: no
door_open_rear: no
```

```
motion_in_living_room: no
motion_in_kitchen: no
motion_in_attic: no
```

With this report in place, the program should run and quit silently:

```
% python home_security.py
%
```

This is what you want a burglar alarm to do if everything is OK!

In the top of Listing 10-5, we define a `SecurityError` exception as a subclass of `Exception`. However, we then go on to define even more specific exceptions and use these to deal with different security problems that arise. Try changing a no to a yes and running the program again, or try removing a line from the report file altogether. You should see different classes of exception being raised depending on what you do in the report file.

The different classes of custom exceptions are useful, because later on, you might decide that some security problems are more important than others. For example, if you bought a cat and kept it in the kitchen while you were out, you wouldn't want motion detection in the kitchen to raise an exception, and motion anywhere else in the house might just mean that your cat has got out of the kitchen! At that point, because you've already used different exception classes, you can quickly rewrite your code to handle some security problems differently from others.

Accessing Properties of the Raised Exception

Sometimes, you will want to access the details of the original exception *object* and not just handle them based on their *class*. The object will contain, at a minimum, the readable message you see when an exception reaches the interactive prompt, but it may also contain extra information depending on how it was first raised. Even with the minimum, you might find it useful, if you're doing a lot of (otherwise silent) discarding of exceptions, to log those messages somewhere. That way, you can check your log files if something is going wrong with your program, and perhaps notice patterns in the exceptions that are occurring.

The script in Listing 10-7 accesses the original exception's human-readable message. Either save it to a file or run it from an interactive prompt to see how this works in practice.

Listing 10-7. *Handling an Exception by Logging Its Message Harmlessly to the Screen*

```
def log_error(err):
    """Simple logging method: writes error's details to standard output"""
    print("LOG:: {0}: {1}".format(err.__class__.__name__, err))

# KeyError: accessing a dictionary key that does not exist
try:
    d = {"foo":  "bar"}
    d["quux"]
except KeyError as e:
    log_error(e)
```

```
# TypeError: trying to perform an operation on incompatible operands
try:
    str = "" + 5
except TypeError as ex:
    log_error(ex)

# NameError: referring to a variable that does not exist
# (Note that neither e nor ex exist outside their "except" clauses above)
try:
    print(ex)
except NameError as exc:
    log_error(exc)
```

Listing 10-7 prints the following message to the screen:

```
LOG:: KeyError: 'quux'
LOG:: TypeError: Can't convert 'int' object to str implicitly
LOG:: NameError: name 'ex' is not defined
```

We have been able in the preceding code to interrogate each exception object and then log its type—its class name—and the message associated with it.

But what if we want to raise more information alongside the exception? You will see later that Python attaches a lot of diagnostic messages to exceptions, so that they can be traced through the code by the programmer. But there might be extra information in the exception's original environment that, for example, helps us clean up after it or otherwise recover from it, helps us track down the precise problem in a configuration file, or helps us decide whether or not to ignore the error.

Along with the message, you can store extra parameters in the exception object by including them as arguments to the Exception() constructor. The parameters are stored in the args attribute of the object. In Listing 10-8, we store an extra parameter on the exception and access it later on during exception handling.

Listing 10-8. *Storing Extra State Information in an Exception*

```
for ignore in (True, False):
    try:
        # Pass a second parameter into the exception constructor
        raise Exception("Ignore is {0}".format(ignore), ignore)
    except Exception as e:
        # Based on that second parameter,
        # work out if the error can be ignored or not
        if(e.args[1]):
            print("I can ignore this error!")
        else:
            print("I canNOT ignore this error!")
```

The preceding script produces the following results:

```
I can ignore this error!
I canNOT ignore this error!
```

Implementing Complex Error Handling

As you saw in the previous section, Python's exception classes form a hierarchy, where the BaseException class is the superclass of every other exception class. All Python's core exceptions are then created as subclasses of Exception or Warning or are nonerror-like conditions like KeyboardInterrupt. These primitive exception classes are, in turn, all subclasses themselves of BaseException.

Why is this relevant? Well, an except clause that claims to handle an exception class *will also handle any of its subclasses.* The first except that matches either the class or any of the superclasses gets to handle the exception. So if we imagine Python's many exception classes as giving us information to distinguish between different errors, then the class hierarchy lets us *ignore the differences* between what we might think of as similar classes of error.

Listing 10-9 gives examples of this. You should see no output from this code!

Listing 10-9. *Handling Exceptions by Referring to Their Superclasses*

```
dict = {}
try: dict['foo']
except KeyError: pass # dictionary-specific lookup problem

try: dict['bar']
except LookupError: pass # lookup problems in dictionaries, tuples and lists

try: dict['quux']
except Exception: pass # any problem, of any sort
except KeyError: raise Exception("Should have been handled by the first match")
```

Almost all exceptions you encounter could be handled by explicitly handling the Exception class; similarly, any dictionary or sequence lookups can be handled with LookupError rather than explicitly handling both KeyError and IndexError. Note again in the last example in Listing 10-9 that they are handled by the first matching except clause found, not the closest match.

Using finally to Clean Up After a Problem

If you don't handle an exception locally, that's generally a signal to the rest of your program that there might be some cleaning up to do. However, sometimes an exception can interrupt your program at such a point that there are other unfinished tasks that are far more easily cleaned up locally, even if the primary exception needs to be handled at a higher level.

An example is closing a file that you've opened in the current method. Your current method might want to write a log to a file. If an exception is raised while the file is still open, only that method has direct access to the file object in order to close it. Leaving the file open could cause problems much later in your program should it try to access that potentially locked file. It's best to be certain that the file object will be closed, whether or not an exception is raised and whether or not it is handled.

To ensure that such operations are always carried out, you can use the **finally clause**. If an exception is raised but not handled, and a finally clause exists in the try statement, the exception is put to one side temporarily, the finally clause is executed, and the exception is raised by Python as usual. If there's no exception, or the exception is handled, the finally clause is still executed. You can see an example of this in Listing 10-10. Run this code in the interactive prompt or from a file.

Listing 10-10. Doing Basic Clean Up with finally, Without Handling the Error Locally

```
def log_data(x, y):
    """Logs some incoming data, plus their division"""
    # Try logging some data to an open file
    try:
        f = open('finally_log.txt', 'a')
        f.write("{0:g} / {1:g} = {2:g}\n".format(x,y, (x/y)))
    # If there's a problem, log it, but then re-raise the error
    # Don't handle it locally
    except ZeroDivisionError:
        f.write("Error: tried to divide by zero\n")
        raise
    # Whatever happens, close the file
    finally:
        f.close()

log_data(12.5,29.1)
log_data(23.0,84.3)
log_data(66.4,55.9)
log_data(58.2,0)
```

You will notice that the ZeroDivisionError is not entirely handled: the logging method partially handles it with a matching except, but then it reraises it with raise. That means the method can write a warning message to the log and then let the surrounding program decide what needs to be done with the exception. Nonetheless, the file is always closed, even when the exception occurs: the finally clause is always run.

Putting Everything Together with else

So far, we've used exception handling to try out some code, handle a number of exception classes, and tidy up after both handled and unhandled exceptions. But what about handling the situation where there is no exception? In that case, the program executes all of the try clause and then goes straight to finally, with no special treatment for the no-exception scenario!

At first sight, this scenario presents no real problem. After all, if there's no exception, our program should just carry on, so we could append our code to the try clause. Consider the pseudocode in Listing 10-11, which demonstrates this idea.

Listing 10-11. An Example of Handling a No-Exception Situation

```
try:
    # This method could raise a SomeError
    perilous()
```

```
        # If it doesn't, then this handler method is called
        handle_no_problem()
    except SomeError:
        # If it does, then this handler method is called
        handle_some_error()
    finally:
        # Whatever happens, this clean-up method is called
        clean_up()
```

On closer inspection, the code in Listing 10-11 won't suffice. If we execute handle_no_problem() in the try clause, depending on its internals, it could raise a SomeError exception, which would then prompt the exception handling to call handle_some_error() before clean_up(). The two handle_ methods might, between them, perform some action twice, so they would have to be coded in a way to make sure that never happened.

In essence, by just putting that line at the end of the try clause, we've actually complicated our code at the next layer down, because these lower-level methods now have to take into account how each other behaves to recover from an internal exception. Although you might generally be able to work around this in your own coding, when you're using other people's code, doing so might be quite difficult.

If we liken our try...except statement to an if statement, then we are able to execute code if an exception is raised, but we also need a way of executing code if *no* exception is raised: we want to have the equivalent of if...else functionality. So, to complete our error-handling functionality, we add one last clause: an **else clause**. This is executed after the try clause but before the finally clause, *only if* no exception is raised.

Confused? That's understandable. Let's take a step back and look at a listing that should illustrate as simply as possible everything that you can do with Python exception handling. Examine and run Listing 10-12, and look at its output:

Listing 10-12. Python's Complete Exception Handling Using try, except, else, and finally

```python
def divide_by_complex(x, y):
    """Division of two numbers with complex exception handling"""
    try:
        print("TRYING : beginning division of {0} / {1}".format(x,y))
        result = x / y
    except ZeroDivisionError:
        print("HANDLED: division by zero!")
    else:
        print("SUCCESS: result is {0:g}".format(result))
    finally:
        print("FINALLY: cleaning up")

# This surrounding try/except block helps clarify when exceptions "escape"
# unhandled from the divide_by_complex method
try:
    # Normal behaviour
    divide_by_complex(2,1)
    print()
    # Internally handled exception
    divide_by_complex(2,0)
```

```
    print()
    # Raised exception
    divide_by_complex(2,None)
except Exception as e:
    print("RAISING: exception {0} not handled; ↵
rising up".format(e.__class__.__name__))
```

```
TRYING : beginning division of 2 / 1
SUCCESS: result is 2
FINALLY: cleaning up

TRYING : beginning division of 2 / 0
HANDLED: division by zero!
FINALLY: cleaning up

TRYING : beginning division of 2 / None
FINALLY: cleaning up
RAISING: exception TypeError not handled; rising up
```

Here's a summary of the full try statements behavior, in more or less plain English:

1. *Try* some potentially dangerous code.

2. If an exception has been raised, look for an except clause that matches

   a.   The exception's class

   b.   Some superclass of the exception

3. If no exception is raised, run the code in the else clause.

4. *Finally*, always run any clean-up code.

5. *If no except clauses have handled the exception, raise it even further in the program until it's handled or it reaches the user.*

The fifth step is core Python behavior for unhandled exceptions, inside or outside a try clause: that's why it's in italics. It corresponds to the very last line of the output for Listing 10-12.

With these four clauses—try, except, else, and finally—plus the concept of unhandled exceptions rising up through the program, Python's exception handling provides complex, flexible, and above all useful methods of flow control. Along with handling errors, the try statement is also similar to the standard if...else flow control. This means you can use exception handling in Python with as much confidence as any other flow control methods: in fact, you are actively encouraged to do so, for reasons which we'll discuss at the end of this chapter.

Using the Traceback If All Else Fails

As you've already seen, unhandled exceptions generate a report when they reach you or another user. This report is called a traceback, and it gives details of the files and the locations within them, where an exception—even if it's been partially handled—has in some way led to the program coming to a halt.

Look back at our very first code example in this chapter, involving a simple division by zero at the interactive prompt. This is a single-stage traceback. It begins by announcing itself as a traceback and then gives a location in line 1 of "<stdin>" (i.e., your typing, or *standard input*). It also specifies any method that the exception is raised in: in this case, it was raised outside of any method and so is considered to have been raised in <module>. For now, treat this as a special signifier for not being inside any method.

Let's generate a more complicated traceback. Save the code in Listing 10-13 to a file called traceback.py, and run it.

Listing 10-13. *Demonstrating a Complicated Traceback*

```
def f1(): f2()
def f2(): f3()
def f3(): foo

# This will raise a NameError, deep in f3
f1()
```

Calling this simple function will produce the following traceback:

```
Traceback (most recent call last):
  File "./traceback.py", line 6, in <module>
    f1()
  File "./traceback.py", line 1, in f1
    def f1(): f2()
  File "./traceback.py", line 2, in f2
    def f2(): f3()
  File "./traceback.py", line 3, in f3
    def f3(): foo
NameError: global name 'foo' is not defined
```

As you can see, the traceback provides you with a complete explanation of the stack of methods calling methods, from the final point where the exception reached you, the programmer (in the <module>), right back to the original source of the exception in f3(). A good rule of thumb if you're also using code from a module (see Chapter 11 for more information on how to do this) is to read a traceback as far as the last thing you wrote yourself, and look there for any mistakes you might have made. Programming errors can also occur in the standard library, of course, but they're quite rare.

You can also use the traceback module to extract tracebacks from errors while you handle them, so that, for example, you can log the full traceback somewhere and then continue with your program. We won't discuss that technique here, but modules are discussed in the next chapter, and Python's standard library of modules is documented in quite a lot of depth and with examples on the Python web site.

Exception Chaining and Tracebacks

Tracing an unhandled exception can get more difficult if one exception is handled, only for another to be invoked in the very try statement that's doing the handling. The biggest worry from the debugger's perspective is that the original exception, having been dealt with, might be inaccessible. However, tracebacks provide a way of establishing from one exception if it was raised in the context of handling a different exception: this is called exception **chaining**.

If one exception is being handled, and another is raised either by accident or through an unconnected raise statement, the first is set as the __context__ attribute of the second. If, however, you want to raise a new exception directly as a result of the one being handled, you can use the raise...from syntax to show the connection: the original exception is set as the __cause__ attribute of the new.

The combination of __cause__ and __context__ lead to complex but useful tracebacks. Save Listing 10-14 as chaining.py, and run it.

Listing 10-14. *Demonstrating Exception Chaining*

```
def return_explicit_chain():
    try:
        # Catch a NameError, and raise a new error "from" it
        try: foo
        except Exception as e:
            raise Exception("Explicitly raised") from e
    # Re-catch the new exception
    except Exception as e2:
        return e2

def return_implicit_chain():
    try:
        # Catch a NameError, but accidentally raise a KeyError
        try: foo
        except Exception as e:
            {}['bar']
    # Re-catch the new exception
    except Exception as e2:
        return e2

# The explicitly raised exception, and its "cause"
ex_ch = return_explicit_chain()
print("Explicit chain:")
print(ex_ch.__repr__())
print(ex_ch.__cause__)

# The implicitly raised error, and its "context"
print("Implicit chain:")
im_ch = return_implicit_chain()
print(im_ch.__repr__())
print(im_ch.__context__)

# Re-raise, to see the corresponding traceback
# raise im_ch # Uncomment this to see the implicit chain
raise ex_ch
```

When you run the preceding code, you'll get these results:

```
Explicit chain:
Exception('Explicitly raised',)
global name 'foo' is not defined
Implicit chain:
KeyError('bar',)
global name 'foo' is not defined
Traceback (most recent call last):
  File "./chaining.py", line 4, in return_explicit_chain
    try: foo
NameError: global name 'foo' is not defined

The above exception was the direct cause of the following exception:

Traceback (most recent call last):
  File "./chaining.py", line 35, in <module>
    raise ex_ch
  File "./chaining.py", line 6, in return_explicit_chain
    raise Exception("Explicitly raised") from e
Exception: Explicitly raised
```

Now, comment out the next-to-last line to see the traceback from an implicit chain:

```
Explicit chain:
Exception('Explicitly raised',)
global name 'foo' is not defined
Implicit chain:
KeyError('bar',)
global name 'foo' is not defined
Traceback (most recent call last):
  File "./chaining.py", line 14, in return_implicit_chain
    try: foo
NameError: global name 'foo' is not defined

During handling of the above exception, another exception occurred:

Traceback (most recent call last):
  File "./chaining.py", line 34, in <module>
    raise im_ch # Uncomment this to see the implicit chain
  File "./chaining.py", line 16, in return_implicit_chain
    {}['bar']
KeyError: 'bar'
```

As you can see, more complex tracebacks will distinguish between explicit and implicit chaining by leaving a newline and then referring to the next exception that was raised *en route* to the eventual traceback.

A Final Note on Pythonic Exception Handling

Some languages try to make exception handling a last resort—the syntax can often be cumbersome and the functionality basic—and the performance of the language interpreter might suffer during its equivalent of try statements. But as you have seen, Python actively *encourages* error handling, through simple syntax with a fully developed flow control based on exception handling. Also, in most Python distributions, exception handling is no slower than simple if...else flow control.

When a language tries to discourage you from using exception handling, it is following a philosophy known as **"look before you leap" (LBYL)**. This means that you should ensure that something is allowed first and do it only if it's allowed. In contrast, the **Pythonic** philosophy of trying something first and then using exception handling to deal with unusual consequences, is often referred to as **"easier to ask forgiveness than permission" (EAFP)**.

In Python, you should always use the EAFP style, rather than LBYL, wherever possible. Listing 10-15 compares simple examples of the LBYL and EAFP programming styles.

Listing 10-15. *LBYL Programming vs. EAFP Programming*

```
# LBYL: not Pythonic
if hasattr(some_object, 'result'):
    return some_object.result()
else:
    return None

# EAFP: Pythonic
try:
    return some_object.result()
except AttributeError:
    return None
```

To people used to looking before they leap, Python's approach can feel dangerous: LBYL is a very risk-averse strategy and implicitly perceives exceptions as risks. But exceptions in Python aren't risks; they're just another part of the language, and so EAFP is entirely suitable in that context. Of course, you have to be careful to keep your error handling tight: in the EAFP example in Listing 10-15, if some_object.result() were itself to raise an exception, then handling all exceptions of class Exception would mean your program is ignorant to any problems occurring inside that method. As it is, an AttributeError from deep within the result() method will be ignored in the example.

To program in a Pythonic way is to follow a number of different interlocking conventions. EAFP itself isn't an important one, but it embodies many of the other Pythonic conventions. These are summarized online in the Pythonic Enhancement Proposal 8 (PEP 0008) and are a subject of much discussion among the larger Python community.

Pythonic conventions are to be encouraged among Python programmers, and many of these have reasons that go to the heart of Python's core principles. So don't be afraid to use exception raising and handling at the heart of your Python programs: your code will only be the more Pythonic for it!

Jargon Busting

Here is some further explanation of the terms presented in this chapter:

- *Chaining*: To chain exceptions, you attach the exception currently being handled by a try statement to any new exception which, whether deliberately or accidentally, occurs during the execution of any of the clauses in the statement. If the new exception is raised using the raise...from syntax, the chaining is said to be explicit. Otherwise, if the exception is raised on its own or occurs because of a programming error, then the chaining is said to be implicit.

- *"Easier to ask for forgiveness than permission" (EAFP) philosophy*: In this programming style, the program always attempts to execute code that might raise exceptions and then handles any of those exceptions afterward. This style implicitly treats exception handling like any other type of flow control (e.g., for loops or if...else statements) and as such is very much suited to languages like Python.

- *else clauses*: This part of a try statement block is executed if there are no exceptions raised by the code in the try clause but before the code in the finally clause is run. The else clause is analogous to except clause but is run in the situation where there is no exception.

- *Exception*: An exception is a Python object, of the BaseException class or any subclass of BaseException, that Python's core exception framework creates when some part of the program encounters an exceptional circumstance that can't be dealt with there and then.

- *Exception handling*: This refers to manipulating exceptions in such a way as to deal with the problems that originally caused them, using Python's core handling structures to turn exceptions and other problematic situations into straightforward control flow.

- *finally clauses*: This part of a try statement block is executed regardless of whether or not an error occurs. Even if the error is not handled by a relevant except clause, the finally clause will still execute. After that, Python's exception framework raises any unhandled errors to the next method up, and so on. These clauses are useful for any tidying up that must be performed locally, regardless of the nature of the error.

- *"Look before you leap" (LBYL) philosophy*: In this cautious programming style, situations that might raise exceptions are tested for in advance and only attempted if they are possible. This philosophy is useful in languages other than Python, where exception handling is either cumbersome or detrimental to program performance.

- *Pythonic*: This term describes a program that is structured in a way that is most amenable to both the ideas and principles that have informed Python's internal development and to the nature of the Python community's established coding conventions.

- *Raise*: When you raise an exception, you both create an exception object and cause Python's core exception framework to begin passing it up from the current method, through the method that called it, and the method calling that one, and so on until the exception is dealt with using exception handling.

- *Traceback*: A traceback is the human-readable report that an unhandled exception creates when it is raised up to either the command prompt or the Python interactive prompt.

- *try statements, try clauses, and except clauses*: These compound statements are the core of Python's exception handling. A try statement consists of a try clause and (usually) one or more except clauses. Execution of the contents of the try clause is attempted, and if an exceptional circumstance causes an exception object to be created, Python looks for an except clause that matches the class of the exception object or one of its superclasses.

Summary

You can now include sophisticated error handling techniques in your Python repertoire. You have seen how the try...except...else...finally statement is used to handle exceptions and you now know how to create exception classes of your own based on the existing exception class. The next chapter looks at some of the most useful modules in Python's standard library.

## CHAPTER 11

Reusing Code
with Modules and Packages

The primary motivation for humans to offload work to computers is that, for a human, the work is boring and repetitive. So it would be a shame if, every time you wanted a new program and you were building to include functionality you'd built before, you had to cut and paste every method and class definition from the earlier program into the new one by hand, or worse, rewrite them from scratch.

Python has a number of indispensible standard methods that your programs can always access. However, you're bound to end up encountering some problems a few times, and their solutions won't be part of Python's core built-in functionality. For example, one of your programs might need a class to interact with spreadsheet files, or another might make use of a method to calculate the distance between two points on the earth's surface.

It would be impractical for Python to have to hand every last bit of functionality you might need. The Python distribution would be enormous, and it would grow over time. The Python interpreter would take a long time to start, as it found all of the functionality and brought it into memory, and again, this procedure would only get longer. And a running interpreter would take up huge amounts of memory. This is clearly not satisfactory, given how rarely the average program would use most of this functionality.

Luckily, Python has a solution for these problems. It provides a flexible, easy-to-use system for modularizing your code: that is, for reusing your own code, for optionally including extra functionality from the standard Python distribution, and for bringing in any other contributed code from other Python developers. The structure of modules and packages lets you keep your projects organized, smaller, and easier to understand.

In this chapter, we'll cover Python's module system so that you can apply it to your own programs. We'll start with a simple module before seeing typical module usage. This will lead us onto packages, which are collections of modules, and some standard Python modules that you can make use of.

Understanding Python Modules

Before we begin, you should understand that *any Python file can be a module*. A **module** is just another Python file. It can include methods, classes, references to other modules, and even executing code. When you bring the module into your program, the methods, classes and modules are made available in your current namespace.

Whether or not Python can find modules and packages depends on their relative location to your current file, as you'll see later. So let's start this chapter's tutorials by creating a separate directory for all the content: call it my_modules for now.

Creating Your First Module

Let's create a fairly simple module with a number of straightforward methods. Often, one of programmers' first modules will contain utility methods that they find themselves writing again and again to perform tasks like advanced string conversion, so we'll build a module of string methods.

Imagine that you wanted to alter some text—the content of your outgoing e-mails, perhaps, or your next blog post—so that it sounded like it was written by a pirate. This might sound odd, but Talk Like a Pirate Day (September 19) has been an Internet phenomenon since the 1990s. On this day, many web sites automatically turn their output text into pirate-speak, which can produce unusual effects depending on the site.

Listing 11-1 details a skeleton module—no piratical pun intended—that you will be able to use in a number of different ways to write like a pirate. You should save it in the my_modules directory, and call it strings.py.

Listing 11-1. *A Module of String Conversion Methods*

```
"""Module of methods to convert strings to pirate-speak"""

def _strip_punctuation(sentence):
    """Strips punctuation and all whitespace off the end of a sentence"""
    return sentence.strip().rstrip("!.")

def piratify(str):
    """Generic piratify of whole paragraphs, by exclaiming everything!"""
    return (str + " ").replace(". ", "! ").replace(".\n", "!\n").strip()

def me_hearties(str):
    """Appends 'me hearties!' to the end of a stub sentence"""
    stub = _strip_punctuation(str)
    return stub.strip() + ", me hearties! "

def yarr(str):
    """Appends 'Yarr' to the start of a stub sentence and piratifies it"""
    stub = _strip_punctuation(str)
    return "Yarr, " + stub[0].lower() + stub[1:] + "! "
```

Make sure you are in the same directory as this file, and run the Python interactive prompt. At the prompt, type the following: you should see the results as shown.

```
>>> import strings
>>> print(strings.piratify("Hello, world."))
Hello, world!
>>> print(strings.yarr("This is a test."))
Yarr, this is a test!
>>> print(strings.me_hearties("It uses the strings module!"))
It uses the strings module, me hearties!
```

After you try this out, look in the my_modules directory. You should now see a new file called strings.pyc (we'll discuss this later in the chapter, in the "Python's Internal Behavior" section).

You can now use this module to convert short sentences into pirate-speak at the Python prompt. But there's a limit to how much you would want to paste into print() statements in this way, and this script will only ever convert one sentence at a time. In short, although the methods are useful in the context of a program, they aren't convenient for the end user. Let's see how to overcome this shortcoming.

Using Your Module in Another Program

Wouldn't it be great if you could embed these low-level conversion methods in another, higher-level method: one that could take a large block of text, decompose it into sentences, and randomly include piratical interjections? Then, you could get it to rewrite your e-mail content before sending it to a friend and celebrate Talk Like a Pirate Day in style. Let's build this next, using the import statement to keep the low-level methods in strings.py.

Look at the code in Listing 11-2, which uses a slightly different form of the import statement, to avoid cluttering up the code. When we used the module in the previous section, the methods were still attached to the strings module: that is, we run them by prefacing each method's name with strings. In Listing 11-2, all the methods are added to the current program's scope, rather than only adding the strings object to the scope and keeping the methods inside it.

Save this code as convert.py, in the same directory as strings.py.

Listing 11-2. Importing from the Module in Listing 11-1

```
"""Module to utilize existing string conversion functions on lots of text"""

# Import the contents of our strings module from the local directory
from strings import *
# Import the Python random module from the standard library
import random

# Probability of calling yarr() and me_hearties() functions
weightings = (0.2, 0.3)

def random_pirate(stub):
    """Randomly turn a stub into a piratified sentence"""
    choice = random.random()
    if choice <= weightings[0]:
        return yarr(stub)
    elif choice <= weightings[0] + weightings[1]:
        return me_hearties(stub)
    return stub + "! "

def to_stubs(text):
    """Convert a string into stub sentences"""
    # Piratify first, to make every sentence an exclamation
    text = piratify(text)
    # Now split, discarding any empty strings
    return [ s for s in (sen.strip() for sen in text.split("!")) if s != ""]
```

```
def convert_string(content):
    """Convert a string to pirate-speak"""
    return "".join([ random_pirate(txt) for txt in to_stubs(content) ])

def convert_file(filename):
    """Convert a file to pirate-speak"""

    return convert_string(open(filename).read())
```

Next, save some text that you'd like to convert to pirate-speak. You can call the file whatever you want, but for the purposes of the example output, I've called it example.txt. Still in the same directory as all of these files, run the interactive prompt, and type the following commands:

```
>>> import convert
>>> convert.convert_string("He sleeps all night and he works all day.")
'He sleeps all night and he works all day, me hearties! '
>>> open('example.txt').read()
"Mister Pudey, the very real problem is one of money. I'm afraid that the Ministry
of Silly Walks is no longer getting the kind of support it needs. You see, there's
Defence, Social Security, Health, Housing, Education, Silly Walks. They're all
supposed to get the same."
>>> convert.convert_file('example.txt')
"Yarr, mister Pudey, the very real problem is one of money! I'm afraid that the
Ministry of Silly Walks is no longer getting the kind of support it needs, me
hearties! You see, there's Defence, Social Security, Health, Housing, Education,
Silly Walks! Yarr, they're all supposed to get the same! "
```

The convert module can now be used, in conjunction with the strings module, to convert large blocks of text to pirate-speak. You can change the weightings variable in convert to make particular piratical conversions more or less likely. It still needs to be used at the interactive prompt, but we'll expand on this module later to make it more useful.

Everyday Module Usage

When you use modules, you'll commonly want some flexibility over how you import them into your applications. Luckily, Python gives you a few options, which we'll look at in the next section. You'll also need to organize your modules so they don't get out of control, so we'll look at that too.

Flexible Importing

Once you've put your code into a module, you have a number of flexible ways of using the import keyword to access the contents of the module. That means you need import only what you require for a particular project.

To automatically import everything from a module, you can use one of two Python constructs. import modulename creates an object called modulename in the current scope, with all the module contents as attributes of that object. Alternatively, from modulename import * puts all methods, classes, or variables from the module into the current scope as separate variables (not quite all, as you will see later).

```
>>> # Import the module 'convert', with methods referenced inside it
... import convert
>>> convert
<module 'convert' from 'convert.py'>
>>> convert.convert_string
<function convert at 0xb7c1b82c>
>>> convert.weightings
(0.20000000000000001, 0.29999999999999999)
>>> # Now import each method from 'convert', into the current scope
... from convert import *
>>> convert_string
<function convert at 0xb7c1b82c>
>>> weightings
(0.20000000000000001, 0.29999999999999999)
```

This is simple enough to use, but it's untidy practice: all of the contents are imported from the module, regardless of whether they are used or not, and in the second instance, some contents might overwrite existing variables. Instead, you can specify each item you want to import, and even what name you want to import it with, using variants on the above from syntax:

```
>>> # Single, basic import clause: one method
... from convert import piratify
>>> piratify
<function piratify at 0xb7c6b0ac>
>>> # Import clause, with 'as' sub-clause to rename the method
... # This avoids overwriting an existing 'convert_string' in the scope... from
convert import convert_string as convertiferize
>>> convertiferize
<function convert_string at 0xb7c0f82c>
>>> # convert itself imports the random module into its own namespace
... # so you can in turn import the random module from convert!
... from convert import random
>>> random
<module 'random' from '...'>
>>> # Several clauses - including renaming - can be separated with commas
>>> from convert import yarr, weightings as weightables
>>> (yarr, weightables)
(<function yarr at 0xb7c6b12c>, (0.20000000000000001, 0.29999999999999999))
```

You can also import from a module at any point in your code. In fact, you can import within conditional statements; that way, under certain conditions, the import never happens at all. However, note that the wildcard version of the import syntax (i.e., from modulename import *) cannot be used anywhere except in the main body of a program or module. If you try to use it in a method, Python will raise a syntax error.

Finally, all of these invocations of the import keyword rely on the internal method __import__. For example, these two statements are equivalent (i.e., their internal representations in Python are similar in structure):

```
>>> import convert as foo
>>> foo = __import__('convert')
```

More information about the arguments to __import__ is available from the help() built-in method for advanced users. You will almost never need to use __import__, but one useful application is to import a module whose name is not known until the program is being run. The module name convert is actually a string in the second example, so it could be set to another variable or even set based on user input:

```
>>> my_module_name = 'convert'
>>> foo = __import__(my_module_name)
```

Structuring Your Modules

Broadly speaking, you don't need to structure your code differently if you want to turn an already functioning program into a module. That means, of course, that your module code must already be syntactically correct! However, there are a number of conventions that you should follow in your modules, if you want to make the full use of Python's modular support.

From the perspective of legibility, it helps if you can put any import statements at the top of the module, so that many of the dependencies of that module on other code are immediately obvious. Conditional import statements must, of course, go within the control structures that optionally execute them. Any important variables, either for exporting or internal use throughout the module, should go next.

Most stylistic conventions for naming variables in Python are just that: stylistic. Python doesn't mind if you name your classes using camel case or lowercase with underscores. One exception, however, is that Python treats any module variables named with a leading underscore slightly differently from other module variables. Such variables are considered to be reserved for internal module use only and will not be imported by from modulename import *. However, you can explicitly import the variable by specifying its name: these variables are therefore called **weakly internal**.

Save the code in Listing 11-3 as internals.py, and run the interactive code after it.

Listing 11-3. *Weak Internal Variables*

```
# An internal value
_config = True

def return_config():
    """Get an internal config value"""
    return _config

def set_config(val):
    """Set an internal config value"""
    # Global means "global to this module", not truly global
    global _config
    _config = val
```

Let's try this out:

```
>>> from internals import *
>>> return_config()
True
>>> set_config({'foo': 'bar'})
>>> return_config()
{'foo': 'bar'}
>>> # _config hasn't been imported: try it!
... _config
Traceback (most recent call last):
  File "<stdin>", line 1, in <module>
NameError: name '_config' is not defined
>>> # Assigning to it locally won't change the module variable
... _config = {'where': 'local'}
>>> return_config()
{'foo': 'bar'}
>>> # And assigning in the module won't change it locally
... set_config({'where': 'internal'})
>>> _config
{'where': 'local'}
>>> # But if you now import it explicitly, the stored module variable appears
... from internals import _config
>>> _config
{'where': 'internal'}
>>> # It's the same object: modifying it locally modifies it in the module
... _config['test'] = ['success']
>>> _config
{'test': ['success']=, 'where': 'internal'}
>>> return_config()
{'test': ['success']=, 'where': 'internal'}
>>> # Local assignment still doesn't change the module object
... _config = {'new': True}
>>> return_config()
{'test': ['success'], 'where': 'internal'}
>>> # Nor vice versa: the local object isn't changed by set_config()
>>> set_config({'even_newer': True})
>>> _config
{'new': True}
```

The interplay of scopes—separate collections of variables inside and outside the module—demonstrated in Listing 11-3 is quite complex, but don't worry: the important point is that here we can see the _config variable hiding inside the module until we explicitly imported it, and you can use this in your own code to hide internal variables from the outside world.

Also, you might notice that Python *remembered* the module's value of _config, to such an extent that when you eventually imported it, Python *didn't* revisit the file and decide it was actually True but used the remembered value. This means that, if you want to reload the content of a module whose text has changed on disk, Python will ignore those changes unless you use the advanced technique described later in this chapter.

Self-documenting code is even more important than usual if you're writing something that other people—or you, in many months' time—will need to be able to understand at a glance, without reading the whole file. If you include documentation strings (discussed in Chapter 6) in your modules, and in the classes and methods contained in them, anyone importing your module into the interactive prompt will have access to a wealth of detail about the module.

When we wrote `strings.py` and `convert.py`, we took care to add documentation strings wherever possible. So either module will produce detailed documentation at the interactive prompt, as you can see in the following example:

```
>>> import strings
>>> help(strings)

Help on module strings:

NAME
    strings - Module to convert strings to pirate-speak

FILE
    /home/jp/ch11/my_modules/strings.py

FUNCTIONS
    me_hearties(str)
        Appends 'me hearties!' to the end of a stub sentence

    piratify(str)
        Generic piratify of whole paragraphs, by exclaiming everything!

    yarr(str)
        Appends 'Yarr' to the start of a stub sentence and piratifies it

(END)
```

Finally, your module can contain a reference to the module variable __name__. This was first discussed in Chapter 8, and its most common use is to put code into your module that only runs if the module is executed on its own at the command prompt.

At the bottom of `convert.py`, add the code from Listing 11-4. Then, you can execute the whole file at the command prompt in different ways, as suggested in the output block below the listing.

Listing 11-4. *Executable Block to be Added at the End of convert.py*

```python
# ... appended at the bottom of convert.py
if __name__ == "__main__":
    import sys
    if len(sys.argv) > 1:
        # Convert file given on command line
        print(convert_file(sys.argv[1]))
    else:
        # Convert any content piped into the program
        print(convert_string(sys.stdin.read()))
```

Let's run this:

```
% python convert.py "Hello, world."
Hello, world, me hearties!
% python convert.py example.txt
Mister Pudey, the very real problem is one of money, me hearties! Yarr, i'm afraid
that the Ministry of Silly Walks is no longer getting the kind of support it needs!
Yarr, you see, there's Defence, Social Security, Health, Housing, Education, Silly
Walks! They're all supposed to get the same!
% python convert.py < example.txt > example_converted.txt
```

We'll discuss how modules are run in Python, and how it therefore uses the __name__ variables to keep track of the context in which code is being executed later on, in the "Python Module Internals" section.

Advanced Module Behavior

Now that you've got the basics of modules, let's look at some slightly more advanced module topics. In particular, we'll cover how to reload modules so that you can test them effectively and will have a look at how Python handles modules internally.

Reloading Module Changes Dynamically

When you're in the middle of developing a module, and you want to keep testing changes to its functionality at the interactive prompt, one of the most frequent problems you'll encounter is that only the first import statement visits the module; later import statements just take a copy of the module stored (or cached) internally in Python's memory allocation and provides you with that instead. It does this to speed up handling import statements across a lot of interconnected modules.

However, the caching means that you'll typically find yourself quitting the interactive prompt and running it again, to clear Python's internal cache of imported modules. Help is at hand, however, in Python's own imp module:

```
>>> import convert
>>> import imp
>>> convert.weightings
(0.20000000000000001, 0.29999999999999999)
>>> # Now edit the weightings in convert.py by hand
... # Save the file to disk and try importing again
... import convert
>>> convert.weightings
(0.20000000000000001, 0.29999999999999999)
>>> # The values haven't changed, so force reload with imp.reload()
... imp.reload(covert)
<module 'convert' from 'convert.py'>
>>> convert.weightings
(0.10000000000000001, 0.59999999999999998)
```

The imp module has other advanced functionality for finding, loading, and handling modules. However, you should generally only need the variations on the import keyword discussed previously in this chapter: the functionality exposed by imp is generally only useful when modules are being re-created or recompiled during a program's execution.

Note also that multiple module reloads are additive: changing a variable name in a module can leave the old one lying around after a reload. For example, if you've imported the convert module, and then you change the name of the convert() method to change() and use imp.reload(), you will see the following behavior:

```
>>> import convert, imp
>>> convert.convert
<function convert at 0xb7c1a82c>
>>> # Rename the convert() method to change() and reload
... imp.reload(convert)
<module 'convert' from 'convert.py'>
>>> convert.change
<function change at 0xb7c6f62c>
>>> convert.convert
<function convert at 0xb7c1a82c>
```

If you also edited the method when renaming it, convert.convert() will still exhibit the old functionality. The old definition is not stored anywhere permanently, though, so if you restart the interactive prompt, the old method will be lost.

If you *have* renamed convert() to change(), you might want to change it back to avoid any confusion when following the examples in this chapter!

Python Module Internals

When you ask Python to import a module, it performs three main tasks: First, it finds the module file on disk by looking in a number of specific directories. Next, it pulls the module into memory, interpreting it into an internal representation. Finally, it executes this representation. Each of these phases is worth a bit of explanation, so you have more of an idea of what Python's doing for you, should anything go wrong.

Python will find any module in a directory on the PYTHONPATH. This has a different use from that of the PATH discussed in Chapter 8, which tells your *operating system* where to find *executable* files. Also, you might not have the PYTHONPATH environment variable set on your system: that doesn't matter, as Python adds its own default values to the path, so it can find files such as its own standard modules.

Try running the following experiments at the command line. Note that we run Python below with the -c option. This tells Python to execute the following string as if it were a Python program. It's a handy shortcut for very short programs that you don't want to either save to a file or run from the interactive prompt.

```
% echo $PYTHONPATH # If it's not set, this just gives an empty newline

% python -c "import sys; print(sys.path)"
['', '/opt/python3.0/lib/python30.zip', '/opt/python3.0/lib/python3.0',
'/opt/python3.0/lib/python3.0/plat-linux2', '/opt/python3.0/lib/python3.0/lib-
dynload', '/opt/python3.0/lib/python3.0/site-packages']
% export PYTHONPATH=/home/jp:/home/jp/bin
```

```
% echo $PYTHONPATH
/home/jp:/home/jp/bin
% python -c "import sys; print(sys.path)"
['', '/home/jp', '/home/jp/bin', '/opt/python3.0/lib/python30.zip',
'/opt/python3.0/lib/python3.0', '/opt/python3.0/lib/python3.0/plat-linux2',
'/opt/python3.0/lib/python3.0/lib-dynload', '/opt/python3.0/lib/python3.0/site-
packages']
```

When Python encounters an `import` statement in the code, it checks each of the entries in `sys.path` in list order: it will import from the first module, which matches the `import` statement. As you can see, the list always begins with an empty string, so Python will always look in the current directory first. Next in the list are the colon-delimited terms in the `PYTHONPATH`, if it has been set. Finally, if no match is found in any of these locations, the **standard library** locations are always appended to the list, so those libraries are always available to Python. However, any similarly named module in the current directory or on the `PYTHONPATH` will override them.

When the module is found, the Python interpreter has to do some work to turn your text into something that matches Python's internal representation of code. This compilation happens before it actually executes the contents of the module and exposes the functionality. As it only needs to be done once—assuming a module is not changed during Python's execution cycle—then it tries to save the compiled version as a `.pyc` file (the `c` is for *compiled*).

You should have seen `.pyc` files while following the examples in this chapter. The compiled files are in **bytecode**, which is platform-independent: this means that they don't depend on your operating system. That's only really useful if your files are on a network share or are otherwise accessible by people running Python under more than one operating system. Note that when Python saves a compiled file, it's just speeding up its future compilation phase, because it doesn't have to recompile the file: Python's actual running speed doesn't change. The converse of this is also true, so if you really have to reload a module or recompile its bytecode version, as long as you don't do it too often, you shouldn't see too much of a performance hit. Python also keeps track of the timestamp of the original text file (it records it in the bytecode). That way, if you edit the text, Python notices the change in timestamp and recompiles the bytecode.

Finally, Python actually executes your module. This might come as a surprise, because you're importing modular code into your program, and you don't want it running itself as if it were a separate process. But don't worry: this is execution in a much broader sense. When Python interprets a `def foo` statement or `class bar` statement, it's actually executing that statement: it bundles up the method or class definition in its internal representation and hangs that bundle off the current scope under the name `foo` or `bar` respectively.

A consequence of this behavior is that all the code in your modules really is executed! Any control flow, method calls, and so forth in your module (outside of class or method definitions) are also executed at this time. Indeed, your module might need to run some setup tasks at the point of import, so this is potentially useful behavior. This is why, if you want to run your module as a standalone file, you have to put that code in an `if-else` statement, which checks to see if the module is being run with `__name__ == "__main__"`. Otherwise, the code in the `if-else` block would be run during module import as well.

Since *execution* in Python can mean following some control flow and sending output to the user or it can mean defining new classes: it's all the same to the interpreter, it's important to remember that no magic is at work in modules: no magic in the `__name__ == "__main__"` block, none in weak internal variables; and none in class or method definitions. It's not magic; it's just Python.

Combining Modules into Packages

Before we can make a package out of our modules, we have to see what a package is, so let's do that now.

Understanding Packages

One way of looking at a **package** is as a hierarchical directory structure containing potentially very many .py files, with similar files found in the same place. Another is as a convenient way of preventing the names of many different modules from conflicting both on disk and also when imported. The two are equivalent.

For example, if you wanted to distribute your pirate-speak code, you would first of all want to put strings.py and convert.py in the same directory purely for convenience; you would also want to avoid subjecting users of your code to problems from two files sharing the same name. Someone might have a string-formatting module called strings or might do a lot of automatic image processing and already have a convert module. That user wouldn't appreciate having to change all the references to those modules, just to be able to use your pirate-speak code!

More precisely, for a collection of files to be a Python package, you need the following:

- A top-level directory, plus any arrangement of subdirectories

- Your .py files somewhere in that directory hierarchy

- A (potentially empty) file called __init__.py in each directory in the package

The __init__.py file tells Python that the directory is part of a package and can contain configuration information and methods.

Building a Pirate-Speak Package

In my_modules, create a subdirectory called pirate. Put strings.py and convert.py in there, and add an empty __init__.py. Then, change your current directory to my_modules, and run an interactive prompt with the following:

```
>>> import pirate
>>> pirate
<module 'pirate' from 'pirate/__init__.py'>
>>> # Now import a submodule explicitly
... from pirate import convert
>>> convert
<module 'pirate.convert' from 'pirate/convert.py'>
>>> # This submodule also gets added to pirate
... pirate.convert
<module 'pirate.convert' from 'pirate/convert.py'>
>>> # But the strings submodule isn't there yet
... dir(pirate)
['__builtins__', '__doc__', '__file__', '__name__', '__package__', '__path__',
'convert']
>>> # If we import that explicitly too, then it appears in pirate
... # Note we can use the dot notation to import it directly
... import pirate.strings
```

```
>>> dir(pirate)
['__builtins__', '__doc__', '__file__', '__name__', '__package__', '__path__',
'convert', 'strings']
```

Importing from packages already has a lot of flexibility. For example, using dot notation, you can import pirate.strings and not worry about what's in pirate.convert. But with an entirely empty __init__.py, importing submodules is hard work: they won't be imported implicitly, and from pirate import * does nothing.

There are two main ways that you can make importing easier: by running import statements in your __init__.py and by defining a list variable in __init__.py called __all__, which is interpreted as matching the import * wildcard form. These are demonstrated by the sample content for __init__.py in Listing 11-5, and the examples at the interactive prompt that follow it.

Listing 11-5. *Sample __init__.py Content*

```
"""Pirate-speak package"""

# Import both modules when this package is imported
import convert, strings

# Just import "convert" with the * wildcard form
__all__ = ["convert"]
```

Let's try it out:

```
>>> import pirate
>>> dir(pirate)
['__all__', '__builtins__', '__doc__', '__file__', '__name__', '__package__',
'__path__', 'convert', 'strings']
>>> from pirate import *
>>> convert
<module 'convert' from 'convert.py'>
>>> strings
Traceback (most recent call last):
  File "<stdin>", line 1, in <module>
NameError: name 'strings' is not defined
```

Note that, as with our discussion of Python execution and Python internals, any content in the __init__.py script is executed by Python when it imports the package. You can see this in the example in the propagation of the variable result of import statements from __init__.py into the resultant code. But try adding print("foo") into your __init__.py, and consider the following output:

```
>>> from pirate import convert
foo
>>> # Importing the root of the package now does nothing
... import pirate
>>> # So let's reload it explicitly
... import imp
>>> imp.reload(pirate)
foo
<module 'pirate' from 'pirate/__init__.py'>
```

```
>>> # Re-importing a sub-module does nothing
... from pirate import convert
>>> # Nor does reloading it
... imp.reload(convert)
<module 'convert' from 'convert.py'>
>>>
```

This is consistent with other package and module behavior: only on the first import, which needs to consult __init__.py, is __init__.py actually executed; to execute it again, you have to reload pirate explicitly. As with module files, there's nothing special about __init__.py files: Python executes them like ordinary code. So they can contain class or method definitions, or package-level variables, or even control flow such as if . . . else statements or exception handling. It will all be executed the first time anything is imported from the package.

The Universe of Python packages

As has been noted throughout this chapter, packages are a great way to offer reusable code and Python itself comes with a number of packages that make your life easier. We'll look at them in the next section and then examine some third-party packages that have been contributed by the Python community.

Standard Modules

Python is distributed with a standard library of modules that provide useful, if basic, functionality. The precise list of modules varies depending on what operating system you are using, primarily in the system modules, for example: Unix and Linux Python distributions have support for POSIX system calls, Unix users and groups, and terminal (command-prompt) functions, whereas Microsoft Windows Python has modules to access the Windows registry and Windows installer files.

However, broadly speaking, the list of standard modules is the same across distributions, and is quite long! This does mean that there's a big toolkit of modules for you to play with. Always check the functionality provided by standard modules before writing your own or downloading contributed code.

Importing from the standard library is as easy as importing from modules you've written yourself: the standard library is on sys.path, so Python's import statements will always be able to find the modules in it. In fact, I snuck the random module from the standard library into Listing 11-2 .

To help you find the functionality you need in the standard library, a comprehensive and up-to-date list of all the modules in it is available in Python's own online documentation. There's code in there to support string formatting and regular expressions, as well as interprocess communication and the operating system. There's also a large library containing functions for date and time parsing and formatting and for working with calendars. You can process audio and video using multimedia functionality, and if you're working with web sites, APIs, and similar mash-up technology, there's a long list of modules to interface with such technologies as HTTP, FTP, and e-mail.

Installing Contributed Packages

Eventually, you will decide that the core library doesn't provide you with enough functionality and that to write it yourself would take you some considerable time. Luckily, the thriving, distributed community of Python developers is already likely solving the problems you experience. The majority of the code they produce is freely available, and much of it is made so under open source licenses, so you're free to examine what the developers have done, and in some circumstances, edit it. Be warned, though: any changes you make will probably not be supported by the community, certainly not unless you contribute them back and they're accepted. Support options will depend strongly on what license the software is made available under.

The most simple **contributed** package is a single module file. When downloaded, it can be placed anywhere on Python's sys.path—even in your program's own directory, if you don't need to use it anywhere else or don't mind keeping multiple copies—and used immediately with import statements. The accepted location for storing downloaded modules is in one of the site-packages directories on sys.path.

Large, complex packages will often be distributed with installation instructions. The most basic distribution is as some type of compressed file, like zip, GZip, or BZip. These will typically unpack to provide a package directory hierarchy, with __init__.py files in each subdirectory. You can sometimes just put the top-level directory somewhere on the sys.path and the package will be discovered by import. Python packages also often use the .egg format, and these can usually just be dropped into a directory on the sys.path as with unzipped packages.

Sometimes ZIP files will contain a setup.py file, or eggs will require special installation: check any README file included with the package. In the first instance, the package has been prepared to the **Distutils Python** standard, and you will generally want to run the setup.py file (ensuring you're using the right version of Python):

```
% cd unpacked_zipfile_directory
% python setup.py install
```

Eggs can be installed with the **Easy Install** Python package manager. This is a whole separate infrastructure for installing Python packages, including the ability to search the online **Python Package Index (PyPI)** by name. Here are a few examples of the Easy Install syntax:

```
% # Install a package in the PyPI, by just specifying a name
% easy_install pylint
% # Install a package from a zipfile or egg on the web
% easy_install http://example.com/NewPackage-1.2.3.tgz
% # Install an egg that you've already downloaded
% easy_install Desktop/Documents/NewPackage.egg
```

Packages may also be distributed as installers for your specific operating system. The developers might provide a Windows installer, RedHat Linux package or Debian/Ubuntu package. These are also straightforward to install, but you should follow the instructions for your operating system.

Note that installing eggs and running any setup.py files may require you to have full administrator access on your machine: you might have to discuss installing such packages with your system administrator if you're developing on shared web hosting, as they can have knock-on effects for all users of Python on the server.

As always, you should only ever install software from sources that you trust. Check that your downloaded software is coming from that source, and you're not accidentally following a link to an untrustworthy site. If in doubt, confirm with the software developers. Also, consider using checksum software to ensure that your downloads are as the original developers expected. Many open source projects publish the checksums of their packages, and their developer communities will have documentation explaining how this works.

Three Examples from the Python Universe

To give you a flavor of the sort of solutions that already exist out there, we'll discuss three straightforward but particularly neat modules below. These were chosen not so much because they're the most impressive modules to be found, but because they're freely available, easy to use, and solve common (and to some extent quite dull) problems, which you might otherwise be tempted to spend a lot of time fixing on your own!

CSV

This module is built to handle the comma-separated variable (CSV) file format. Most spreadsheet data can be exported to CSV, which produces text-only files. However, there's no recognized standard for CSV, so along with other operations this module lets you worry less about whether or not your Python file is dealing with some particular variant.

A number of other modules do exist, which can deal with more complex types of spreadsheet files, but the csv module is part of the core Python distribution. Given that it'll be immediately available to you, and that much of the data in a spreadsheet can be exported to CSV format, csv is a useful tool for importing or exporting structured data from your program.

Listing 11-6 contains an example CSV spreadsheet, representing a number of purchases. The first column is item name; the second column is the number of items, and the third column is the per-item price. Save this to a file called purchases.csv.

Listing 11-6. *Example CSV Spreadsheet for Parsing with Listing 11-7*

```
Gromit,5,0.57
Widget,2,1.20
Splatchet,10,0.27
Snorklet,3,0.99
```

You can manipulate this CSV file using the code in Listing 11-7. Save this file to csv_demo.py, and run it from the command line: you should see the output shown following Listing 11-7.

Listing 11-7. *The csv Module*

```python
import csv

# Set up some store variables
total = 0
priciest = ('',0,0,0)

# Loop over CSV rows
r = csv.reader(open('purchases.csv'))
for row in r:
    # Work out the total cost of this row and add it to running total
    cost = float(row[1]) * float(row[2])
    total += cost
    # If this is the priciest row so far, replace the priciest
    if cost > priciest[3]:
        priciest = row + [cost]
```

```
# Report on the total and the priciest purchase
print("You spent {0}".format(total))
print("Your priciest purchase was: {0[1]} {0[0]}s, at a total cost of
{0[3]}".format(priciest))
```

Let's try it out.

```
% python csv_demo.py
You spent 10.92
Your priciest purchase was: 3 Snorklets, at a total cost of 2.97
```

The csv module can also be used to write CSV files, and you can use either the online documentation or help(csv) in the interactive prompt to give you more information on how csv can parse different variations of the CSV format.

datetime

Handling dates and times is always a difficult problem in any language, and it's tempting for the new programmer to develop all sorts of string-munging libraries to do quite specific tasks. datetime exists in Python's core libraries so that you can resist that temptation, should it ever arise.

The datetime module contains a lot of functionality that we won't cover explicitly here. However, Listing 11-8 demonstrates its core features: parsing, creating, and manipulating date and time objects. Save this code to datetime.py, and run it from the command line.

Listing 11-8. The datetime Module

```
import datetime

# Date parsing
# Original data in a fairly human-readable format
guess = "19 Feb 2001, 08:23"
# Parsing into a Python object
time_obj = datetime.datetime.strptime(guess, "%d %b %Y, %H:%M")
# Printing the object generates a slightly different readable format
print("Python thinks that '{0}' is '{1}'".format(guess,time_obj))

# Date manipulation
# Define a time interval of five days
interval = datetime.timedelta(5)
day = datetime.date.today()
for i in range(1,10):
    # Count back in intervals of five days
    day -= interval
    print("{0} days ago was {1}".format(i*5,day))
```

In Listing 11-8, we have to give strptime() a format mask, which it uses to try to parse the guess string into the relevant fields for day, month, year, and so on. If strptime() can't parse the date using the format specified, it raises a value error exception. Chapter 10 explained how to use exceptions to your advantage: in this case, you could specify a different date format and try again!

The datetime module should do much of your heavy lifting if you need to work with time-related input or output. Date and time objects can be created, manipulated, and time-shifted with timedelta objects. Methods like strptime() can parse many different formats of timestamps. If you want even more advanced date and time handling, you might want to look at the contributed mxDateTime module, available on the Web (http://www.egenix.com/products/python/mxBase/mxDateTime/).

Beautiful Soup and urllib

Fetching and understanding HTML is a common problem for web-enabled programs. Sometimes, you'll be lucky and be able to retrieve data in a structured format like rich-document format (RDF), XML, or from spreadsheets or even a database, but often, data will be spread over multiple web pages, some of them with poor or invalid markup. Beautiful Soup is an intelligent HTML parser, which can take markup of quite variable quality and turn it into an object-oriented Python interface.

When provided with some HTML—not necessarily completely valid HTML or even a full HTML document—Beautiful Soup turns it into an internal Python representation and returns a single object that gives you access to that representation. Exactly how the internals work isn't important, but from your perspective, the HTML has been turned into a hierarchy of objects, each corresponding to a plain-text string or a HTML element within the original document. The hierarchy means that, once you've got the Beautiful Soup object corresponding to the <body> tag, you can access tags like paragraphs <p> within it. Similarly, a paragraph object lets you access such tags within the paragraph as <em> or <a>. Beautiful Soup also provides you with many simplifying methods: some of these slice through the hierarchy, meaning you don't have to always drill down explicitly into the depths of paragraphs to find <a> tags (and maybe not find them if they're in <li> or <div> tags) but could instead grab all the <a> tags in the document straight away.

Beautiful Soup is not part of Python core but is contributed software. The module is only a single Python file: as discussed previously, single-file modules are easy to install. However, at the time of this writing, the module is still not available in a separate Python 3 version from its maintainer. You can work out how to convert the Python 2.x module using documentation included with the download, and it's very straightforward, certainly on Linux/Unix systems. But to make life easier for you in the meantime, Apress has provided the Python-3–compatible module on the Source Code/Download page for this book at www.apress.com.

Once you've downloaded the file from the Apress web site, you can extract the file BeautifulSoup.py and store it anywhere on Python's sys.path, and it will be available for use.

A quick example follows to show you how easy it is to start obtaining useful information from HTML. Note, though, that the Python home page has quite probably changed since the time of this writing, so this might no longer work as expected. But BeautifulSoup is a flexible and usable module, so you should be able to easily adapt this code to your own requirements.

```
>>> import urllib.request, BeautifulSoup
>>> # Connect to the remote site and read the content
... r = urllib.request.urlopen('http://python.org/')
>>> text = r.read()
>>> # Parse into BeautifulSoup
... soup = BeautifulSoup.BeautifulSoup(text)
>>> # Stepping around the tree
... soup.contents[0]
'DOCTYPE html PUBLIC "-//W3C//DTD XHTML 1.0 Transitional//EN"
"http://www.w3.org/TR/xhtml1/DTD/xhtml1-transitional.dtd"'
>>> soup.contents[2].name
```

```
'html'
>>> soup.contents[2].contents[1].name
'head'
>>> # How many links does the document have?
... len(soup("a"))
91
>>> # Finding content by element name and class
... soup("h1", {'class': 'pageheading'})[0].renderContents()
b'Python Programming Language -- Official Website'
>>> # Going up and down the tree
... soup("div", {'id': 'search'})[0].fetchParents()[0].name
'form'
```

urllib in the preceding example fetches a remote web page. Automatically retrieving content over the Web is another common task these days, and it's worth having urllib up your sleeve. Think of it as a bonus fourth example for you!

A Package for Everything—Eventually

Python 3 is still a relatively new dialect of the Python language. As such, it doesn't necessarily have the same breadth and depth of third-party package support as Python 2.x. At the time of this writing, many of the more popular modules have been ported or are being ported to Python 3, thanks to the effort of the core Python developers in providing tools to aid automatic migration to the new dialect of the Python programming language.

Ultimately, it's likely that the majority of 2.x-only code will gradually migrate to 3.x soon. In the long term, only underused or legacy packages will remain in 2.x-only versions. That means that, eventually, you should be able to find a Python package out there somewhere to solve most of your day-to-day problems: PDF creation, integration with other proprietary file formats, image conversion, and more.

Here's the trick: whatever you find yourself about to build, consider if other people might have been in a similar situation in the past. If so, they may well have packaged up their code, and you should be able to find it on the Web.

Python has an active and dedicated community of both core coders and end-use programmers, and it makes sense for you to take as much advantage of that as you can. But once you've felt the benefit of this community, you might wish to consider giving back wherever possible: through discussing, testing, and providing feedback on other people's projects and maybe even one day contributing code with your own programming skills.

Jargon Busting

Here are the terms from this chapter:

- *Bytecode*: This compiled equivalent of a textual Python script is turned into an internal computer-readable representation and, where possible, stored on disk in a .pyc file so that Python can omit the compile process in future.

- *Contributed*: This term describes code that is available on the Web separately from the Python installation. Contributed modules are maintained by the Python developer community.

- *Distutils*: This is the first of two standard methods of installing contributed Python software.

- *Easy Install*: This is the second of two standard methods of installing contributed Python software.

- *Egg*: This archived format for Python packages allows you to download and install them as a single file for simplicity.

- *Import*: When you import, you put the objects from a module into the current scope so they can be accessed by other objects in that scope, and you execute any other contents of the module when doing so.

- *Module*: This Python file contains methods, classes, or other variables that can be reused.

- *Package*: This collection of Python modules is conveniently stored in a directory hierarchy, so modules of similar function are stored in the same directories. Each directory has an __init__.py, so Python knows it's part of the package, and each __init__.py can contain configuration code and variables for that particular subpackage.

- *PyPI*: This is the abbreviation for the Python Package Index, an online searchable repository for Python software. Easy Install can retrieve software from PyPI by specifying the package name.

- PYTHONPATH: This environment variable, configured by your operating system but modifiable at a command prompt, contains a list of directories. Python first checks these directories when an import statement causes it to look for a suitable candidate module, before checking in the contributed and standard libraries.

- *Standard library*: This is the set of packages with which Python is distributed; they are always available to your programs.

- *Weak internal use indicator*: When a variable in a module is named with a leading underscore, Python treats it as being for internal use only: this weak variable will not be imported unless explicitly specified.

Summary

Python comes with a lot of useful functionality, but it can't do everything. To make up for this, it gives you the ability to add whatever functionality you want in the form of modules. This allows you to organize and reuse your code and to use modular code provided by other Python developers.

We had a good look at Python's module system and built modules of our own to see how easy it is. This allowed us to talk about the different ways to import and use modules, another flexible aspect of Python modules. We also covered some of the more advanced aspects of modules, such as reloading them and how they work internally.

The power of Python modules can be seen when you consider the wealth of material provided by the Python community. It's fair to say that almost any piece of functionality is out there in the form of a Python module (and if it's not, then get to work on it and get it out there).

CHAPTER 12

■ ■ ■

Simple Windowed Applications

Now that you have a working understanding of the whole Python language, you have the knowledge required to start creating graphical applications. As you have seen, rather than trying to code everything from scratch, many tasks are covered by modules in Python's standard library, which provides a more-or-less friendly programming interface for you to use in your own programs.

There are quite a few different tool kits available to help you create a graphical user interface (GUI) interface that interacts with the program code behind the scenes. Therefore, this chapter serves as a survey of some of the different kits and how to get started using them. Of course, there could be a whole book on each of these kits, so this chapter is in no way an exhaustive treatise on the subject of GUI tool kits.

Most of the programs you use on your computer have a GUI—when you click an icon, a new window opens on your screen, which can display data in a graphic format and provide buttons and menus for the various commands that you might want to run on that data. This relationship of data and commands strongly suggests a class structure; what we need is some means of easily creating graphic containers for displaying data and other graphic objects representing commands. Python has interfaces available for several graphical toolkits, including: Tkinter, PyGTK, Glade, and tepache. GIMP, on which PyGTK is based, is an open source image manipulation program similar to Photoshop.

We'll mainly focus on PyGTK and Tkinter, with a little on Glade and tepache at the end of this chapter. First, let's look at Tkinter as it is the simpler of the two major toolkits. One of the more interesting aspects of building a GUI interface for a Python program is that the resulting program would be a cross-platform GUI application—a truly powerful aspect of Python.

■ **Note** The examples in this chapter use Python 2.5 rather than Python 3, because Python 3 support for graphical interfaces wasn't complete at the time of this writing. Some of the issues relating to Python 3 and GUI code can be found in the discussion at http://mail.python.org/pipermail/tutor/2009-February/067443.html.

Using Tkinter

Before you can use **Tkinter**, you need to have the python-tk package installed. Once the tkinter module has been imported, it provides all the necessary building blocks to make text areas, menus, buttons and so on, and to hook them up to the commands you want to run. These graphical building blocks connected to program functions are known as **widgets** (presumably because calling them *watchamacallits* or *dubreywotsis* would have sounded silly). The most obvious example of a widget is a button, but in fact, every part of what you see is some kind of widget or other. (Does this sound familiar?) Even the containing box into which all the other widgets are packed—usually in a top-bottom and then left-right fashion—is a widget. This approach to widgets is a little ungainly, but it makes for a fairly quick way to get graphic applications up and running, as you can see in Listing 12-1.

Listing 12-1. *hellotk.py*

```
#! /usr/bin/env python

"""HelloTk: Example windowed application.

Usage: HelloTk.py
Target System: GNU/Linux
Interface: tkinter
Functional Requirements: Display a GUI window containing two buttons,
which write a message to stdout when pressed.
"""

__version__ = 0.1
__maintainer__ = "maintainer@website.com"
__status__ = "Prototype"
__date__ = "12-01-2009"

# Import modules

import Tkinter

class HelloTk:

    def __init__(self, master):

        # First create a frame
        # This fills the main window of the application
        frame = Tkinter.Frame(master)
        # Everything has to be packed into place before it can be displayed.
        frame.pack()

        # Create the 'Hello' button.
        self.hello_button = Tkinter.Button(frame, text="Hello",
                                           command=self.say_hi)
        self.hello_button.pack(side=Tkinter.LEFT)

        # Create the 'Quit' button.
        self.quit_button = Tkinter.Button(frame, text="QUIT", fg="red",
                                          command=frame.quit)
        self.quit_button.pack(side=Tkinter.LEFT)

    def say_hi(self):
        print "hi there, everyone!"
```

```
root = Tkinter.Tk()
app = HelloTk(root)
root.mainloop()
```

Listing 12-1 will create a window with two buttons in it, as shown in Figure 12-1. In order to understand how it works, you will need to run it from a terminal emulator screen. Basically, two class objects are created: root, an instance of Tkinter.Tk(), and app, an instance of HelloTk() with root as its only argument. The root object provides a method called mainloop(), which displays an instance of the window defined in HelloTk() and waits for user input in the form of mouse clicks and key pressing. Clicking the Hello button will cause a message to be printed on the terminal screen.

Figure 12-1. *Hello World Tkinter style*

To initialize Tkinter, you must first create a Tk root widget. This is an ordinary window, with a title bar and other decorations provided by your window manager. You should create only one root widget for each program, and it must be created before any other widgets.

The rest of the application has been gathered up into the HelloTk class. As the class is constructed, the window becomes populated with widgets. The first item is a frame, which will contain the two buttons. The first argument is the container this widget is to be packed inside; in this instance, it's the root window. The Tkinter.Frame instance is stored in a local variable called frame. Calling the pack() method on frame tells it to size itself to fit the contents and then make itself visible. A similar process is used to create the buttons, except that Tkinter.Button() takes more arguments: buttons need to have some text or an image to use as a label to indicate their usage, and they also need a command to be run when they are clicked. The first button runs the self.say_hi() method, and the second runs the frame.quit() method of the Tkinter.Frame object, which quits the application. You can specify the direction of packing using the side option; here, the buttons are packed as far to the left as possible. If this option is left out, side defaults to Tkinter.TOP. Having set all that up, we just need to launch the root window, with all the widgets you just packed into it, and to enter into the Tkinter event loop, which handles events from the user and those queued by Tkinter itself. The program will stay in the event loop until you close the window, which you can do by clicking the Quit button.

Tkinter supports 15 core widgets, which are explained in Table 12-1.

Table 12-1. *Tkinter Widget Classes*

Widget	Description
Button	A simple button used to execute a command or other operation.
Canvas	This widget can be used to draw graphs and plots, create graphics editors, and to implement custom widgets.
Checkbutton	Represent a variable that can have two distinct values. Clicking the button toggles between the values.
Entry	A text entry field.
Frame	A container widget. The frame can have a border and a background and is used to group other widgets when creating an application or dialog layout.
Label	Displays a text or an image.
Listbox	Displays a list of alternatives. The list box can be configured to get radio button or checklist behavior.
Menu	A menu pane. Used to implement pull-down and pop-up menus.
Menubutton	A menu button used to implement pull-down menus.
Message	Displays text similar to the label widget but can automatically wrap text to a given width or aspect ratio.
Radiobutton	Represents one value of a variable that can have one of many values. Clicking the button sets the variable to that value and clears all other radio buttons associated with the same variable.
Scale	Allows you to set a numerical value by dragging a slider.
Scrollbar	Standard scrollbars for use with canvas, entry, list box, and text widgets.
Text	Formatted text display. Allows you to display and edit text with various styles and attributes and supports embedded images and windows.
Toplevel	A container widget displayed as a separate, top-level window.

If you want to develop applications further using Tkinter, The full documentation can be found at `http://www.pythonware.com/library/tkinter/introduction/index.htm`.

Saying "Hello" with PyGTK

Tkinter can be used to make functional interfaces, but the presentation is rather basic. Python's Gtk bindings provide access to the themeable and potentially prettier **PyGTK** graphic toolkit. You need to have python-gtk2 installed; from there, you'll follow a process similar process to the one you used with Tkinter: import the module into your program, and use the methods and widgets it provides. Again, the main application is abstracted into the HelloGtk class (see Listing 12-2), and the object it creates is represented by the main window, which is displayed on the screen.

Listing 12-2. *hellogtk.py*

```
#!/usr/bin/env python

"""HelloGtk: Example windowed app.

Usage: hellogtk.py
Target System: GNU/Linux
Interface: Gtk
Functional Requirements: Display a GUI window containing two buttons,
which write a message to stout when pressed.
"""

__version__ = 0.1
__maintainer__ = "maintainer@website.com"
__status__ = "Prototype"
__date__ = "12-01-2009"

# Import modules

import gtk

class HelloGtk:

    # This is a callback. The data passed to this method is printed to stdout.
    def callback(self, widget, data):
        print "Hello again - %s was pressed" % data

    # This is another callback, which exits the application.
    def delete_event(self, widget, event, data=None):
        gtk.main_quit()
        print "Bye!"
        return False

    def __init__(self):
        # Create a new window
        self.window = gtk.Window(gtk.WINDOW_TOPLEVEL)

        # Set the title of the window to "GUI"
        self.window.set_title("GUI")
```

265

```
        # Create a handler for delete_event that immediately quits GTK.
        self.window.connect("delete_event", self.delete_event)

        # Set the border width of the window.
        self.window.set_border_width(6)

        # Create a box to pack the widgets into. The box is an invisible
        # container, which is used to arrange the widgets inside it.
        self.box1 = gtk.HBox(False, 0)

        # Put the box into the main window.
        self.window.add(self.box1)

        # Create a new button with the label "Hello".
        self.button1 = gtk.Button("Hello")

        # Now when the button is clicked, the self.callback method is called
        # with a text string "the Hello button" as its argument.
        self.button1.connect("clicked", self.callback, "the Hello button")

        # Instead of add(), we pack this button into the invisible box,
        # which has been packed into the window.
        self.box1.pack_start(self.button1, True, True, 0)

        # Always remember this step, this tells GTK to actually display the
        # button.
        self.button1.show()

        # Do these same steps again to create a second button
        self.button2 = gtk.Button("Quit")

        # This time, delete_event is called and the window exits.
        self.button2.connect("clicked", self.delete_event, "the Quit button")
        self.box1.pack_start(self.button2, True, True, 0)

        # The order in which the buttons are shown is not really important,
        # but it is recommended to show the window last, so that everything
        # displays at once.
        self.button2.show()
        self.box1.show()
        self.window.show()

def main():
    gtk.main()

if __name__ == "__main__":
    hello = HelloGtk()
    main()
```

This script is longer than the equivalent using Tkinter, partly because Gtk provides more options. Essentially, it does the same thing. When the HelloGtk class is instantiated a new Gtk window is created with the argument gtk.WINDOW_TOPLEVEL. This argument makes a window that is under the control of your window manager with the usual decorations and buttons. You can set the title of the window using the gtk.Window.set_title() method and attach commands to the window using gtk.Window.connect().

The gtk.Hbox widget works similarly to Tkinter.Frame, in that it creates a container for widgets, which are packed horizontally. To get more complex layouts, you can nest several gtk.Vbox widgets, which pack their contents vertically, inside a gtk.Hbox widget, or vice versa. Then, you create the buttons, connect them to the appropriate callback methods, and pack them into the box. You need to call the show() method on each widget in order for it to be displayed, starting with the details, like the buttons, and moving out to the main window last. Calling main() invokes the Gtk main event processing loop, which handles mouse, keyboard, and window events. So finally a little Gtk window should open on your desktop like the one shown in Figure 12-2.

Figure 12-2. *A little Gtk window*

Catching Signals

Gtk not only provides nice graphical building blocks, but it also monitors user input and other events. Each widget can respond to different **signals**, such as mouse clicks and text input. Gtk provides a huge number of widgets, which are detailed at http://www.pygtk.org/pygtk2reference/gtk-class-reference.html. Get used to understanding the contents of this reference. Each page gives a brief description, a list of the methods available to the widget object, a list of its properties with explanations, and a list of signals that it can receive. The full syntax of each method is explained at the end of the page.

In order to understand the arguments given to the various gtk.Button methods used previously, you need to go to the gtk.Button page. First, you should read the "Constructor" section. You should also make a note of the signals it can receive (such as click and right-click). You will see that gtk.Button can take three optional arguments: label, stock, and use_underline. Mostly, you'll just want to stick a label on it, and a label is a plain text string. The stock argument is for using preformatted stock Gtk icons; the list of available options is at http://www.pygtk.org/pygtk2reference/gtk-class-reference.html. The use_underline is a function that allows you to underline letters in the label as a mnemonic for key combinations.

To find the syntax for some methods, you to trace the ancestry of some of these objects. For example, the origin of the connect() method lies way back in the gobject.GObject class, which is the parent of all graphic objects used in Gtk. gobject.GObject.connect(detailed_signal, handler, . . .) is the given syntax: detailed_signal is a text string identifying the signal to be acted upon. The gtk.Button widget can understand activate, clicked, enter, leave, pressed, or released in this context (in Listing 11-2 the value "clicked" is used). The handler method that you have already specified is the command to be run when the signal is received. The handler is the self.callback method in this instance. All subsequent arguments are passed on to the method.

The show() method is inherited from gtk.Widget and mercifully takes no arguments. Because of the way the class hierarchy is organized, you can assume that all widgets have connect() and show() methods, which work in exactly the same way.

The buttons are packed using the gtk.Box.pack_start(child, expand, fill, padding) method inherited by gtk.Hbox: child is the widget to be packed, and expand and fill are Booleans indicating whether or not the child widget fills the available space in each direction according to the packing direction of the container. And padding is the number of pixels between each widget.

This graphical Hello World example isn't particularly big or clever, but it does provide a nice visual representation of how an object oriented graphical application works. The principles scale well for small to medium-sized applications, and the Gtk library provides the majority of the functionality you would expect from a standard windowed application, so building bigger applications is simply a question of adding more building blocks.

Building Complex Interfaces

Now, you know how to put a tiny window with a couple of buttons in it on the screen. The point of creating graphic interfaces is to provide a reassuring user-friendly window that the user can point and click within, instead of having to follow some arcane command-line procedure. For the final example in this chapter, I'm going to show you how to wrap up some command-line instructions in a smart Gtk interface.

My main functional requirement is that the application should display some system information in a window. I also want to be able to save that information as a text file. I have a Bash script that I've been using to provide diagnostics for my audio system. This script is all well and good for those who are accustomed to the command line, but this audio information that could be useful to complete beginners too, so I want to create a graphical point-and-click version.

I'm going to use the bits of Bash script as they are, by importing the commands module; commands.getoutput() allows me to run Bash commands and pass the results back to Python. This program will also use os.system() to launch external applications.

The pseudocode outline for such an application might look like this:

```
# Assign BASH commands to strings named <option>_func.
# Create GUI.
    # Create Icons.
    # Create clipboard.
    # Create a new window.
        # Create menubar.
        # FILE menu.
            # Save -> Create save As dialog & specify file to open for writing.
            # Quit -> Quit the application.
        # EDIT menu.
            # Copy -> Copies selected information to the clipboard.
        # HELP menu.
            # About -> What it says on the box.
            # Help -> Launch browser with help page.
    # Create option list panel.
        # Create list of options.
        # get selection from option list.
        # Create command line according to option chosen.
        # Execute command line and display in text output panel.
```

```
        # Create text output panel.
        # Create QUIT button.
# Display GUI and wait for user signals
```

The immediate issue that needs facing here is that this design is going to require several additional files to be available to the application: several icon images and an HTML help page. For want of a better name, I'm going to call this program GtkInfo, so to organize the files, I have created a folder in ~/Projects called gtkinfo (see Figure 12-3).

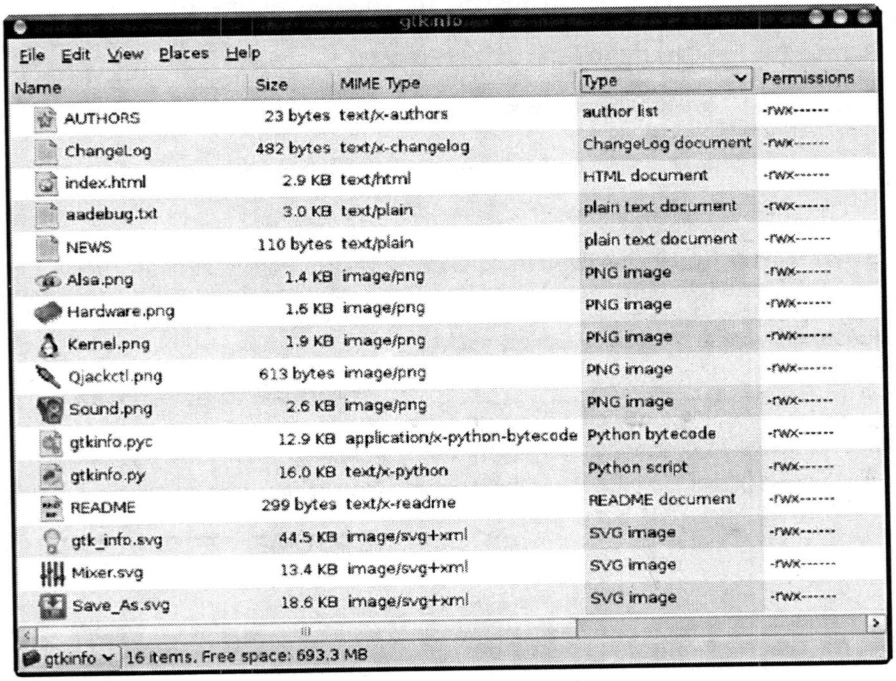

Figure 12-3. The gtkinfo directory

The original Bash commands were taken from http://alsa.opensrc.org/index.php/Aadebug; all I have done is turn the sequences of Bash instructions into Python strings.

Creating the GUI

As in the previous example, the entire graphic interface is defined as a single class, GtkInfo(). The graphic interface is built by the constructor method GtkInfo.__init__(). The first thing I do is create some icon images using gtk.gdk.pixbuf_new_from_file(path), which creates Gtk picture buffers to hold the images in a format that Gtk, and therefore Python, can use. These will come in handy later. I aliased the method as image to save on typing and similarly defined path to be the full path to the gtkinfo directory.

Creating a clipboard is simple using gtk.Clipboard(). Once the clipboard's created, I create a text buffer, which will hold the output messages for the right-hand pane of the main window display using gtk.TextBuffer(None). The text can be formatted by creating a text tag. This tag uses the pango library, which also needs to be separately imported. Here, I am using it to create a simple headline format. The next commands get the position of the cursor and place the output items at the cursor position to create the formatted output.

With all that done, I can now start to construct the graphic components. First, the main window needs creating; this is the outer box that provides the title bar and iconify, maximize, and quit buttons for the application. I can set various properties of the main window here and connect any delete_event received by the window to my GtkInfo.delete_event() method. The compiler will complain if I try to reference a method that doesn't exist yet, so I need to create a stub for this method, which will show me whether the signal is being caught and allow me to fill in the details later.

```
def delete_event(self, widget, event, data=None):
    """Quits the application"""
    print "You called a", event, ": Bye!"
    return False
```

Now, I can begin to fill in the details on the canvas provided by the main window. Gtk organizes the graphical components of the interface by packing them into boxes, which are aligned either vertically or horizontally and can be packed from left to right, top to bottom, right to left, or bottom to top. This type of organization means careful planning. I started by dividing the space vertically, inserting an invisible vertical box in which the main areas of the interface can be stacked.

■ **Note** The vbox has to be added to the window, so that Gtk knows where to place it. Later in this stanza, it is necessary to explicitly call self.vbox1.show() to tell Gtk to actually display the widget—even though it's invisible.

The first item in the window is the menubar, which is constructed in a fashion similar to stacking Russian nested dolls. First, the headers for the three menus are constructed, and submenus are set for each header. After that, the individual menu entries are constructed as separate widgets. As with the delete_event command, I constructed stubs for these methods, so I could get on with building the GUI first and worry about the functionality later.

■ **Note** Each menu still has to be specifically appended to the menubar and its show() method run. The menubar also has to be packed into place. The exact command varies from widget to widget, but the principle remains the same.

Next, I made a container for the two main panels of the application: on the left is a list of options, and the right-hand pane displays the retrieved information. The process of filling the space proceeds in a similar manner to the menus. First, I created two scrolled windows to contain the views, setting the to gtk.POLICY_AUTOMATIC so that the scrollbars will disappear if the information fits inside the space. In order to display the list of options, I will use the gtk.TreeView object, which provides a file-browser-like display. Actually, I'm just going to use it to display a list rather than a tree, but that doesn't matter immediately. I can fill it with information later. Next, I connect the "cursor-changed" signal to a self.on_treeview1_cursor_changed() method stub, so I can get a response when the user clicks a different option. All this functionality is packed into place and then filled with relevant information by self.create_treelist().

The second scrolled window is filled with a gtk.TextView widget, which displays the text buffer that I created earlier. Again, all the widgets are packed into place, and the horizontal box is displayed. The last piece in the puzzle is a Quit button, which is packed into the bottom of the vertical box, and the remaining items are displayed, with the main window coming up last.

Once the basic framework for the GUI has been constructed, it is necessary to fill it with some information. GtkInfo.create_treelist() creates a gtk.ListStore to structure the information that is to be displayed in treeview1, the left-hand options panel, as shown in Figure 12-4. Again, a nest of items is created started with the columns, and these are populated with individual cells. Next, the icons are put in place by the make_pixbuf() method and then packed into the columns. The liststore is associated with treeview1 using the treeview1.set_model(model=self.liststore) method.

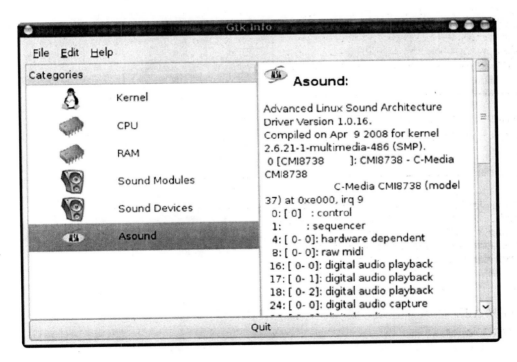

Figure 12-4. The panel on the left is a treeview

Making the Commands Do Something Useful

The next step is to turn the stub methods into commands that actually do something. To remember what these methods were supposed to do, I need to go back to the original pseudocode.

The resulting Python file is fairly substantial but not unmanageable, as shown in Listing 12-3. For larger programs, you would probably want to split the program up into smaller files, possibly separating the form from the functionality. I've omitted large chunks for brevity and clarity, so you can see the important bits of the program; the complete example can be found in the code download.

Listing 12-3. gtkinfo.py

```
#! /usr/bin/env python

"""Example windowed app.

Usage: gtkinfo.py
Target System: GNU/Linux
Interface: Gtk
Functional Requirements: Display some system information in a window.
"""

__version__ = 0.1
__maintainer__ = "maintainer@website.com"
__status__ = "Prototype"
__date__ = "12-01-2009"

# Import modules

import gtk
import pango
import os, commands

class GtkInfo:
        # Code removed for clarity. See the download for full listing.

        # Create a new window
        self.window = gtk.Window(gtk.WINDOW_TOPLEVEL)
        self.window.set_title("Gtk Info")
        self.window.set_border_width(6)
        self.window.set_default_size(600, 400)
        self.window.set_resizable(True)
        self.window.connect("delete_event", self.delete_event)

        # Create a vertical box to pack the widgets into.
        self.vbox1 = gtk.VBox(False, 0)
        self.window.add(self.vbox1)

        # Create menubar
        self.menubar1 = gtk.MenuBar()
        self.menubar1.set_pack_direction(gtk.PACK_DIRECTION_LTR)
        self.menubar1.set_child_pack_direction(gtk.PACK_DIRECTION_LTR)
```

Here is where we start creating the separate menus and wiring the application together. Note how we connect each action to a method. Each method will be explained as we work our way through the rest of this example's code.

```
# FILE menu
self.file = gtk.MenuItem(label="_File", use_underline=True)
self.file_menu = gtk.Menu()

self.save_as = gtk.ImageMenuItem(stock_id="gtk-save")
self.save_as.connect("activate", self.on_save_as)
self.file_menu.append(self.save_as)
self.save_as.show()

self.quit = gtk.ImageMenuItem(stock_id="gtk-quit")
self.quit.connect("activate", self.on_quit)
self.file_menu.append(self.quit)
self.quit.show()

self.file.set_submenu(self.file_menu)
self.file_menu.show()

# EDIT menu
self.edit = gtk.MenuItem(label="_Edit", use_underline=True)
self.edit_menu = gtk.Menu()

self.copy = gtk.ImageMenuItem(stock_id="gtk-copy")
self.copy.connect("activate", self.on_copy)
self.edit_menu.append(self.copy)
self.copy.show()

self.edit.set_submenu(self.edit_menu)
self.edit_menu.show()

# HELP menu
self.help = gtk.MenuItem(label="_Help", use_underline=True)
self.help_menu = gtk.Menu()

self.about = gtk.ImageMenuItem(stock_id="gtk-about")
self.about.connect("activate", self.on_about)
self.help_menu.append(self.about)
self.about.show()

self.hhelp = gtk.ImageMenuItem(stock_id="gtk-help")
self.hhelp.connect("activate", self.on_help)
self.help_menu.append(self.hhelp)
self.hhelp.show()

self.help.set_submenu(self.help_menu)
self.help_menu.show()

# Don't forget to add them to the menubar.
```

273

```
        self.menubar1.append(self.file)
        self.file.show()
        self.menubar1.append(self.edit)
        self.edit.show()
        self.menubar1.append(self.help)
        self.help.show()

        # Then pack the menubar into place.
        self.vbox1.pack_start(self.menubar1, False, True, 0)
        self.menubar1.show()

        # Create the main panels
        self.hbox1 = gtk.HBox(False, 0)

        # Create option list panel
        self.scrolledwindow1 = gtk.ScrolledWindow()
        self.scrolledwindow1.set_policy(gtk.POLICY_AUTOMATIC,
                                        gtk.POLICY_AUTOMATIC)
        self.treeview1 = gtk.TreeView()
        self.treeview1.connect("cursor-changed",
                               self.on_treeview1_cursor_changed)
        self.scrolledwindow1.add_with_viewport(self.treeview1)
        self.treeview1.show()
        self.scrolledwindow1.show()
        self.hbox1.pack_start(self.scrolledwindow1, True, True, 0)

        # Fill it with relevant info
        self.create_treelist()

        #Create text output panel
        self.scrolledwindow2 = gtk.ScrolledWindow()
        self.scrolledwindow2.set_policy(gtk.POLICY_AUTOMATIC,
                                        gtk.POLICY_AUTOMATIC)
        self.textview1 = gtk.TextView(self.textbuffer)
        self.textview1.set_wrap_mode(gtk.WRAP_WORD)
        self.textview1.set_editable(False)
        self.textview1.set_left_margin(6)
        self.textview1.set_right_margin(6)
        self.scrolledwindow2.add_with_viewport(self.textview1)
        self.textview1.show()
        self.scrolledwindow2.show()
        self.hbox1.pack_start(self.scrolledwindow2, True, True, 0)
        self.hbox1.show()

        self.vbox1.pack_start(self.hbox1, True, True, 0)

        # Create QUIT button
        self.button2 = gtk.Button("Quit")
        self.button2.connect("clicked", self.delete_event, "the Quit button")
        self.vbox1.pack_start(self.button2, False, False, 0)
        self.button2.show()
```

```
        self.vbox1.show()
        self.window.show()

    def create_treelist(self):
        """create_treelist

        Create list of options
        """
        # Add some messages to the window

        # Omitted for clarity
        return

    def make_pixbuf(self, tvcolumn, cell, model, tier):
        """make_pixbuf

        Create icons for TreeView menu.
        """

        # Omitted for clarity
        return
```

The get_selection() method catches selections in the options list and displays the system information that I was after; it is called by on_treeview1_cursor_changed(). The selection itself is retrieved by treeview1.get_selection(). This selection is then dropped into a command string, which is evaluated using eval(). Finally, the output is prepared for sending to the textbuffer in much the same way as before.

```
    def get_selection(self):
        """get_selection

        Creates text appropriate to choices
        """
        # get selection from listview
        self.choice = self.treeview1.get_selection()
        self.choice.set_mode(gtk.SELECTION_SINGLE)
        self.model, self.row_reference = self.choice.get_selected()
        self.choice = self.liststore.get_value(self.row_reference, 0)

        # Create command line
        command_ref = "self." + self.choice.replace(' ','_') + "_func"
        command = eval(command_ref)

        # GUI output
        # Make clean textbuffer
        self.textbuffer = gtk.TextBuffer(None)
        # Create headline style
        self.headline = self.textbuffer.create_tag('headline',
                            weight=700, scale=pango.SCALE_LARGE)
        # navigate to start of buffer
        place = self.textbuffer.get_start_iter()
```

```
    # Create pixbuf icon reference
    icon = eval("self." + self.choice.replace(' ','_') + "_image")
    # Insert icon at top of page
    self.textbuffer.insert_pixbuf(place, icon)
    # Print appropriate text underneath
    text = " " + self.choice + ": \n\n" + commands.getoutput(command)
    self.textbuffer.insert_at_cursor(text)
    iter0 = self.textbuffer.get_iter_at_line(0)
    iter1 = self.textbuffer.get_iter_at_line(1)
    self.textbuffer.apply_tag(self.headline,iter0,iter1)
    self.textview1.set_buffer(self.textbuffer)
    return
```

The menu item File ➤ Save is connected to the on_save_as() method, which is supposed to create a
Save As dialog to specify file to open for writing. Fortunately, Gtk provides a handy
gtk.FileChooserDialog() method with which to perform this function; the dialog retrieves the filename
using the get_filename() method. Running the dialog also returns a response, which needs to be
handled. If the dialog receives the OK signal from the user, it fetches the output from the Bash commands
for each of the headings and writes them out to a text file, displaying a helpful message in the GUI when
it's done. If the dialog receives the 'Cancel' signal, nothing is done. Either way, dialog.destroy() is
called to get rid of the now-extraneous window.

```
def on_save_as(self, widget):
    """Save

    Opens a dialog asking you where you want to save the information
    as a plain text file.
    """
    print "Exporting aadebug information"
    # Create save As dialog & specify file to open for writing
    dialog = gtk.FileChooserDialog(title='Save Multimedia Info to file',
                                   action=gtk.FILE_CHOOSER_ACTION_SAVE,
                                   buttons=(gtk.STOCK_CANCEL,
                                       gtk.RESPONSE_CANCEL,
                                       gtk.STOCK_OPEN,
                                       gtk.RESPONSE_OK))
    dialog.set_current_name('aadebug.txt')
    response = dialog.run()
    outfile_name = dialog.get_filename()
    print "response: " + str(response)
    print "outfile: " + str(outfile_name)

    if response == gtk.RESPONSE_OK:
        # Write out items
        a_out = """Multimedia System Information (%s)

""" % (__version__,)
        headings = ['Kernel','CPU','RAM','Hardware','Modprobe',
                    'Sound_Modules','Sound_Devices','Asound']
        a_list = [a_out]
        for heading in headings:
```

```
                command = eval("self." + heading + "_func")
                a_ = """***** %s *****
%s

""" % (heading, commands.getoutput(command))
                a_list.append(a_)
            a_out = ''.join(a_list)
            # write out System info to file
            output_file = open(outfile_name,'w')
            output_file.write(a_out)
            output_file.close()
            print "aadebug info written out"

            # Create GUI output
            # Make clean textbuffer
            self.textbuffer = gtk.TextBuffer(None)
            # Create headline style
            self.headline = self.textbuffer.create_tag('headline',
                            weight=700, scale=pango.SCALE_LARGE)
            # navigate to start of buffer
            place = self.textbuffer.get_start_iter()
            # Create pixbuf icon reference
            icon = eval("self.save_image")
            # Insert icon at top of page
            self.textbuffer.insert_pixbuf(place, icon)
            # Print appropriate text underneath
            text = """Saving Information ...

To file:
%s""" % (outfile_name,)
            self.textbuffer.insert_at_cursor(text)
            iter0 = self.textbuffer.get_iter_at_line(0)
            iter1 = self.textbuffer.get_iter_at_line(1)
            self.textbuffer.apply_tag(self.headline,iter0,iter1)
            self.textview1.set_buffer(self.textbuffer)
        elif response == gtk.RESPONSE_CANCEL:
            print "Save As cancelled"
        dialog.destroy()
        return
```

The code for on_quit() is easy. As I have already defined a delete_event() method, this method can be used by the File ➤ Quit menu entry as well.

```
def on_quit(self, widget):
    """Quit the application"""
    self.delete_event("Quit", "Quit")
    return
```

Edit ➤ Copy turns out to be a one-liner also. The textbuffer has a built-in method to transfer its contents to the clipboard, named sensibly enough textbuffer.copy_clipboard(self.clipboard).

```
    def on_copy(self, widget):
        """Copy

        Copies selected information to the clipboard
        """
        self.textbuffer.copy_clipboard(self.clipboard)
        return
```

Gtk has another preformed dialog for the About dialog box, so I can fill in the on_about() stub using that. For the help pages, I used a different approach. The os.system() method allows external applications to be launched in a fairly straightforward way; it just takes the command-line as an argument. After all that trouble packing widgets into boxes, making them functional turned out to be much easier.

```
    def on_about(self, widget, *args):
        """About Dialog

        What it says on the box
        """
        print "About Gtk Info"
        logo = self.icon
        dialog = gtk.AboutDialog()
        dialog.set_name('Gtk Info')
        dialog.set_version(str(__version__))
        dialog.set_authors([__maintainer__])
        dialog.set_documenters([__maintainer__])
        dialog.set_logo(logo)
        comment = 'A graphical interface for displaying system information'
        dialog.set_comments(comment)
        response = dialog.run()
        if response == -6:
            dialog.destroy()
        return

    def on_help(self, widget, *args):
        """Help

        Launches help page in a web browser.
        """
        os.system('/usr/bin/sensible-browser index.html')
        return
```

The on_treeview1_cursor_changed() method is called when a new selection is made, and it calls get_selection(), which you saw previously. The delete_event() method is called when the Quit menu option is clicked.

```
    def on_treeview1_cursor_changed(self, widget, *args):
        """Option panel
```

```
        Gets the icon that received the click
        and displays relevant information
        """
        self.get_selection()

    def delete_event(self, widget, event, data=None):
        """Quits the application"""
        gtk.main_quit()
        print "You called a", event, ": Bye!"
        return False
```

Finally, we start the application.

```
def main():
    gtk.main()

if __name__ == "__main__":
    application = GtkInfo()
    main()
```

Using Glade and tepache to Build Interfaces

Only certain sorts of programmers find building GUIs from scratch exciting, and there is a kind of logic in the idea that graphic interfaces should be made in a graphic interface. If you are using Linux, you can create your GUI using **Glade** and use a utility called tepache to generate a Python framework from it. You then just have to fill in the blanks, such as menu names and error messages.

```
$ tepache guixample.glade
written file guixample.py
```

The preceding code snippet will produce a page of code like the following, as well as a file called SimpleGladeApp.py. The .py file builds the GUI according to the instructions in the corresponding .glade file.

```
#!/usr/bin/env python
# -*- coding: UTF8 -*-

# Python module guixample.py
# Autogenerated from guixample.glade
# Generated on Thu Jan 22 17:30:21 2009

# Warning: Do not modify any context comment such as #--
# They are required to keep user's code

import os

import gtk

from SimpleGladeApp import SimpleGladeApp
from SimpleGladeApp import bindtextdomain
```

```
app_name = "guixample"
app_version = "0.0.1"

glade_dir = ""
locale_dir = ""

bindtextdomain(app_name, locale_dir)


class Window1(SimpleGladeApp):

    def __init__(self, path="guixample.glade",
                 root="window1",
                 domain=app_name, **kwargs):
        path = os.path.join(glade_dir, path)
        SimpleGladeApp.__init__(self, path, root, domain, **kwargs)

    #-- Window1.new {
    def new(self):
        print "A new %s has been created" % self.__class__.__name__
    #-- Window1.new }

    #-- Window1 custom methods {
    #   Write your own methods here
    #-- Window1 custom methods }

    #-- Window1.on_window1_delete_event {
    def on_window1_delete_event(self, widget, *args):
        print "on_window1_delete_event called with self.%s" % widget.get_name()
    #-- Window1.on_window1_delete_event }

    #-- Window1.on_new1_activate {
    def on_new1_activate(self, widget, *args):
        print "on_new1_activate called with self.%s" % widget.get_name()
    #-- Window1.on_new1_activate }

    #-- Window1.on_open1_activate {
    def on_open1_activate(self, widget, *args):
        print "on_open1_activate called with self.%s" % widget.get_name()
    #-- Window1.on_open1_activate }

    #-- Window1.on_save1_activate {
    def on_save1_activate(self, widget, *args):
        print "on_save1_activate called with self.%s" % widget.get_name()
    #-- Window1.on_save1_activate }

    #-- Window1.on_save_as1_activate {
    def on_save_as1_activate(self, widget, *args):
        print "on_save_as1_activate called with self.%s" % widget.get_name()
    #-- Window1.on_save_as1_activate }
```

```python
    #-- Window1.on_quit1_activate {
    def on_quit1_activate(self, widget, *args):
        print "on_quit1_activate called with self.%s" % widget.get_name()
    #-- Window1.on_quit1_activate }

    #-- Window1.on_cut1_activate {
    def on_cut1_activate(self, widget, *args):
        print "on_cut1_activate called with self.%s" % widget.get_name()
    #-- Window1.on_cut1_activate }

    #-- Window1.on_copy1_activate {
    def on_copy1_activate(self, widget, *args):
        print "on_copy1_activate called with self.%s" % widget.get_name()
    #-- Window1.on_copy1_activate }

    #-- Window1.on_paste1_activate {
    def on_paste1_activate(self, widget, *args):
        print "on_paste1_activate called with self.%s" % widget.get_name()
    #-- Window1.on_paste1_activate }

    #-- Window1.on_delete1_activate {
    def on_delete1_activate(self, widget, *args):
        print "on_delete1_activate called with self.%s" % widget.get_name()
    #-- Window1.on_delete1_activate }

    #-- Window1.on_about1_activate {
    def on_about1_activate(self, widget, *args):
        print "on_about1_activate called with self.%s" % widget.get_name()
    #-- Window1.on_about1_activate }

    #-- Window1.on_treeview1_cursor_changed {
    def on_treeview1_cursor_changed(self, widget, *args):
        print "on_treeview1_cursor_changed called with self.%s" % widget.get_name()
    #-- Window1.on_treeview1_cursor_changed }

    #-- Window1.on_button1_clicked {
    def on_button1_clicked(self, widget, *args):
        print "on_button1_clicked called with self.%s" % widget.get_name()
    #-- Window1.on_button1_clicked }


#-- main {

def main():
    window1 = Window1()

    window1.run()

if __name__ == "__main__":
    main()

#-- main }
```

This method makes developing new graphic interfaces remarkably quick, although you will still need to get your hands dirty with the Gtk library to make the most of what it provides. Using Glade and tepache like this, you can create sophisticated interfaces able to cope with most requirements you may dream up.

Jargon Busting

Here are the terms from this chapter:

- *Glade*: This user interface designer for GTK is available at http://glade.gnome.org/.

- *GTK*: This is a cross-platform GUI toolkit available at http://www.gtk.org/.

- *Signal*: An event, such as a mouse down or hover, triggers a signal to a widget to call an appropriately assigned function for the event.

- tepache: This utility generates a Python framework from a Glade design.

- *Tkinter*: This is GUI interface building toolkit available at http://tkinter.unpythonic.net/wiki/FrontPage.

- *Widget*: This graphical user interface (GUI) element displays information or provides controls to the user, such as a window, button or text box.

Summary

Award yourself the rest of the day off, or failing that, your favorite beverage and a light snack. You've just finished the final chapter in the book. We covered a fair amount in this chapter too, including four major tools for building GUIs in Python. It's clear that Python 3 isn't yet the best language to use for GUI programming, but this chapter will give you enough to look into it when Python 3 is ready for GUIs.

As for the book as a whole, you know Python. You will probably be more aware of what you still don't know about programming than when you started reading this book. Good. Over the coming months, you will want to familiarize yourself with the parts of Python's standard library that look like they might be useful. Just take one module at a time, and construct an application that does what you want it to do. As we've done in this book's examples, start with a pseudocode design or flowchart, and improve the design until you have ticked all your user requirements boxes. Once you have done that, move on to the next thing.

You now know how to go about designing applications with command-line, windowed, and web-based interfaces from a basic set of requirements. As you progress, you will develop your own methods through experience and come into contact with more sophisticated programming ideas, which you may want to integrate. I hope this book provides a first step on the path of programming that you can always come back to when you want to remind yourself of the basics.

Happy programming!

Index

You Need the Companion eBook

We believe this Apress title will prove so indispensable that you'll want to carry it with you everywhere, which is why we are offering the companion eBook (in PDF format) for $10 to customers who purchase this book now. Convenient and fully searchable, the PDF version of any content-rich, page-heavy Apress book makes a valuable addition to your programming library. You can easily find and copy code—or perform examples by quickly toggling between instructions and the application. Even simultaneously tackling a donut, diet soda, and complex code becomes simplified with hands-free eBooks!

Once you purchase your book, getting the $10 companion eBook is simple:

❶ Visit **www.apress.com/promo/tendollars/**.

❷ Complete a basic registration form to receive a randomly generated question about this title.

❸ Answer the question correctly in 60 seconds, and you will receive a promotional code to redeem for the $10.00 eBook.

THE EXPERT'S VOICE™

233 Spring Street, New York, NY 10013

Offer valid through 4/10.

CPSIA inf...
Printed in th... ...ion can be obtained at www.ICGtesting.com
LVOW09025...A
311549L...212
...0029B/597/P